JEREMY BENTHAM
AND REPRESENTATIVE DEMOCRACY

For Maria,
Gregory, and Alexander

JEREMY BENTHAM AND REPRESENTATIVE DEMOCRACY

A Study of the *Constitutional Code*

FREDERICK ROSEN

CLARENDON PRESS OXFORD

*This book has been printed digitally and produced in a standard specification
in order to ensure its continuing availability*

OXFORD
UNIVERSITY PRESS

Great Clarendon Street, Oxford OX2 6DP

Oxford University Press is a department of the University of Oxford.
It furthers the University's objective of excellence in research, scholarship,
and education by publishing worldwide in

Oxford New York

Auckland Bangkok Buenos Aires Cape Town Chennai
Dar es Salaam Delhi Hong Kong Istanbul Karachi Kolkata
Kuala Lumpur Madrid Melbourne Mexico City Mumbai Nairobi
São Paulo Shanghai Taipei Tokyo Toronto

Oxford is a registered trade mark of Oxford University Press
in the UK and in certain other countries

Published in the United States
by Oxford University Press Inc., New York

ISBN 0-19-822656-X

Preface

This study of the political theory of Jeremy Bentham has grown out of the work of editing the first volume of Bentham's *Constitutional Code* for the new edition of the *Collected Works*. As I began to emerge from a preoccupation with textual and historical problems with the completion of the text, I realized that Bentham had set forth a major theoretical work on representative democracy, which, for numerous reasons, had remained largely unknown to students of political ideas. This book represents an attempt to restate and assess this theory and to show that its perspectives and arguments remain of interest today.

I have received generous financial support from the Social Science Research Council in the form of a Personal Research Grant which has enabled me to complete this study. Smaller useful grants were received from the University of London Research Fund and the London School of Economics Staff Research Fund. The staff at the Bentham Project have over the years offered great assistance and encouragement for which I am grateful. In particular, I wish to thank Dr Martin Smith, Miss Claire Gobbi, and the General Editor, Dr J. R. Dinwiddy. Dr C. Bahmueller, the Assistant General Editor, read the whole of the book in manuscript. I am especially indebted to him for his careful comments, and although we do not agree on a number of points, his criticisms have led to a great improvement in the quality of the text. Mr Geraint Williams of Sheffield University read chapters IX and X on James Mill and J. S. Mill, made several useful suggestions, and pointed out a few mistakes. Over many years I have discussed virtually every passage of the *Constitutional Code* with Professor J. H. Burns in our joint attempt to establish the meaning of the text we set out to edit. Although we seldom had time to reflect on the significance of what we were trying to sort out, my familiarity with Bentham's text and arguments depends in part on these numerous meetings. He bears no responsibility however, for the arguments and conclusions presented here.

I am grateful to the Librarian and staff of the British Library of Political and Economic Science of the London School of Economics for its generous policy of loaning books to staff which enabled me to proceed without undue interruption in my research. This policy demonstrates above all the support for research which animates this great library. I am also indebted to the Librarian and staff of University College London, the Trustees of the British Library, and the Director, Bibliothèque Publique et Universitaire, Geneva, for permission to quote from manuscripts and other valuable assistance.

Many scholars have over the years favoured me with advice, encouragement, and assistance for which I am grateful: Professor M. W. Cranston, Professor H. L. A. Hart, Dr L. J. Hume, Dr M. H. James, Dr Pedro Schwartz, Professor G. Jones, Dr I. Asquith, and Mr J. Geldzahler. I also acknowledge with thanks the typing assistance of Mrs Paula da Gama Pinto who typed a full draft of the text and part of another, Miss Sally Bergin who completed the text and notes, and Miss Pauline Job.

London School of Economics   Fred Rosen
January 1982

Contents

Chapter I

Introduction

Jeremy Bentham's contribution to a theory of representative democracy has never been fully explored. The main work of his later years, the massive, unfinished *Constitutional Code*, has not received much detailed attention either from friends or from critics.[1] There are few scholars who have reached the actual text of the *Code* as opposed to the introductory essays collected by Richard Doane for the Bowring edition.[2] The new edition of the *Code* and especially the first volume (which corresponds to the only volume Bentham himself published in 1830) will for the first time provide scholars with an accurate, readable text to explore Bentham's main ideas on constitutional democracy.[3]

It would be foolish to suppose that the improved format will overcome the numerous obstacles which Bentham places in the path of the most diligent scholar. The long,

[1] For brief discussions of some features of the *Constitutional Code* (subsequently referred to as the *Code*), see Thomas Peardon, 'Bentham's Ideal Republic', *Canadian Journal of Economic and Political Science*, xvii (1951), 184-203, reprinted in *Jeremy Bentham*, ed. B. Parekh, London, 1974, pp. 120-44; E. Halévy, *The Growth of Philosophic Radicalism*, trans. Mary Morris, London, 1928, pp. 403-32; J. Steintrager, *Bentham*, London, 1977, pp. 97-116; C. W. Everett, 'The Constitutional Code of Jeremy Bentham', *Jeremy Bentham Bicentenary Celebrations*, London, 1948, pp. 1-29. L. J. Hume, *Bentham and Bureaucracy*, Cambridge, 1981, provides an extensive discussion of the *Code*, but unfortunately his book was published after this book was substantially written. I have, however, used Hume's book in this chapter and have discussed it more generally in the Appendix.

[2] *The Works of Jeremy Bentham, published under the superintendence of John Bowring*, 11 vols., Edinburgh, 1838-43. References to this edition are to Bowring, followed by the volume number in roman and the page number in arabic numerals. The actual text of the *Code*, more or less as Bentham intended, appears in Bowring, ix. 146-647. The introductory material, some of which was not intended for the *Code*, is printed as 'Book I' (Bowring, ix. 1-145). For a discussion of Bentham's original plan of the *Code* and the Bowring version, see F. Rosen, 'The Constitutional Code: The New Version', *The Bentham Newsletter*, ii (1979), 40-3.

[3] See J. Bentham, *Constitutional Code*, vol. I, eds. F. Rosen and J. H. Burns, *Collected Works of Jeremy Bentham*, Oxford, 1983, which corresponds roughly to: *Constitutional Code; for the use of All Nations and All Governments professing Liberal Opinions* vol. i, London, 1830 (Bowring, ix. 146-333).

often obscure sentences, the technical language, the numerous digressions, and the legalistic framework act as strong deterrents to both Bentham scholars and students of political ideas.[4] This book is intended to overcome some of these difficulties by providing a guide to Bentham's *Code* and an assessment of his achievement. The book is intended, perhaps in contrast with Bentham himself, to be a brief and concise guide to his work. It does not pretend to be an exhaustive study of the *Code* or of Bentham's later writings. These tasks must await the publication of further *Code* volumes, additional related volumes on such themes as penal law, judicial procedure, parliamentary and legal reform, and the correspondence of the period. The task attempted here is a different one. Bentham's *Code* is studied primarily as a work of political theory. It is argued that the *Code* is the classic utilitarian text on representative democracy, far superior in scope, depth, and subtlety to those of James Mill and J. S. Mill, and that it contains arguments and insights of great importance to democratic theory today.

I

Most of Bentham's ideas which are brought together and take a special form in the *Code* had already been developed in different contexts many years earlier. But he had never before made an attempt on this scale to bring these ideas together and apply them to the basic organization and rationale of representative democracy. We might distinguish four main themes which form the background to the *Code*: (a) codification and the construction of the *pannomion* (complete code of laws); (b) economy and reform in government administration; (c) parliamentary reform and political radicalism; and (d) reform of judicial institutions and procedure.

Bentham's interest in codification existed throughout his life and formed the rationale for his earliest writings. *An Introduction to the Principles of Morals and Legislation,*

---

[4] L. Stephen, *The English Utilitarians,* 3 vols., London, 1900, i, p. 283; 'In this book Bentham's peculiarities of style reach their highest development, and it cannot be recommended as light reading.'

prior to its separate publication in 1789, was originally
intended by Bentham to introduce a detailed 'Plan of a Penal
Code'.[5] Dumont's *Traités* of 1802, based on earlier manuscripts, was concerned almost exclusively with codification
and with the principles of the penal and civil codes.[6] Bentham
himself recognized that he had not yet developed the principles of a constitutional code as a distinct code in this early
period, although it has been argued that he was 'falsely
modest' in making this admission.[7] In *A Fragment on Government* he had explored, though largely through the critique
of Blackstone, a number of political and constitutional
questions, and at the time of the French Revolution he wrote
some notable manuscripts containing arguments which
he subsequently abandoned in support of representative
democracy.[8] By 1811 he had offered James Madison, President of the United States, a full set of codes, a *pannomion*,
and in 1814 he made a similar offer to Alexander I of Russia.[9]
In his letter to Alexander I, Bentham referred to two codes
promulgated by Napoleon in France and Bavaria which
contained statements of praise of his work, but *'approbation
is one thing; adoption is another'*.[10] Although they praised
him, he admitted that the codes adopted were based on

[5] See *An Introduction to the Principles of Morals and Legislation*, eds. J. H.
Burns and H. L. A. Hart, London, 1970 (*CW*), pp. xxxviii–xxxix. The abbreviated
reference to *CW* is to the *Collected Works of Jeremy Bentham*, London, 1968- .

[6] *Traités de législation, civile et pénale*, ed. P. E. L. Dumont, 3 vols., Paris,
1802.

[7] See *An Introduction to the Principles of Morals and Legislation*, XVII. In
(*CW*), p. 281n, and Bentham to the Earl of Shelburne, 18 July 1781, *Correspondence*, iii. ed. I. Christie, London, 1971 (*CW*), pp. 28–9. See also Hume,
pp. 77–8: 'But he had convinced himself that constitutional law was a proper
and necessary part of his system and he had begun to deduce some of its general
characteristics and even a few of its details.'

[8] See *A Comment on the Commentaries and A Fragment on Government*,
eds. J. H. Burns and H. L. A. Hart, London, 1977 (*CW*), pp. 391–501. On Ben-
tham's writings at the time of the French Revolution, see Mary Mack, *Jeremy
Bentham, An Odyssey of Ideas 1748–1792*, London, 1962, pp. 432 ff; J. H.
Burns, 'Bentham and the French Revolution', *The Transactions of the Royal
Historical Society*, 5th series, xvi (1966), 95–114; and M. H. James, 'Bentham's
Political Writings 1788-95', *The Bentham Newsletter*, iv (1980), 22–4.

[9] See *Papers relative to Codification and Public Instruction: including Correspondence with the Russian Emperor, and Divers Constituted Authorities in the
American United States*, London, 1817 (Bowring, iv. 451–533).

[10] *Ibid.*, p. 514. Bentham commonly uses italics for emphasis, and the italic-
ized words will be reprinted here without further acknowledgement or comment
except where a change in the text is considered necessary.

Roman jurisprudence rather than on the principles of his *Traités*.[11] *The Papers relative to Codification* was published in 1817 and followed by *Codification Proposal* in 1822.[12] The latter contained a section consisting of testimonials and letters from England, Geneva, Spain, Portugal, Italy, France, United States, Russia, and Poland to support his claim to be able and willing to draft codes for 'All Nations Professing Liberal Opinions'.[13] Bentham thus had been fully prepared for the work of codification for more than a decade before he began the *Constitutional Code* and the other codes of the *pannomion* in the 1820s.

The second theme, economy in government and management, may also be traced to Bentham's early writings and especially to his writings in the 1790s on panopticon and the poor.[14] His early position reflected both his adherence to the principles of classical political economy and his concern with the economic management of public enterprises. With his conversion to radicalism, economy in government became an increasingly important theme in his writing, serving as a major object of radical reform. The two earliest essays collected in Bentham's *Official Aptitude Maximized; Expense Minimized* (1830) were 'Defence of Economy against Burke' and 'Defence of Economy against Rose', first published as pamphlets in 1817 but based on manuscripts written in 1810.[15] These essays developed in a practical and polemical way a strong attack on prevailing attitudes towards economy in government. They also reflected the principles Bentham had evolved in manuscripts on reward which were published in 1811 as part of Dumont's *Théorie des Peines et des Récompenses*.[16] At the same time he began to develop his ideas on the virtues of competition as a means to enhance

---

[11] Ibid.

[12] *Codification Proposal, addressed by Jeremy Bentham to All Nations Professing Liberal Opinions*. London, 1822 (Bowring, iv. 535-94).

[13] Bowring, iv. 564-94. A Supplement was added in 1827 containing additional testimonials from Portugal, Greece, and South America. See Bowring, iv. 566.

[14] See *Panopticon; or, The Inspection House*, London, 1791 (Bowring, iv. 37-172); and the material on the poor laws in Bowring, viii. 359-461.

[15] Bowring, v. 278-328.

[16] 2 vols., Paris, 1811. See the English translations made by Richard Smith, *Rationale of Reward*, London, 1825 (Bowring, ii. 189-266) and *Rationale of Punishment*, London, 1830 (Bowring, i. 388-525).

aptitude in office.[17] He turned more directly to economy in government in writings associated with parliamentary reform. Some manuscripts, headed 'Official Economy' were written in 1818, and in May and June 1822, he wrote a long manuscript headed 'Economy as to Office' to which he referred in a letter to Dumont as 'a forerunner and in part of my *Constitutional Code*'.[18] Although these manuscripts were never published, the themes of maximizing aptitude and minimizing expense in government dominated vast portions of the *Constitutional Code*.[19]

Bentham's conversion to radicalism has been the subject of considerable speculation. Although he wrote in support of representative democracy at the time of the French Revolution, his subsequent 'retreat' has led John Dinwiddy to return to 1809 as the crucial date in Bentham's development, when he began drafting manuscripts on parliamentary reform, some of which were published in 1817 and 1819.[20] Although the factors which led Bentham to advocate parliamentary reform were numerous and complex, the important influence of James Mill in this process has also been confirmed.[21] The *Plan of Parliamentary Reform* (1817) was the first published work where Bentham presented the radical doctrine of 'virtual' universal suffrage and representative government.[22] This was developed in the *Radical Reform Bill* of 1819 where annual, secret, universal, and equal suffrage was set forth in the form of a detailed Election

---

[17] See Hume, op. cit., pp. 200-1.

[18] For the 1818 manuscripts, see, for example, UC clx. 6-27 (November 1818). 'UC' refers to the Bentham Manuscripts in the University College London Library. The manuscript headed 'Economy as to Office' is at UC cxiii. 1-159; Bentham to Dumont, 26 May 1822, Dumont MSS, MS 33/v, fo. 25, Bibliothèque Publique et Universitaire, Geneva.

[19] See, for example, the *Extract from the Proposed Constitutional Code, Entitled Official Aptitude Maximized, Expense Minimized*, London, [1826] which contains a version of ch. IX, §§ 15-17 (*CW*), pp. 297-329, 337-46, 362-4. See also Bowring, v. 278.

[20] J. R. Dinwiddy, 'Bentham's Transition to Political Radicalism', *Journal of the History of Ideas*, xxxvi (1975), 683. On Bentham and the French Revolution, see the references at note 8 above. Dinwiddy (p. 684) notes that Bentham wrote approximately 1,000 pages of manuscript on parliamentary reform and 500 pages on 'sinecures' in the twelve months after August 1809.

[21] Dinwiddy, loc. cit., p. 684.

[22] *Plan of Parliamentary Reform, in the Form of a Catechism*, London, 1817 (Bowring, iii. 433-557).

Code.[23] Bentham later attempted (though not with satisfactory results) to incorporate this Election Code into the *Constitutional Code*.[24] With Bentham's radicalism firmly established by 1817, much of his writing after this time possessed a shrill rhetoric, as he attacked the numerous institutions and practices opposed to representative democracy. The unrelenting attack on the English monarchy and aristocracy—a theme of the *Code* and related writings —also appeared earlier following his conversion to radicalism. Thus, both Bentham's devotion to representative democracy and his elaborate critique of institutions opposed to it were developed considerably before he began the *Code*.

The final major theme of the *Code* to which we shall call attention here, that of judicial organization and the reform of judicial procedure, was also a concern of Bentham from his earliest writings. It is difficult to think of any period in Bentham's life when he was not writing about a range of problems connected with the organization of the judiciary and the numerous procedures of the law. His critique of the Common Law and its 'arch-defender', Blackstone, continued throughout his life.[25] It formed one of the main stimulants for Bentham to engage in the arduous task of codification. *The Draught of a Code for the Organization of the Judicial Establishment in France* (1790) was a major work with a detailed plan of judicial organization.[26] Halévy noted that Bentham's ideas on judicial procedure were stated 'in [their] definitive form' in *Scotch Reform* (1808)[27] and repeated in *An Introductory View of the Rationale of Evidence* (1812),[28] Dumont's *Traités des Preuves Judiciaires* (1823),[29] and the *Rationale of Judicial Evidence* (1827)[30] before being tackled again in the Procedure Code written to

[23] *Bentham's Radical Reform Bill, with Extracts from the Reasons*, London, 1819 (Bowring, iii. 558–97).

[24] Ch. VI, §§ 4–17 (*CW*), p. 48. See also the Introduction to *Constitutional Code*, vol. I, (*CW*), pp. xxv–xxvi, for a full discussion of this problem.

[25] Bentham returned to draft another (unpublished) critique of Blackstone in 1828–9. See UC xxx. 60–164; xxxi. 1–220.

[26] Bowring, iv. 285–406.

[27] Bowring, v. 1–53.

[28] Bowring, vi. 1–187.

[29] 2 vols., Paris, 1823. An English translation, *A Treatise on Judicial Evidence* was published in London in 1825.

[30] Bowring, vi. 189–585; vii. 1–599.

accompany the Constitutional Code.[31] In addition, Bentham wrote numerous works (e.g. *Elements of the Art of Packing*) which were highly critical of various practices in English law and the law of other nations, and which contain numerous proposals for judicial reform.[32] What was most surprising about Bentham was not that he began so massive a work as the *Constitutional Code* in 1822, at the advanced age of seventy-four, but that he had delayed starting it when many of his ideas were already well developed. The impulse which prompted him to begin the *Code* was the acceptance by the Portuguese Cortes of his offer to draft penal, civil, and constitutional codes in April 1822.[33] The invitation was the best he had received since he became involved with the new liberal regimes of Spain and Portugal. In the end neither state adopted one of his proposed codes, but when his interest in Spain and Portugal faded, his hopes were raised with the prospect of drafting some codes for Greece.[34] Bentham went so far as to send an early draft of the *Constitutional Code* to Greece in 1823-4, but when his chances there began to diminish by 1825, he was still hopeful that one of the new states of Latin America would adopt it. He had been in correspondence for many years with a number of leaders of Latin American governments including Bernardino Rivadavia, President of Argentina, José del Valle of Guatemala, and Francisco de Paula Santander and Simon Bolivar, both of whom served as President of Colombia.[35]

These contacts and prospects for his various codes provided important stimulation for Bentham throughout the 1820s. Although his *Code* was written for 'All Nations and All Governments professing Liberal Opinions', his hopes

[31] E. Halévy, op. cit., p. 376.
[32] Bowring, v. 61-186.
[33] See Bowring, iv. 576. See also Bowring, ix. p. iii.
[34] Bowring, iv. pp. 580-92. See also F. Rosen, 'Bentham's Letters and Manuscripts in Greece', *The Bentham Newsletter*, v (1981), 55-8.
[35] See P. Schwartz, 'Bentham's Influence in Spain, Portugal and Latin America', *The Bentham Newsletter* i (1978), 34-5; Alamira de Avila-Martel, 'The Influence of Bentham on the Teaching of Penal Law in Chile', Theodora L. McKennan, 'Benthamism in Santander's Colombia', Antonio-Enrique Pérez Luño, 'Jeremy Bentham and Legal Education in the University of Salamanca during the Nineteenth Century', ibid., v (1981); M. Williford, *Bentham on South America*, Baton Rouge, 1980. See also *The Iberian Correspondence of Jeremy Bentham*, ed. P. Schwartz, 2 vols., London-Madrid, 1979.

for its adoption by one state enabled him to proceed fairly steadily in the laborious task of drafting it. He was also sustained in his work by his belief that if he died or was unable to finish the work, one or more of his numerous disciples could do it for him.[36] The first volume (chapters I-IX on the electorate, legislature, prime minister, and administration) was printed in 1827 and distributed to various political figures and friends.[37] Its 'publication' in 1830 was hardly noticed; for example, no reference to it appeared in either the *Westminster Review* or the *Edinburgh Review*.[38] Bentham died in 1832 before he published the second volume, although chapter X on the Defensive Force was in print by 1830. Richard Doane, one of Bentham's former secretaries, performed the difficult task of completing the *Code* in 1841 for the Bowring edition.[39]

Bentham ran into two major problems with the later chapters. Soon after he had begun, he found that he could not complete the chapters on the judiciary (roughly chapters XII-XXV) without settling first the basic principles of judicial procedure. He began the Procedure Code as early as August 1823 and worked on it intensively between 1824 and 1827.[40] It too was not completed and Doane also prepared a version of it for the Bowring edition.[41] Furthermore, in working on the unfinished chapter on the thirteen individual ministers (chapter XI), Bentham wrote so much on the army and navy ministers that he expanded this material to form the general chapter on the 'Defensive Force' (chapter X).[42] He was assisted in the final preparation of this text by T. Perronet Thompson, together with Leicester Stanhope and James Young. The expansion of chapter X led Bentham

---

[36] Besides Dumont, the following assisted Bentham in this way on his various works: James Mill, John Stuart Mill, Peregrine Bingham, Richard Smith, George Grote, Francis Place, Richard Doane, T. Perronet Thompson, Leicester Stanhope, James Young, George Bentham, and Edwin Chadwick.

[37] See, for example, Bentham to Brougham, 2 November 1827, UC Brougham MSS 26,007.

[38] According to accounts Bentham received from Robert Heward, the publisher, fifty copies were boarded and sewn in 1830 with three copies reported sold in 1830 and ten in 1831. See BL Add. MS 33,553 fos. 301-2, 309-10.

[39] See Bowring, ix. pp. iii-iv.

[40] See UC liia, liib, liii, lv, lvi, lvii, lxi.

[41] 'Principles of Judicial Procedure' (Bowring, ii. 1-188).

[42] See the brief discussion of this material in chapter VIII below.

to conceive of the *Code* as a three-volume work with the
chapters on the military and the individual ministers forming
the second volume and the chapters on the judiciary and local
government, the third. Although chapter X was printed
before Bentham died, he did not complete the rest of the
second volume nor the third. He also devoted considerable
time to drafting the penal and civil codes which constituted
the final two of four major parts of the *pannomion*, but these
were never finished and the civil code was barely begun.

In 1822, just after he began to work on the *Code*, Bentham drafted a number of lengthy essays on constitutional
principles. Some of the material was taken from manuscripts
written earlier for other works, but much of it was drafted
especially for the *Code*. When Bentham settled down to draft
the more definite sections and articles of the *Code*, he set
these essays aside, but in the introduction to the first volume,
he referred to them and other material as possibly forming an
introduction to the three-volume text of the *Code*.[43] Doane
attempted to follow Bentham's wishes and selected a portion
of this material for the Bowring edition to constitute what he
called 'Book I' with the whole three-volume *Code* following
under the title of 'Book II'. Doane's 'Book I' was poorly
constructed and the text reflected neither the amount of
material nor the character of the essays which Bentham had
written. Although this material is drawn on at several points,
concentration is mostly on the actual text of the *Code* itself
to which Bentham devoted most of his energy. Doane's
arrangement of this material into a 'Book I' has resulted in
many scholars ignoring 'Book II' which in fact contains the
main text of the *Code*.

The influence of the *Code* on other thinkers and on
reforms in England and abroad is difficult to estimate.[44]

[43] See *Constitutional Code*, vol. I (*CW*), p. 2.

[44] See the debate over Bentham's influence on the administrative reforms in
England in the 1830s and 1840s and interpretations of the *Code* as representing
a *laissez-faire* or interventionist perspective: J. B. Brebner, 'Laissez Faire and
State Intervention in Nineteenth-Century Britain', *Journal of Economic History*,
viii (1948), 59-73; O. MacDonagh, 'The Nineteenth-Century Revolution in
Government: A Reappraisal', *Historical Journal*, i (1958), 52-67; D. Roberts,
'Jeremy Bentham and the Victorian Administrative State', *Victorian Studies*,
ii (1959), 193-210, reprinted in *Jeremy Bentham*, ed. B. Parekh, pp. 187-204;
H. Parris, 'The Nineteenth-Century Revolution in Government: A Reappraisal
Reappraised', *Historical Journal*, iii (1960), 17-37; J. Hart, 'Nineteenth-Century

Preliminary research suggests that Bentham may have had considerable influence in Latin America where he eventually thought his *Code* might be adopted.[45] But it is difficult to distinguish between Bentham's influence generally and that of the *Code* in particular, especially when Dumont's *Traités* was widely read on the Continent and in Latin America. Bentham was in direct contact, either personally or through an elaborate correspondence with numerous political leaders, codifiers, and fellow-reformers, and the extent of these contacts will become more evident as the later volumes of his correspondence are published as part of the *Collected Works*.

But even when the extent of his contacts and correspondence is revealed, it will not be easy to state what it was that brought so many practical, political men to the eccentric philosopher and hermit of Queen's Square Place. Nor is it easy to see now why so many friends and disciples were willing to devote an enormous amount of time and energy to editing the various works which he himself was unable or did not bother to complete.

Bentham was surrounded largely (though not exclusively) by lawyers and politicians. Unlike the numerous literary figures or representatives of the dissenting clergy who advocated parliamentary reform, Bentham could speak directly to lawyers who tended to be conservative in outlook and distrustful of change. He persuaded many that major legal reform was necessary and feasible and that reform on this scale could be achieved without revolution and even with the object of making the persons and property of those affected by reform more secure than before. He also bestowed on enthusiastic reformers a 'method' which became the hall-

Social Reform: A Tory Interpretation of History', *Past and Present*, xxxi (1965), 39–61; V. Cromwell, 'Interpretations of Nineteenth-Century Administration: An Analysis', *Victorian Studies*, ix (1966), 245–55; L. J. Hume, 'Jeremy Bentham and the Nineteenth-Century Revolution in Government', *Historical Journal*, x (1967), 361–75. This author favours the views of Parris, Hume, and Lord Robbins (*Bentham in the Twentieth Century*, London, 1965 and elsewhere) who rate Bentham's influence as considerable and regard the *Constitutional Code* as representing neither *laissez-faire* nor collectivism. The theme of the extent of government intervention in the economy is not raised to any extent in the *Code* and for this reason is not discussed very much here. L. J. Hume, op. cit., pp. 93 ff. traces the theme through Bentham's economic and political writings and provides a useful discussion.

[45] See note 35 above.

mark of subsequent legal and administrative reform. He brought to the study of law an analytic skill and an attention to detail not seen before. He also displayed great imagination and creativity in the numerous reforms he proposed through the years. He encouraged others to think afresh about political and legal problems. When David Roberts suggests that Chadwick was not influenced by Bentham because he investigated numerous subjects for himself, Roberts fails to appreciate that Bentham would have encouraged Chadwick to make these independent investigations.[46] This *is* the influence of Bentham—careful, independent, empirical studies of problems and detailed, workable proposals for reform. And if Chadwick displayed these traits before he met Bentham, he would have found in Bentham confirmation that these characteristics were indeed valuable and useful in planning and implementing major enterprises of reform.

In this book the *Code* is approached largely as a neglected work among Bentham's writings but important both for its ideas and as the culmination of his life and thought. It is a work which must be rediscovered and looked at in a new light, which, though containing dated references and some absurd ideas, may still be important as a classic and hence enduring text on the difficult subject of representative democracy.

II

There are a number of reasons why Bentham's *Code* should appeal to the student of contemporary democratic thought. It is true that Bentham is usually discussed as one of several 'classical' theorists of democracy, and such a classification does not necessarily serve as a recommendation. Even by showing the superiority of Bentham to James Mill and J. S. Mill, it will not necessarily be established that the *Code* contains ideas and arguments of relevance to contemporary theory. Nevertheless, in recent years the gulf between 'classical' and contemporary theory has greatly diminished, as the relevance of the former and the limits of the latter have

[46] D. Roberts, 'Jeremy Bentham and the Victorian Administrative State', in Parekh, op. cit., p. 193.

been appreciated.[47] Bentham has a good deal to add to this development. Firstly, as 'empirical' political science has discovered that it contains within itself a prescriptive bias which cannot disappear with neutral and technical termino- logy, it is interesting to find in Bentham a similar concern with neutrality of language, classification, and empirical data, but set within a prescriptive system. 'Bentham's major aim in seeking an empirical social science', writes Ian Budge, 'was the production of better policy-proposals.'[48] As political science has turned more from abstract theory to a policy orientation, Bentham's approach to theory remains an important guide. His classifications and his concern with facts are usually developed within the context of recom- mendations of policy (in this case constitutional arrange- ments). The prescriptive framework operates to keep in check and give direction to what otherwise would be an endless refinement of terms and categories with little relevance to actual political arrangements. Furthermore, Bentham's approach to theory avoids the charge that his empirical work contains a hidden ideological bias. His assumptions about politics are clearly set forth; they are embedded in the principles he seeks to establish. He is also willing to defend his prescriptions to the extent that they can be defended by referring them to the greatest happiness principle and the hierarchy of subordinate ends. Thus, he avoids the problem of covert ideological bias by using his values consciously to direct his theory.

Secondly, Bentham's approach to democratic politics incorporates what has been called a theory of élites. A major thesis underlying his argument is that all rulers, however they are chosen, form a class apart by virtue of their wealth and political power and are potentially at odds with the people whose happiness they are supposed to secure. This tendency is not overcome, in Bentham's view, by democratic govern- ment, and his overriding task in the *Code* is to determine various means to reduce the power of these élites to rule in their own interests. What is important in Bentham, however,

---

[47] See, for example, D. Thompson, *John Stuart Mill and Representative Government*, Princeton, 1976.

[48] I. Budge, 'Jeremy Bentham: A Re-evaluation in the Context of Empirical Social Science', *Political Studies*, xix (1971), 20.

is not that he anticipates élite theory but that he does so
without neglecting the constitutional doctrines of the 'classical' democratic tradition, i.e. universal suffrage, majority
rule, secret ballot, and constitutional government. He does
not see the two approaches as being antagonistic.

Thirdly, it is well known that Bentham's political theory
is related to his economic theory. Some make the connection
very strong and see in his political theory little more than a
model of the capitalist market economy consisting of individuals with conflicting interests.[49] As we shall see, he does
not approach politics as some have claimed, solely from the
perspective of a set of isolated individual consumers and
appropriators. The starting-point is more sociological and
lies in the distinction between the 'ruling few' and 'subject
many' in society. His emphasis on the individual complements
and helps resolve the political problems raised by the opposition of ruling few and subject many. His view of politics
also includes a political dimension which is distinct from and
to a great extent more comprehensive than the economic
dimension. His conception of democracy controls and directs
his economic theory even though his view of the economy
plays an important role in his political theory.

Fourthly, Bentham in several ways seems to broaden the
scope of democratic theory. He removes the emphasis one
finds in contemporary writing on the electoral system and
representation and places it on a number of diverse though
related practices designed to maximize the accountability of
ruling élites. These range from the organization of the civil
service and army, the use of records and publicity, and the
structure of bookkeeping, to the critical role of a free press.
In what is called here the 'strategy of reform' he provides an
important alternative to the party system which, in contemporary theory, is regarded as the fundamental institution
in representative democracies. Furthermore, his theory of
democracy seems to embrace different strands which have
been recently emphasized as standing opposed in the tradition of democratic thought. For example, in his emphasis

[49] See C. B. Macpherson, *The Life and Times of Liberal Democracy*, Oxford,
1977 which is discussed at length in chapter XII below. For a more moderate
version, see J. Dunn, *Western Political Theory in the Face of the Future*, Cambridge, 1979, pp. 41-2.

on security and accountability, Bentham's theory has been depicted as serving a 'protective' function as opposed to a participatory one.[50] We shall see here that his theory performs both functions without sacrificing either of them. The strategy of reform is conceived as involving the full participation of citizens in the political life of society.

Finally, Bentham provides a link for modern democratic theory not only with earlier 'classical' theories, but with the longer tradition of the legislator, enshrined in ancient thought in Solon and Lycurgus and resurrected in the political thought of the Enlightenment.[51] His transformation of Hume's descriptive utilitarianism into a critical doctrine, which none the less does not lose the empirical orientation he so admires, also places Bentham close to Aristotle. Although the philosophical differences between Bentham and Aristotle are far greater than the affinities, in one sense Bentham's careful analysis of constitutions, conceived in a wide political sense, and his search for the constitution which will bring happiness to the community it serves, renders Bentham's *Code* a worthy companion, if not a successor, to Aristotle's *Politics*. Bentham himself might have objected to the company of Aristotle, but this may only be evidence, not of a limited perspective, but of an urge to confront the problems of constitutional politics in a fresh and original fashion.

III

This book begins with a chapter on Bentham's emphasis on public opinion and the continual pressure for reform which constitutes the dynamic force within his conception of democracy. Within this context his discussions of the main classes in society, the role of the Public Opinion Tribunal, and his conception of the public interest are examined. Bentham is so identified with legal reform that it may seem natural to identify him with the view that the law is the main instrument of reform. This chapter argues that public opinion, not law, plays this important role.

Chapter III turns to the basis of Bentham's constitutional

---

[50] C. Pateman, *Participation and Democratic Theory*, Cambridge, 1970, p. 20.

[51] See J. H. Burns, *The Fabric of Felicity: the Legislator and the Human Condition*, London, 1967.

thought and begins by examining the theme of sovereignty and the way he reconciles sovereignty with democracy. The chapter also includes a discussion of his rationale, based on a conception of interests, for placing sovereignty in the people. There are few arguments in political theory which justify popular sovereignty and Bentham's argument, taken from unpublished manuscripts, is of considerable interest.

In chapter IV, Bentham's treatment of constitutional rights in the *Code* and other later writings is examined. Besides exploring his objections to bills of rights, the chapter is devoted to a detailed consideration of 'securities for appropriate aptitude', the doctrine which in the *Code* replaces constitutional rights. Although Bentham's objections to moral and natural rights are well known, little attention has been paid to the important theme of securities, developed in his later writings and especially in the *Code*.

In the chapter on 'Power' (chapter V) three related themes in the *Code* are taken up: the way constitutional power is translated into functions; the discussion of administrative chains of command; and the analysis of the place of reward and punishment in government. These important themes are examined in terms of Bentham's attempts to transform power into accountable government.

Chapters VI and VII are largely devoted to an exposition of Bentham's complex and original ideas on the problems of controlling expense and providing for full publicity for government activities. In chapter VI, the main emphasis is placed on the way he links economy to democracy and reform, and how he incorporates a democratic 'dimension' into his pursuit of the minimization of expense in government. The 'disappointment-prevention' principle, which is developed in his later writings, is discussed as a principle of justice especially relevant to cutting government expenditure in the name of reform. In chapter VII an attempt is made to show the full range of issues that he thinks is relevant to communication in government including inspection, keeping records, public criticism, and publicity.

Chapter VIII contains an exposition of the major institutions of the *Code*. Those more interested in ideas than institutions may disregard this chapter, but it is included, because no one has yet presented a summary of Bentham's main institutions. The emphasis is on material not discussed in earlier chapters, such as qualifications for suffrage and office, the organization of the army, the judiciary, and local government.

In chapters IX and X, Bentham's *Code* is compared first with James Mill's *Essay on Government* and then with J. S. Mill's *Considerations on Representative Government*. In the former an attempt is made to establish that Bentham's discussion of representation is superior to that found in Mill and, in addition, that Bentham escapes from many of the criticisms that Macaulay makes of James Mill's *Essay*. The chapter on John Stuart Mill contains a detailed comparison between the *Code* and Mill's *Considerations*. It is the first time, we believe, that a comparison of these two major utilitarian texts on representative government has been attempted.

Chapter XI is devoted to the limited object of discussing Bentham's treatment of the greatest happiness principle in the *Code* and concentrates on three issues: the 'parochial' limitation on the greatest happiness principle recently discussed by David Lyons;[52] the relationship between self-interest and sympathy; and the theme of equality. The book ends with an assessment of Bentham's contribution to contemporary democratic thought and shows how he can reply to many of the criticisms made of his theory.

In writing this book the author has been conscious of a tendency to distinguish between an earlier and later Bentham with the latter developing after 1809-10, but especially from 1817 with the publication of the first of his writings on parliamentary reform. This is not a distinction we should wish to press or see establshed in the sense that we speak of the early and late Marx. With Bentham there is remarkable continuity of thought for a man whose published writings span nearly sixty years and whose manuscripts and published works testify to an enormous output of ideas and theories. Nevertheless, there are several reasons for calling attention to the fact that the *Code* was the major work of his last years. He develops and refines the ideas and institutions of representative democracy here in a way which does not appear in the earlier writings. Even brief support for the

---

[52] *In the Interest of the Governed*, Oxford, 1973.

French Revolution and for reform in England at the time of the Revolution does not provide materials to equal the later *Code* writings in breadth or depth.[53] At the minimum, no reasonable account of Bentham's political theory or his theory of democracy should ignore the material in the later writings and especially the *Constitutional Code*.[54] Furthermore, because of the gradual deterioration of Bentham's handwriting, the manuscripts associated with the later writings have not been widely or fully explored. Bentham's attempts at devising a technical language suitable for legal codes make his later published works also difficult to read. As a result, there has been a tendency to ignore these writings in favour of the earlier ones. By calling attention to the writings of this period, it is hoped that a previous imbalance will be corrected.

The attempt has been made to approach Bentham's *Code* as a constitutional document rather than as a treatise on government written in an eccentric fashion. This has meant paying some attention to the various articles and sections and whether they are intended to be enacted or serve as suggestions or arguments in justification of enacted provisions. In the *Code* Bentham uses five different headings to the various articles: enactive (legal enactments), expositive (giving definitions), exemplificational (providing examples), ratiocinative (giving reasons), and instructional (giving instructions to the legislators). At times these become somewhat confused, but, for the most part, the different headings guide the reader to the various parts of the *Code*. Only the enactive provisions, a relatively small part of the total *Code*, would be actually adopted as laws by a state, and the other articles would provide an interpretation of and commentary on the small number of articles with the 'enactive' headings. This arrangement is part of Bentham's attempt to bring clarity to the law and to avoid widespread judicial

---

[53] See note 8 above.
[54] This has been common among many writers on Bentham's political theory. See, for example, J. Plamenatz, *The English Utilitarians*, Oxford, 2nd ed., 1958, pp. 63, 82–4; W. I. Davidson, *Political Thought in England, the Utilitarians from Bentham to J. S. Mill*, London, 1915, pp. 74–9; G. H. Sabine, *A History of Political Theory*, London, 3rd ed., 1963, pp. 694–9; H. M. Magid, 'Jeremy Bentham and James Mill', *History of Political Philosophy*, eds. L. Strauss and J. Cropsey, Chicago, 1963, pp. 621–4.

interpretation. By accepting that the *Code* is a legal document of this kind, one is able to provide a better interpretation of Bentham's ideas by working within the system as he would have it established. At numerous points, for example, a distinction is made between his enactments and his suggestions, and the use of this distinction allows us to see Bentham as less dogmatic and more creative and experimental than he often appears.

The references in the text to the *Code* are to the chapters, sections, and articles of the new edition of the first volume in the *Collected Works*. References to other texts and parts of the *Code* not yet published in the new edition are made directly, where possible, to the Bowring edition.

Chapter II

Public Opinion and the Strategy of Reform

Bentham is well known as an advocate of legal and political reform, but little attention has been paid to the emphasis he places on a continual process of reform, supported by public opinion, as an essential condition for the success of constitutional democracy.[1] The starting-point for this chapter is the way Bentham conceives the main classes or divisions in society and how he defines the task of reform. The institution of the Public Opinion Tribunal is then explored in terms of its role as the main engine of reform and in relation to Bentham's conception of the public interest. Finally, the problem of the fragility of constitutional democracy is examined and the grounds for optimism, which Bentham has in believing that reform towards democracy is possible, are assessed.

I

When Bentham speaks of the major divisions in society, he usually refers to the 'ruling few' and 'subject many' or to the 'opulent few' and 'unopulent many'. Every society possesses, he believes, a 'power-holding class'. A democracy is distinguished from a non-democracy by its power-holding

---

[1] Two useful articles by Warren Roberts anticipate some of the arguments developed here. See 'Bentham's Conception of Political Change: a Liberal Approach', *Political Studies*, ix (1961), 254-66; 'Behavioural Factors in Bentham's Conception of Political Change', *Political Studies*, x (1962), 163-79. Roberts, however, uses the more modern, neutral notion of change rather than reform. His conclusions that Bentham (a) does not believe in the inevitability of progress, (b) is an empiricist, (c) does not believe in perfection, and (d) appreciates the complexity and importance of human character, institutions, traditions, and history are basically correct, and similar ground will not be covered here. Roberts also points to Bentham's emphasis on the 'ruling few', on the importance of public opinion, and to the blend of optimism and pessimism to be found in Bentham's writings, but he does not develop these themes to any extent. His account of power in Bentham, as will be seen, differs from the one developed here.

class possessing an aptitude for the functions it performs.[2] In non-democracies, that is to say, most existing societies at the time Bentham was writing, the opulent, ruling few were unapt and ruled at the expense of the subject many.

The concept of class does not play as important a role in Bentham's thought as it does in Marx, for example, and Bentham does not clearly spell out who is included in the opulent or ruling few. But he continually dwells on this fundamental division in society which has both an economic and political dimension. It is worth noting that Bentham does not promote the interests of the middle classes as did James Mill in his *Essay on Government* which was published prior to the *Constitutional Code*.[3] Bentham simply employs the contrasts of few and many, rich and poor. In one passage in the *Code*, where Bentham is writing about the subversion of the general interest, he lists several 'subclasses' opposed to the welfare of the many.[4] These consist of the 'misemployed' and the 'unemployed'. For the former, he lists the lawyer, mercantile, and official subclasses; for the latter, the 'unemployed', he lists those possessing or expecting to possess a peerage. This list seems to include important sections of the middle class as well as the aristocracy. Where Bentham depicts the subject many, he at one point includes the 'productive classes' (including those concerned with distribution) which would incorporate elements of both the middle and lower classes.[5] Members of the middle classes may, in principle, belong to the ruling few or the subject many depending on whether or not they possess political power and do or do not produce useful goods.

The wealthy ruling class in most societies thus contains elements from both the middle class and the aristocracy. This class forms the main obstacle to reform towards constitutional democracy. In 'Securities Against Misrule', Bentham mentions

---

[2] Ch. IX, § 25, Art. 48 (*CW*), p. 433.

[3] James Mill's *Essay on Government* originally appeared in the *Supplement* to the fifth edition of the *Encyclopaedia Britannica*, iv, September 1820, less than two years before Bentham began to write the *Constitutional Code*. See *Utilitarian Logic and Politics*, eds. J. Lively and J. Rees, Oxford, 1978, pp. 51-2, 93-4. See also James Mill, *Selected Economic Writings*, ed. D. Winch, Edinburgh, 1966, p. 13.

[4] Ch. IX, § 25, Art. 47 (*CW*), p. 433. See also *Codification Proposal* (Bowring, iv, 558 and n).

[5] See Roberts, 'Behavioural Factors', p. 174 and n; Bowring, ix. 43.

the 'ultra-indigent' as well as the 'ultra-opulent' as sources of depredation in society.[6] But even here, the ultra-indigent are said to act on a very small scale when compared with the opulent. However, Bentham believes that even a good democracy must protect itself against 'popular commotion', and in the *Code* he favours the creation of a professional police force, supported by a professional army, to deal with such situations.[7] But the wealthy ruling class is corrupt, wasteful, indolent, and unwilling to accept responsibility. Bentham's problem is to persuade those who have the most to gain from the status quo to relinquish their power. This task of persuasion might be seen as one reason for the sustained shrill attack on the ruling few which runs throughout the *Code*. The rhetoric of the *Code* is designed so that those in power see what *they* take to be the tradition of ruling to which they are the rightful heirs as simply the power-seeking exploitation of the poor for the satisfaction of their own narrow interests. Bentham's attack on public support for the arts and sciences or his declaration that liberality is waste should be understood not as expressions of a philistine temperament but as part of his attack on those in public office taxing the poor or relatively poor to fund projects for the enjoyment of the rich.[8] The opulent, ruling few must abandon their veneration of established institutions and practices in light of the 'realities' which Bentham exposes.

Discrediting the rich and powerful is only part of Bentham's strategy of reform. Paradoxically, he must also enlist their support, as the success of constitutional democracy depends on the active participation of the wealthy and educated in government.[9] The poor are effectively barred from office by the pecuniary competition system where equally qualified persons compete to take office at the least

---

[6] Bowring, viii. 569. The manuscript, 'Securities against Misrule' (UC xxiv. 96-377), was written in 1822 for Hassuna D'Ghies for use in Tripoli, a state ruled by an absolute Mohammedan prince. Part of the manuscript was printed in Bowring, viii. 555-600. See also L. J. Hume, 'Preparations for Civil War in Tripoli in the 1820s: Ali Karamanli, Hassuna D'Ghies and Jeremy Bentham', *Journal of African History*, xxi (1980), 311-22.

[7] Ch. IX, § 26, Arts. 46-7 (*CW*), pp. 454-5.

[8] Ch. VII, § 4 (*CW*), p. 139; ch. IX, § 15, Art. 7 (*CW*), p. 299.

[9] See Steintrager, *Bentham*, p. 107.

salary.[10] Bentham is so anxious to induce the wealthy to participate in the system of instruction and examination for government office that while he precludes a food or lodging allowance for students on Malthusian grounds, he is inclined to support a clothing allowance to prevent 'the comparatively opulent from being excluded from the benefit of instruction, by disgust produced from the spectacle of deficiency or uncleanliness, on the part of the comparatively indigent.'[11] He also thinks of the wealthy who may otherwise be too indolent for public office as potential legislative deputes (those who act as substitutes for the legislator when he is absent or ill).[12] This enlistment of the wealthy and powerful is a prime task of the strategy of reform. The rich must be induced to calculate the advantages for themselves in participating in the democratic system.

In the *Code* Bentham not only regards society in terms of these basic divisions but also as an aggregate of self-interested individuals. The very structure of the *Code* with its careful enumeration of functions and securities would be unintelligible without the assumption that society is composed of separate individuals who are primarily self-interested and ever prone to corruption and delusion because of this partiality. Furthermore, this individualistic view of society does not preclude Bentham's other conception of society as being divided into two basic classes, and the two perspectives, one social and the other initially psychological, may easily be taken to complement each other.[13]

This view of the individual and society has always been subject to criticism. Henry Sidgwick thought that Bentham's view of man as primarily selfish would defeat the task of ever combining a group of egoists into a democratic government.

[10] Ch. IX, § 17, Arts. 53 (*CW*), pp. 352-4.

[11] Ch. IX, § 16, Arts. 53-4 (*CW*), p. 327.

[12] Ch. VI, § 23, Art. 24 (*CW*), p. 65.

[13] Cf. L. J. Hume, 'The Political Functions of Bentham's Theory of Fictions', *The Bentham Newsletter*, iii (1979), 20 ff., where it is argued that there is a shift in Bentham's later, social and political theory, as, for example, in the *Constitutional Code*, to depicting society 'as a set of interacting groups, offices, and relationships' rather than 'a mass of self-motivated individuals'. However, there is no reason why the two views are incompatible and cannot exist side by side. In qualifying his argument, Hume virtually admits that they do. Hume seems to confuse Bentham's views about the distribution of power in society with his account of human psychology.

'The difficulty that Hobbes vainly tried to settle summarily by absolute despotism', he wrote, 'is hardly to be overcome by the democratic artifices of his more inventive successor.'[14] Even though, as David Lyons has most recently shown, Bentham's limited altruism places him closer to Hume than to Hobbes, Sidgwick's comment is a familiar one in the long tradition of criticism of utilitarian thought.[15] It is true that Bentham finds that altruism plays only a small role in politics and notions of moral and civic virtue (in the Aristotelian sense) are not even entertained. But it does not follow that Bentham's ascription of egoism to individual character defeats the possibility of democratic government. Men will, for Bentham, act in the interests of the community from a number of self-interested motives, such as the desire for security or subsistence, the desire for increased power or reputation, or the fear of punishment. Egoism is no bar to action to advance the general interest.

Another factor in Bentham's thought on which most commentators do not dwell is the attitude or disposition towards reform itself which might serve to bind the democratic polity together and even replace earlier notions of civic virtue and simple patriotism. The spirit of reform is more rational than patriotism and less vague a notion than civic virtue. It is a critical, calculating spirit, manifest in a disposition to subject institutions and practices to critical scrutiny. It aims at improvement and has an optimistic, creative dimension. It is a spirit in which most people can share. The optimism of the spirit of reform is an important counterweight to the pessimistic view of man as primarily self-interested and self-aggrandizing which pervades Bentham's theory of democracy. It also enables Bentham's theory to overcome in a second sense the difficulty which Sidgwick found in Hobbes.[16]

---

[14] H. Sidgwick, 'Bentham and Benthamism in Politics and Ethics', *Miscellaneous Essays and Addresses*, London, 1904, p. 163. In 'Bentham and Democratic Theory', *The Bentham Newsletter*, iii (1979), 58, Sidgwick's criticism is raised in the conclusion, but no answer to it is provided. Here, and in chapter XI below the argument is taken a step further.

[15] Lyons, *In the Interest of the Governed*, pp. 64–9.

[16] It might be argued that the spirit of reform is already present in Hobbes's conception of reason.

II

For Bentham, the spirit of reform is most prevalent in the emanations of public opinion, and public opinion reflects and represents the public interest. We shall now examine these important themes in Bentham's political theory. Both the appeal to public opinion as a standard of legitimacy and the stimulation of public opinion as political strategy was an acknowledged part of the programme of Philosophic Radicalism in Bentham's day.[17] Throughout his writings he places considerable emphasis on public opinion and the related themes of publicity and freedom of the press. The moral or popular sanction appears with the other sanctions early in his writings, and the theme of critical inspection, central to his conception of Panopticon, might be seen as an early formulation of the principle of the Public Opinion Tribunal.[18] The Public Opinion Tribunal itself appears only in Bentham's later writings but it represents an extension of ideas held by Bentham throughout his life to constitutional democracy and politics generally.

The *Constitutional Code* contains a striking passage about the power and importance of public opinion:

To the pernicious exercise of the power of government it is the only check; to the beneficial, an indispensable supplement. Able rulers lead it; prudent rulers lead or follow it; foolish rulers disregard it. Even at the present stage in the career of civilization, its dictates coincide, on most points, with those of the *greatest happiness principle*; on some, however, it still deviates from them: but, as its deviations have all along been less and less numerous, and less wide, sooner or later they will cease to be discernible; aberration will vanish, coincidence will be complete.[19]

Two points are especially worth noting about this passage. Firstly, Bentham does not say that law, the rule of law and constitutions are the main checks to the pernicious exercise of power. Public opinion and not law plays this role. Secondly, he contends that expressions of public opinion more often

---

[17] See J. Hamburger, *James Mill and the Art of Revolution*, New Haven, 1963.
[18] See *An Introduction to the Principles of Morals and Legislation*, III. 2, 5 (*CW*), pp. 34–5; ch. IX, § 26, Art. 20n (*CW*), pp. 445n–5n; *Panopticon; or The Inspection House* (Bowring, iv. 37–172). See also chapter VII, note 2 below.
[19] Ch. V, § 4, Art. 4 (*CW*), p. 36.

than not coincide with what is for the greatest happiness of the greatest number. With respect to the first point, as the *Code* was written for a democratic government, Bentham does not fully explore here how public opinion can resist despotic government, but he does so in 'Securities Against Misrule' which was written with this problem in mind.[20] Bentham begins there by stating that publicity is the only applicable remedy against despotic government. Obviously, the remedy of legal reform is precluded by the fact that the despotic regime makes the laws. Publicity, given both to the acts of the rulers and to the opinions of the people, allows public opinion to act as a judge in relation to rulers 'and in this way exercising rule over, the rulers themselves'.[21] This 'rule' is not by 'direct mandate and coercive powers' but by 'indirect and gentle power, or in one word, influence: for in this way do our children, at an age in which nature places them under the absolute dominion of their parents, operate on the conduct of those same parents.'[22]

Nevertheless, public opinion does possess some more potent sanctions when it suffers extreme oppression. This body may be moved to action in a negative sense in withdrawing obedience from the ruler and thereby extinguishing his power or in a positive sense in ordering the 'extinction of the life of the oppressor-in-chief'.[23] Although public opinion forms an 'irregular' tribunal, it is superior to any regular, lawful tribunal of the oppressive regime in so far as it pursues the greatest happiness of the greatest number. These remarks by Bentham lend some credence to Joseph Hamburger's thesis about 'intimidation tactics' and the 'language of menace' utilized by the Philosophic Radicals.[24] But they seem somewhat out of character with the rule Bentham gives to public opinion of exercising a gentle influence over rulers. In the *Constitutional Code* Bentham does not refer to these ultimate sanctions.

Turning to the second point stressed in Bentham's depiction of public opinion in the passage above, the way it generally

---

[20] See Bowring, viii. 561-72.
[21] Ibid., p. 561.
[22] Ibid.
[23] Ibid., p. 562.
[24] See Hamburger, op. cit., pp. 48-111, esp. p. 51.

coincides with the greatest happiness, we must ask if such a statement is based on unwarranted 'enlightenment' assumptions about progress and civilization which have little credence in the twentieth century. In a similar vein Bentham suggests in the *Code* that public opinion is not corruptible.[25] To make these suggestions may seem nowadays highly naïve and even dangerous.[26] Nevertheless, Bentham's position is not without some merit. In the first place, in consulting public opinion one is more likely, even if he does not consult a majority in society, to consult more people than the members of the ruling few. In this sense public opinion might be closer to what the greatest number would consider would make them happy than would be the case with the opinion of the rulers. Secondly, Bentham may be speaking in a matter-of-fact way about popular movements for reform which in his view pressed for changes (universal suffrage, annual parliaments, etc.) which he believed could be justified in terms of the greatest happiness of the greatest number.[27]

Thirdly, and most importantly, in saying that public opinion is incorruptible, Bentham may mean simply (a) that the people lack the specific instruments of corruption possessed by rulers, and (b) that it is impossible to corrupt, i.e. to buy off, for example, everyone in society. Only a few in society can actually be corrupted. Bentham would admit that the people can be downtrodden, kept in ignorance, and deluded by regimes antipathetic to their interests. But corruption requires political and economic power, and the subject many can be distinguished from the ruling few by the fact that they do not possess the power to corrupt others.

Bentham calls the instrument through which public opinion is expressed the Public Opinion Tribunal. He is aware that such an institution is a 'half and half imaginary tribunal' and to speak of it as a judicial body or as functioning

---

[25] Ch. IX, § 15, Art. 34 (*CW*), p. 304.

[26] Cf. Bentham's *The Book of Fallacies*, London, 1824 (Bowring, ii. 453-4), where Bentham criticizes the Burkean view that the people are corruptible or possess some kind of original sin.

[27] In 'Securities Against Misrule', Bentham admits that there are divisions within public opinion, but he feels that these will be overcome with increased literacy and urban life. See Bowring, viii. 569-70.

analogously to a judicial body is 'the offspring of imagination and language'.[28] In Bentham's terminology, the Public Opinion Tribunal is a fiction, though a useful one.[29] He uses the conception to depict the main force for reform in both democratic and non-democratic societies. It consists of all members of society and everyone who might have an interest in the society.[30] At times Bentham depicts its relationship to the community as analogous to the relationship between the 'committee of the whole house' and the House of Commons in English parliamentary practice.[31] The Public Opinion Tribunal is thus a committee to which everyone in society belongs. It expresses itself through a series of sub-committees, for example, audiences at legislative and judicial sittings, audiences at public meetings and theatrical performances and through those who in speeches and writings take up political matters.[32] The most important institution is that of the press through which the Public Opinion Tribunal functions most effectively.[33] In listing the functions of the Public Opinion Tribunal within a constitutional democracy, Bentham emphasizes four: the statistic, censorial, executive, and melioration-suggestive.[34] The statistic function is exercised by gathering facts and evidence 'of a nature to operate, as grounds for judgment, of approbation or disapprobation, in relation to any public institution, ordinance, arrangement, proceeding or measure, past, present, or supposed future contingent, or to any mode of conduct, on the part of any person, functionary or non-functionary, by which the interests of the public at large may be affected.'[35] The censorial function is exercised by expressions of approval or disapproval made on the basis of the evidence collected through the

---

[28] Ibid., 561, 563.

[29] Ibid., p. 563.

[30] In 'Securities Against Misrule', Bentham seems to limit membership of the Public Opinion Tribunal to members of the particular community (ibid., 566), while in the *Constitutional Code* (Ch. V, §4, Art. 2, *CW*, p. 35), anyone in the world interested in a particular issue may be considered a member.

[31] Bowring, viii. 561-2.

[32] Ch. V, §4, Art. 3 (*CW*), pp. 35-6.

[33] See ch. VI, §25, Art. 50 (*CW*), pp. 86-7; ch. IX, §25, Arts. 29-30 (*CW*), p. 427.

[34] Ch. V, §5, Arts. 1-4 (*CW*), pp. 36-7. Bentham later adds the inspective function in ch. IX, §25, Art. 12 (*CW*), p. 423.

[35] Ch. V, §5, Art. 1 (*CW*), p. 36.

exercise of the statistic function.[36] By the executive function Bentham means the action of public opinion as moral reward and punishment taking place within the law and consisting of performing or withholding good or evil actions.[37] Finally, the melioration-suggestive function is exercised by proposing new arrangements where practices or institutions are found in need of reform.[38]

Bentham depicts the Public Opinion Tribunal as a judicial body which applies the moral sanction to people and institutions. At times, he develops the analogy further. At one point he speaks of the Public Opinion Tribunal in terms of a jury; at another, of public opinion itself as a system of law superior to the Common Law.[39] Seen as a judicatory, Bentham believes that the Public Opinion Tribunal acquires the substance of reality in spite of its fictitious appearance.[40]

One important aspect of Bentham's treatment of public opinion is the way he speaks of it in a 'collective' sense. It is true that in 'Securities Against Misrule', he declares that public opinion is formed by the aggregate of the opinions of the members of society.[41] Nevertheless, he seems to regard the 'sub-committees' of the whole Public Opinion Tribunal as though the parts of the whole express themselves in a way that reflects the disposition of the whole body of public opinion. That is to say, an audience at a public meeting, for example, will tend not to express a particular interest but will represent the public interest. Or, at the minimum, its particular interest will on many points coincide with the public interest. In the *Code* Bentham does not explain how the sub-committees of the Public Opinion Tribunal represent or speak for the public interest. Nevertheless, the Public Opinion Tribunal becomes the unique force for reform in society by representing the public interest. To gain some further insight into this problem we shall now consider Bentham's treatment of interests and especially his conception of the public interest.

---

[36] Art. 2 (*CW*), p. 36. On the significance of the censorial in Bentham, see D. Baumgardt, *Bentham and the Ethics of Today*, Princeton, 1952, pp. 24–33.

[37] Art. 3 (*CW*), p. 37.

[38] Art. 4 (*CW*), p. 37.

[39] See Bowring, ix. 41; ch. V, §4, Art. 4 (*CW*), p. 36.

[40] Bowring, viii. 563.

[41] Ibid., pp. 561–2.

III

In the *Code* Bentham presents no analysis of the concept of an interest. In one brief passage, he states that desire for pleasure and aversion to pain create motives, and motives for action create interests.[42] He makes no attempt to assess the relative importance of various pains and pleasures in giving rise to motives and interests. He simply employs the language of interests: particular interests, sinister interests, self-regarding interests, the universal interest, the general interest, the public interest, etc. Terms such as these appear frequently in the *Code* (as in Bentham's other writings) and Bentham assumes that they are perfectly comprehensible without further explanation. Bentham often uses these terms as contrasting notions to distinguish, for example, particular or sinister interests from the general or universal interest. At times, particular and sinister interests are opposed by the Public Opinion Tribunal. For example, if sinister interests frustrate and retard the introduction and progress of the system of instruction, the Public Opinion Tribunal is called upon to urge its commencement and progress.[43] The Public Opinion Tribunal thus represents the public interest.

It is well known that for Bentham the public interest is the sum of the interests of the members of the community, but it does not follow that the aggregate of whatever the individual members see as being in their interest at a particular time is in the public interest. The interests of the members of the society at a given time is an empirical conception to be discovered by consulting these individuals. The public interest is a normative conception defined in terms of the greatest happiness of the greatest number. The link between individual interests and the public interest is established by Bentham by his argument that at least four ends, subordinate to the greatest happiness of the greatest number, are in each person's interest and also in the public interest: security, subsistence, abundance, and equality. Of these, security and subsistence are primary and equality and abundance are secondary. Although Bentham favours equality, it is subordinate as an end to security and to maintain security may

---

[42] Ch. IX, § 25, Art. 1 (*CW*), p. 419.
[43] Ch. IX, § 17 (conc. inst.) Art. 1 (*CW*), pp. 362-3.

require considerable inequality in society. Similarly, subsistence is a more basic goal than abundance.[44]

Bentham believes that security and subsistence and then
abundance and equality can be justified as being in the
public interest. He also believes that the greatest number in
society do in fact desire these goals as well. They may not know
how to achieve them; they may be misled by unscrupulous
rulers; and they may even seek for a time to pursue their own
self-interest at the expense of others' security, subsistence,
etc. But these facts would not, for Bentham, defeat his
contention that for the most part and for most of the time
the majority in a society would seek goals like security and
subsistence. He often contrasts with this aspiration the
tendency of existing ruling classes to favour other goals like
glory, honour, and empire.

It is important to note that Bentham does not expect
the individual to sacrifice his private interest to that of the
public interest. This is, for Bentham, 'the language of senti-
mentalism'.[45] When it is said that a person has sacrificed
his private interest for the public good (e.g. when a man takes
a reduction in salary in order to assume public office), Bentham would contend that he is merely substituting one
private interest (in power and reputation) for another
(wealth). He does not deny that it is possible to make such
a sacrifice, but only that it is extremely rare for any genuine
sacrifice to be made. Thus, the individual who has an interest
in glory or empire only substitutes one private interest for
another when he seeks security or abundance as goals. But
in seeing his interest in security, for example, his private
interest coincides with the public interest, and the actions
he takes to maximize his security will benefit both himself
and the public.

The question which naturally arises at this point is the
extent to which Bentham thinks that government has to
compel men to see that their private interests coincide with
the public interest on the several points we have identified.

[44] See, for example, the discussions in *Leading Principles of a Constitutional
Code, for any State*, London, 1823 (Bowring, ii. 269-72)); and Bowring, ix.
11-18. Further discussions of security and the relationship between security and
liberty appear in chapters IV, XI, and XII below. Chapter XII also takes up the
problem of reconciling individual interests with the general interest.
[45] Ch. IX, § 26, Art. 36 (*CW*), p. 451.

Bentham obviously believes that it is the task of government to join duty with interest where no natural identity of interests occurs. Given the close conceptual connection between security and a negative view of liberty (freedom from oppression, want, etc.) one might argue that compelling an individual to regard security rather than theft or killing, for example, as being in his interest is, in forcing him to be secure, 'forcing him to be free'. 'Was the radical individualist', asks J. A. W. Gunn, 'really a precursor of what is sometimes called "totalitarian democracy"?'[46]

Bentham himself would not have wished for such an outcome to his theory. He believes that the people themselves will largely seek security and subsistence as ends so long as they are not misled by corrupt government and sinister interests. This might be seen as a correlate to the view stated above that the people lack power and hence would naturally seek security as a defence against possible oppression. Bentham believes that the main problem for the people is to ensure that governments secure ends like security and subsistence rather than ends which are detrimental to the public interest. The problem of sinister interests lies more with governments than with the people.

Nevertheless, M. H. James has recently argued that Bentham may not have been sufficiently aware of the possibility of coalitions of sinister interests in a reformed democratic system based on universal suffrage. The majority in such a regime might not represent the public interest.[47] It is true that Bentham believes that through the use of the secret ballot in legislative elections, electors will tend to consider the public interest rather than sinister interests.[48] If voting is not secret those dependent on the rich and powerful for employment, as tenants, or in other respects might hope to advance their personal interests by selling their votes or might serve a particular interest by voting as they are told. But with the secret ballot, no one can be certain of how a

[46] J. A. W. Gunn, 'Jeremy Bentham and the Public Interest', *Canadian Journal of Political Science*, i (1968), 408.

[47] M. James, 'Public Interest and Majority Rule in Bentham's Democratic Theory', *Political Theory*, ix (1981) 49–64. As Thompson, pp. 68–9 has pointed out, this criticism of Bentham appears earlier in J. S. Mill. See also p. 72.

[48] Ch. VIII, § 11, Art. 6 (*CW*), pp. 163–4; *Bentham's Radical Reform Bill* (Bowring, iii. 558–9).

person votes (whatever he may say), and a voter will see no advantage in trying to advance his interest in buying or selling votes at the expense of the general interest. Thus, the secret ballot will tend to lead the voter away from concern with immediate profit for himself and may incline him to consider his interests in relation to the public interest in security, subsistence, prosperity, and equality. Although Bentham believes that the secret ballot, together with the system of representation and other influences, give rise to an opportunity to advance the public interest at the expense of sinister interests, he does not preclude the possibility of sinister interests attempting to use such a system to advance their ends. For this reason, he does not depend on the electoral system alone to secure the greatest happiness of the greatest number in society.

Even with regard to voting, Bentham is less sure about using the secret ballot in others kinds of elections, because its use precludes the scrutiny and influence of the Public Opinion Tribunal. In the *Code* he proposes to experiment with both secret and open voting and a combination of the two to see which produces the best results.[49] In discussing whether or not to use secret or open voting in the election of the prime minister by the legislature, Bentham can see advantages in open voting which enables the Public Opinion Tribunal to exercise its influence on behalf of the public interest. Under a secret ballot Bentham notes that the vote is subject to the 'seductive influence' of other deputies and candidates. In an unpublished manuscript connected with the part of the *Code* dealing with examinations and choice of candidates for the civil service, Bentham suggests two maxims. If personal interest is not likely to be adverse to the interest of the majority of the community, the secret mode is preferable. The regard for the public interest will have 'nothing to antagonise with'. Where personal interest is likely to be adverse to the interest of the majority, the open mode is preferable so that control by the Public Opinion Tribunal can enter.[50] In these examples, we can see how much emphasis Bentham places on the influence of the Public Opinion

---

[49] See ch. VIII, §8, Arts. 1-6 (*CW*), pp. 157-9; ch. IX, §16, Arts. 24-32 (*CW*), pp. 318-21.
[50] UC xxxix, 50-1 (16 April 1824).

Tribunal as representing the public interest. His unqualified support for the secret ballot in legislative elections is based on the belief that the Public Opinion Tribunal cannot supervise the electorate. Nevertheless, it is the Public Opinion Tribunal which represents the people (including the electorate) as the main champion of the public interest. In his discussion of sinister interests, James omits to consider the important role of this institution in a democracy in opposing coalitions of sinister interests.

IV

Bentham's Public Opinion Tribunal is thus a major force for reform in most societies and has a special role to play within a democratic society (as depicted in the *Constitutional Code*) in securing the people against oppression and corruption even from their democratically elected rulers. In providing these securities, it is clear that he believes the Public Opinion Tribunal to be as important as, if not more important than, the electoral system itself in securing the democratic system and in representing the public interest. Throughout the *Code* at every opportunity where publicity, keeping records, and inspection is possible and useful, Bentham invokes the Public Opinion Tribunal to act in the public interest.

Nevertheless, Bentham is well aware of the difficulty of establishing democratic regimes and in maintaining them once they are established. In new democratic states (he hoped that his *Code* would be adopted in Greece and in South America), he realizes that men of ability and experience are rare though the need for them is especially great. Those able to lead revolutions and establish new governments possess some ability, but are often deficient in what Bentham calls moral aptitude. They tend to favour themselves and their personal connections at the expense of the public generally.[51] They also tend to perpetuate themselves in office by various devices in connivance with the administration and judiciary so that what begins as a representative democracy progresses

---

[51] Ch. VI, § 25, Arts. 42-3 (*CW*), pp. 83-4.

to a Monarchico-Aristocratical form of Government, working by fear and corruption, and thence to a despotic Monarchy, with its standing army, working by fear alone, without need of corruption: every thing going on from comparatively good to bad, and from bad to worse, till the maximum of what is bad is reached, and, bating the chance of a violent revolution, perpetuated.[52]

Besides the difficulty of finding and educating men of ability to govern in new states, Bentham at times suggests, in a way reminiscent of Book V of Aristotle's *Politics*, how simple changes in a constitution amount to changes in regime. If, for example, the legislature fails to elect a new prime minister before the expiration of his term of office, the constitutional democracy tends to become a monarchy or aristocracy.[53] If the secret ballot is compromised and legislative elections made public, 'a constitution, democratical in *appearance*, may be aristocratical in effect'.[54] If the prime minister possesses the power arbitrarily to confer titles of honour, 'sufficient then might this one instrument be, for the conversion of the here-proposed commonwealth into an arbitrary monarchy'.[55]

Bentham proposes no institutional safeguards to prevent the legislature from passing laws which might undermine the constitution.[56] He specifically precludes the judicial review of legislation, even where the legislation might appear to diminish the power of the constitutive authority. Judicial control over legislation conflicts with legislative 'omni-competence' and the latter principle is paramount. The people, themselves, are left to remove and, if necessary, initiate the legal punishment of members of the legislature who support anti-constitutional offences.[57] It is thus up to the people to identify and oppose anti-constitutional measures. In one passage in the *Code*, Bentham identifies as an example of an anti-constitutional offence any attempt to prohibit, restrict, or tax political literature and especially newspapers and periodicals.[58] It is here that the people and especially

---

[52] Art. 46 (*CW*), p. 85.
[53] Ch. VIII, §5, Art. 4 (*CW*), p. 156.
[54] Ch. VIII, §11, Art. 6 (*CW*), p. 164.
[55] Ch. IX, §15, Art. 35 (*CW*), p. 305.
[56] See ch. VI, §2, Art. 2 (*CW*), p. 45, but see the discussions of sovereignty and securities below, in chapters III and IV.
[57] Ibid.
[58] Ch. V, §6, Art. 3 (*CW*), pp. 40-1.

the Public Opinion Tribunal find their strength and weapons. Nevertheless, as we have seen, Bentham does not pretend that these weapons are sufficient to enable democratic constitutions to resist determined efforts at destruction or internal corruption.

In spite of his belief in the fragility of constitutional democracy, Bentham also believed that a number of factors supported a widespread movement towards reform and democracy. Firstly, there was the example of the United States (called by Bentham the 'Anglo-American United States'), where a democratic constitution was established and functioning well. Bentham realized that in many respects the case of the United States was unique. He made an exception of it when he described the numerous difficulties of other new states, as it 'sprung peaceably, as if in the way of child-birth, out of already established parent states, under the Anglo-American Confederacy.'[59] Throughout the *Code* Bentham often referred to state and national constitutions, but he did not use the United States as a model on which his own *Code* was based. His positive references to American constitutional practice were usually designed to show that certain provisions which he advanced were realistic and practical. For example, in arguing for a short legislative term, he referred to the practice in state constitutions where none was longer than a year, and to the House of Representatives which had a two-year term only because of the difficulties of distance and travel.[60] In proposing that the civilian prime minister had extensive powers as commander-in-chief of the defensive force, Bentham referred to still more unlimited powers possessed by the American president who was also not necessarily a military man.[61] He found support for his proposal that the prime minister proposed laws to the legislature in a similar American practice.[62]

He treated in the same way the American practices of one cabinet head for each department, simplicity in the diplomatic structure, and the minimization of expense in grades in the

---

[59] Ch. VI, §25, Art. 43 (*CW*), pp. 83-4. See D. P. Crook, *American Democracy in English Politics 1815-1850*, Oxford, 1965, pp. 11-68.
[60] Ch. VI, §22, Art. 6 (*CW*), p. 59.
[61] Ch. VIII, §2, Art. 11n-12 (*CW*), p. 151 and n.
[62] Ch. VIII, §3, Art. 6n (*CW*), p. 153n.

military service.[63] This view of Bentham's use of the American
example is confirmed when we look at the criticisms he made
of it. He blamed a good deal of the failings of the American
constitution on 'unreflecting imitation' of English practices,
such as in spending less than two-fifths of the year in attendance at the legislature or in the adoption of the Common
Law and consequent elevation to importance of the 'lawyer
class'.[64] In the same vein may be placed his considerable
attack on the practice of two legislative chambers.[65] But not
all of his criticism was based on the slavish imitation of
dubious English constitutional practices. Regarding the Alien
and Sedition Acts, Bentham wrote: 'The *Anglo-American
States*, now so happily confirmed in the possession of a form
of Government, the only as yet fully settled one, which in an
enlightened age, deserves the name of a Government—were
for years within an ace of losing it.'[66] And when it came to
the choice of terms employed in the *Code*, Bentham presented good reasons for preferring the English 'prime minister'
to the American 'president'.[67]

The second important factor was the example of England.
Largely due to the influence of the House of Commons,
Bentham could write: 'Of all forms of Government that ever
were in existence, till *that* of the Anglo-American United
States became visible,—*that* of England, with all its corruptions, was, beyond comparison, the least adverse to the
only defensible end of Government.'[68] However, any positive
words Bentham had to say about England were based on the
efficacy of the Public Opinion Tribunal rather than on any
law or institution. Under the law, wrote Bentham, the
monarch 'may kill any person he pleases, violate any woman
he pleases; take to himself or destroy any thing he pleases.'[69]
He was prevented from doing so only by the Public Opinion
Tribunal which, though lacking the power to punish or

---

[63] Ch. IX, §3, Art. 16 (*CW*), p. 177; §5, Art. 16 (*CW*), p. 206; Arts. 39, 41
(*CW*), pp. 211, 212-13.
[64] Ch. VI, §20, Art. 18 (*CW*), p. 54; §31, Arts. 28-9 (*CW*), p. 124.
[65] See J. Bentham, 'Anti-Senatica', ed. C. W. Everett, *Smith College Studies
in History*, xi (1926), 209-67.
[66] Ch. VI, §25, Art. 50 (*CW*), pp. 86-7.
[67] Ch. VIII, §1, Arts. 8-10 (*CW*), pp. 148-9.
[68] Ch. VI, §27, Art. 49 (*CW*), pp. 106-7.
[69] Ch. II, Art. 24 (*CW*), p. 25.

resist the monarch, could annoy him. And it was the Public Opinion Tribunal and not the legal system which prevented oppression in relations between government officials and the public.[70] His other main compliment to English practice, if it can be called a compliment, was that the ruling few were susceptible to receive favourably systems of education, as they ruled by delusion and corruption but ·not by keeping the people in ignorance.[71] The House of Commons, the Public Opinion Tribunal, and the absence of hostility by rulers to education were important stimulants for reform. In spite of Bentham's well-known attack on English institutions and practices throughout the *Code* as being corrupt and despotic, it is these few exceptions to the general scene of corruption which are of interest. For they lend support to Bentham's view that reform was possible, even in so corrupt a society as England.

Thirdly, Bentham was stimulated by the opportunities provided by new states in South America and the Mediter·ranean to influence the direction and content of their republican constitutions. In the original preface to the 1830 volume of the *Code*, he stated that his complete code of laws (the *pannomion*) of which the *Constitutional Code* was the most important part, was designed to benefit communities 'which have grown out of the wreck of the Spanish monarchy (not to speak as yet of 'the Portuguese) in the American hemisphere'.[72] He also hoped that in the future his work might be applicable to the British Empire.[73] Throughout the 1820s Bentham maintained an elaborate correspondence with a number of political leaders of new states in the hope of influencing the course of constitutional development. It is fair to say that the one major stimulus for progress with the *Constitutional Code* in 1823 was the prospect of its use in Greece. His hopes were not fulfilled.[74] But he was not naïve in his expectations. As we have seen, he was fully aware of the difficulties not only in persuading leaders to adopt his *Code* or other schemes but also, and more

---

[70] Ch. IX, §25, Art. 54 (*CW*), p. 436.
[71] Ch. IX, §17 (conc. inst.), Art. 1n (*CW*), p. 362n.
[72] (*CW*), p. 4.
[73] Ibid.
[74] For a full account of Bentham's hopes for the adoption of the *Code*, see the Introduction to *Constitutional Code*, vol. I (*CW*), pp. xi ff.

importantly, in the establishment of any form of successful constitutional democracy. Nevertheless, the presence of these new states attempting to establish democratic constitutions made Bentham's efforts in proposing new constitutional practices much more realistic than they might otherwise appear.

Finally, there was a widespread movement towards reform and improvement generally throughout society which Bentham translated into political terms. For example, in developing his conception of pecuniary competition for government office, he pointed to the recent widespread acceptance in England of the principle of competition with respect to the price of labour and commodities.[75] Thus, his somewhat eccentric notion of pecuniary competition can be seen more realistically as the simple application of a generally accepted principle to a new sphere. Indeed, Bentham's main complaint was that rulers often accepted that principles like this should be applied to others but not to themselves.[76]

V

A common criticism of Bentham is that he places 'an almost absolute trust in the power of logical ratiocination to persuade, and to persuade to action.'[77] If Bentham believes that the arguments and proposals of the *Constitutional Code* can in themselves, as a rational programme, be persuasive to rulers or the people, he would indeed be guilty of the naïve view which is often imputed to him. His *Code* might better be seen as a response to various movements of reform manifest through public opinion, where the reason of the legislator is joined to the aspirations of the people through the cement of reform. The view of Bentham simply using logic to persuade to political action reduces the importance of public opinion and the Public Opinion Tribunal in his thought. Nevertheless, if Bentham believes that the task of the legislator is to respond to movements of reform, it might be asked why he designs complete codes of law for whole societies. 'Bentham did not want slow, limited innovations

---

[75] Ch. IX, § 17, Art. 45 (*CW*), p. 348.
[76] Ibid., Art. 46.
[77] J. M. Robson, *The Improvement of Mankind*, London, 1968, p. 19.

that would continue to be made always', suggests Shirley Letwin, 'but one grand sweep.'[78] Bentham's strictures against the Common Law and his creation of the *pannomion* seem to suggest that his real object is not gradual reform. But his innovations, though extensive and comprehensive, are not designed simply to be imposed on a society. They are utopian creations, awaiting the dynamic force of reform to put them into practice. Bentham does not believe that the comprehensiveness of his *Code* is incompatible with a slow process of reform. The *Code* represents the end and reform, the means.

Admittedly, Bentham's conception of the Public Opinion Tribunal, on which reform depends, is not altogether clear. He might have explained more fully how he conceived of the Public Opinion Tribunal as a judicial body. Was it simply a useful analogy to suggest a critical spirit or did he take seriously his own proposal to regard public opinion as a substitute for the Common Law? An even greater difficulty arises with his argument that the Public Opinion Tribunal in some way expresses the public interest. The Public Opinion Tribunal expresses itself in many different forms and seems composed of disparate elements. What does a middle-class intellectual writing for the press necessarily have in common with a popular movement on the streets intending to execute a corrupt monarch? Bentham argues, largely from the premiss that the people lack the power to corrupt, that they are more likely to represent in their opinions the public interest. But how can these differing sources of public opinion be considered fused in a single body called the Public Opinion Tribunal? And how can the voice of the Public Opinion Tribunal be more than a confused outpouring of conflicting and disparate voices?

Bentham does not seem to have resolved these problems, but his failure does not extend to an over-optimistic view of the power of the people to rule. Unlike Aristotle, Marx, and some radical proponents of participatory democracy, he rejects claims on behalf of the people to rule or to take important decisions on policy. For Bentham, the people can have security and accountability through the constitutional system. They can share in politics to an extent by voting.

[78] S. R. Letwin, *The Pursuit of Certainty*, Cambridge, 1965, p. 6.

But the main task of the people is to direct their rulers, through public opinion and the vote, to accept reforms and advance policies that can be justified in terms of the greatest happiness of the greatest number.

Chapter III

Sovereignty and Democracy

In the text of the *Constitutional Code* Bentham does not dwell on the problem of sovereignty. Although a chapter is devoted to the subject, it is the briefest in the *Code* and consists of a few terse sentences: 'The sovereignty is in *the people*. It is reserved by and to them. It is exercised, by the exercise of the Constitutive Authority.'[1] These assertions are intended by Bentham as prescriptions as to where sovereignty ought to reside and in themselves provide no account of sovereign power. Bentham does not say that sovereignty *is* in the people, but only that it *ought* to be there. In 'Securities Against Misrule', for example, he recognizes that in absolute monarchies, sovereign power resides with the prince who makes the laws.[2] He does not find that the acceptance of this fact conflicts with his placing sovereignty in the people in representative democracies. However, Bentham's commitment to democracy requires him to separate sovereign power from the power to legislate. Some modern critics find that a version of sovereignty such as this is incompatible with the 'classical theory' of sovereignty as it appears in Bodin and Hobbes and which may be defined as 'an unlimited, supreme, coercive power which has a will and expresses itself through legislation'.[3] In this conception of sovereignty, the emphasis is placed on the necessity of a single, unified supreme power to legislate and coerce in the state. Even before he became a democrat, Bentham rejected this view of sovereignty, and we can see this rejection most clearly in the early *Fragment on Government.*

---

[1] Ch. III, Art. 1 (*CW*), p. 25.
[2] Bowring, viii. 557.
[3] *In Defense of Sovereignty*, ed. W. J. Stankiewicz, New York, 1969, pp. 3-4. 'If one believes in pure democracy, it is hard to believe in sovereignty in the classic sense. If one believes that the logic of the classical theory is essentially sound, it is hard to believe in democracy, unless the ambiguous and unsatisfactory notion of "popular sovereignty" is introduced. Perhaps a complete reconciliation is not possiblè here' (p. 6).

I

'The true scope of the Fragment on Government', writes
F. C. Montague, 'may best be expressed by calling it an essay
upon Sovereignty.'[4] However, Bentham does not in fact
dwell on the notion of sovereignty in the *Fragment*, and this
may be of some importance in understanding his position.[5]
In the well-known and often quoted passage in which
Bentham defines 'political society'—'When a number of
persons (whom we may style *subjects*) are supposed to be in
the *habit* of paying *obedience* to a person, or an assemblage
of persons, of a known and certain description (whom we
may call *governor* or *governors*) such persons altogether
(*subjects* and *governors*) are said to be in a state of *political*
SOCIETY'—the terms 'sovereign' and 'sovereignty' do not
appear.[6] Nor can the passage easily be taken out of the
context in which it appears, that is, the criticism of Blackstone's use of the terms 'society', 'state of nature', and
'original contract'. After noting a number of confusions in
Blackstone's use of these terms, Bentham reformulates Blackstone's position by defining the positive notion of 'political
society' and the negative notion of 'natural society'. What
distinguishes these two forms of society is the presence or
absence of the 'habit of obedience'. The notion of a habit
of obedience is Bentham's matter-of-fact substitute for
Blackstone's limited attempt to employ the notion of the
original contract. Bentham replaces Blackstone's formulation
with the simple observation that wherever subjects usually
are in a habit of obedience to a determinate set of rulers,
political society may be said to exist. One consequence of
this formula is that it takes the emphasis off the problem
of the origin of political society where Blackstone has tended
to place it. Bentham does take up the problem of sovereignty
later in the *Fragment* but here he is responding to Blackstone's treatment of the theme, and he does not present his

---

[4] J. Bentham, *A Fragment on Government*, ed. F. C. Montague, Oxford,
1891, p. 59.
   [5] See H. L. A. Hart, 'Bentham on Sovereignty', in *Jeremy Bentham, Ten
Critical Essays*, ed. B. Parekh, London, 1974, pp. 148 ff. Originally published
in *The Irish Jurist*, ii (1967).
   [6] *A Comment on the Commentaries and A Fragment on Government*, I.
10 (*CW*), p. 428.

own analysis. The most important discussion occurs in chapter IV where he considers Blackstone's contention that in every state there must exist a supreme authority which possesses an absolute authority to make laws.[7] After ridiculing Blackstone's rhetoric and logic, he turns to a passage which he singles out especially for comment: 'However they began, or by what right soever they subsist, there *is* and *must be* in all of them a *supreme, irresistible, absolute, uncontrolled* authority, in which the *jura summi imperii*, or the rights of sovereignty, reside.'[8] Bentham declares that here Blackstone reveals his central concern but that he does it in an obscure manner.[9] This concern is with the adjustment of claims between liberty and government. In Bentham's view Blackstone's statement regarding sovereignty does little to resolve the matter and, more importantly, would lead to inevitable conflict. On the one hand, Blackstone's declaration of sovereignty serves only to gain submission from those who seek resistance to the law. On the other hand, his earlier remarks about laws of nature and revelation encourage resistance. Between Blackstone's two positions Bentham believes that no solution is possible: at one pole, absolute sovereignty; at the other, a right of resistance. At this point we might expect Bentham to advance his own conception of sovereignty, but instead he first argues that the employment of the principle of utility can resolve the problem created by Blackstone's concept of sovereignty. The principle of utility requires a calculation of the 'probable mischiefs' of resistance as opposed to the 'probable mischiefs' of submission to any particular law.[10] This calculation can be discussed by opposing parties, evidence from the past and relevant facts can be set forth, and, in theory as well as practice, a dispute such as this about a law is more likely to be settled.

Just as with the earlier treatment of political society, Bentham does more than replace Blackstone's formulation with a clearer one. He replaces what has become in

---

[7] Ibid., IV.1-2, p. 474.
[8] Ibid., IV.13, p. 480, quoting from W. Blackstone, *Commentaries on the Laws of England* (1765-9), I.48-9.
[9] Ibid., IV.14-15, p. 480.
[10] Ibid., IV.21, p. 484.

Blackstone's hands at best an *a priori* doctrine or at the worst mere rhetorical assertion with a matter-of-fact account of the same phenomena. Political society is not founded on an original contract or similar principles, but rather we can easily say that a political society exists so long as the habit of obedience persists. Similarly, the conflict between liberty and government power need not be an unresolvable conflict of principle, but is a resolvable one of utilitarian calculation. This transformation of the problem of sovereignty is perhaps more important than Bentham's suggestions regarding the character of sovereignty. Although Bentham does not reject the association of sovereignty with a supreme coercive authority or with a supreme legislative authority, he seems anxious to avoid rigid categories and especially to avoid placing himself in a position similar to that of Blackstone where sovereign power on the one hand confronts individual rights on the other. Bentham's few remarks on the character of sovereignty reveal it to be a more flexible notion designed to serve more modest ends. H. L. A. Hart has noted that Bentham's early view of sovereignty (unlike that of Austin) incorporates the notions of the legal limitation and division of sovereign power and the possibility of a plurality of sovereigns with each possessing full sovereign power.[11] Bentham incorporates these ideas because he recognizes that there are or were states where these characteristics of sovereignty have existed and his conception of sovereignty is sufficiently flexible to cover these actual cases.

II

For the most part sovereignty means for Bentham the authority to make laws.[12] However, once Bentham in the *Code* places sovereignty in the people, he can no longer see sovereignty in this light. Instead he declares that the legislature is 'omnicompetent':

The Supreme Legislature is omnicompetent. Coextensive with the territory of the state is its local field of service; coextensive with the field of human action is its logical field of service.—To its power,

---

[11] Hart, 'Bentham on Sovereignty', in Parekh, op. cit., p. 147.
[12] *Of Laws in General*, ed. H. L. A. Hart, London, 1970 (*CW*), p. 1.

there are no limits. In place of limits, it has checks. These checks are applied, by the securities provided for good conduct on the part of the several members, individually operated upon.[13]

The term 'omnicompetent' may well have been invented by Bentham, and the first use recorded in the *Oxford English Dictionary* is Bentham's. And if, by chance, he did not invent the term, he must surely have been the first person to use it in place of sovereignty.[14] In calling the legislature omnicompetent, Bentham avoids any direct reference to absolute power. The omnicompetent legislature is not omnipotent. The main feature of sovereign power which he ascribes to the legislature is that it is unlimited. It is not limited territorially within the state and may legislate regarding any activity in it. More importantly, possessing unlimited power, no act of legislation should be considered null and void. The legislature is not bound by the constitution or by any enactments of previous legislatures. Nevertheless, the unlimited power of future legislatures places certain limits on the present one in that no existing legislature can necessarily legislate for the future.[15] Furthermore, Bentham proposes that acts of previous legislatures are confirmed unless the present legislature acts to change them.[16] But, if a legislature makes a contract with a person or another government, and afterwards does not see fit to observe it, it cannot be compelled to do so by any court.[17] The only remedy lies with the sovereign constitutive authority which can remove the legislators from office.

Bentham justifies his provision for unlimited legislative authority by arguing that an omnicompetent legislature is most directly responsive to the electorate. With omnicompetence there need be no delay by the legislature or any excuse which would prevent action being taken in accordance with the will of the electorate. Nevertheless, it might be argued that in

[13] Ch. VI, § 1, Art. 1 (*CW*), pp. 41-2.
[14] Dicey, for example, has to distinguish between two kinds of sovereignty, political and legal, in making a similar distinction between sovereign electors and a sovereign parliament as two sources of supreme power in the state. A. V. Dicey, *Introduction to the Study of the Law of the Constitution*, London, 5th ed. 1897, pp. 69 ff., 358.
[15] Ch. VI, § 1, Art. 2 (*CW*), p. 42.
[16] Ibid., Art. 3.
[17] Ch. VI, § 2, Arts. 1-11 (*CW*), pp. 45-7.

giving omnicompetence to the legislature but retaining sovereignty in the people, Bentham is falling into the same difficulty that he earlier found in Blackstone. The omnicompetent legislature may see its role as one of directing the people rather than being directed by them. And the people might conceive of their power in terms of rights which they possess. Bentham does not deny that the legislature might substitute omnipotence for omnicompetence, but it is the latter and not the former which he grants to it. And the obstacle to omnipotence being assumed by the legislature lies not with rights but with what Bentham has called 'securities for appropriate aptitude'. Securities, as we shall see in chapter IV, are devised by Bentham to replace rights which directly limit legislative power. Securities are indirect means of preventing the legislature from abusing its power. The Public Opinion Tribunal, acting through widespread publicity and criticism, as we have seen, is an important source of securities against the legislature. The proposed short term of office for legislators is another, as is the power of the electorate to remove individual legislators from office.[18]

Bentham does not claim that in every state there is an omnicompetent legislative power. He would not agree with S. I. Benn's location of 'omnicompetence' in the amending organ of the American constitution (Congress plus three-fourths of the States).[19] For Bentham, the legislature ought to be omnicompetent, but most legislatures were not. He was well aware that his doctrine conflicted with the constitutional separation of powers, bill of rights, and federal system of the United States, but he believed that an omnicompetent legislature was superior and could be justified on utilitarian grounds. However, it would be pointless to look for an omnicompetent legislature in every state as if omnicompetence was a necessary characteristic of legislatures. Legislatures might possess the authority to make laws while sharing this authority with other bodies. The legislature would not be omnicompetent but it would still be a legislature.

---

[18] A full list of securities applying to the legislature may be found at ch. VI, § 31, Arts. 42-5 (*CW*), pp. 130-3.

[19] S. I. Benn, 'The Uses of "Sovereignty"' *Political Studies*, iii (1955), reprinted in Stankiewicz, op. cit., pp. 76-7. Note that Benn adopts Bentham's term.

III

It was perhaps inevitable that once Bentham favoured representative democracy, he would have difficulty combining the association of sovereignty both with the power to legislate and with a supreme directing power in the state. But because he did not formulate this notion of a supreme power in as rigid a manner as Blackstone did, he found little difficulty in depicting the people as sovereign and the legislature as omnicompetent. J. H. Burns has argued that some important aspects of Bentham's transfer of sovereignty to the people in the *Constitutional Code* were anticipated as early as the *Introduction to the Principles of Morals and Legislation*. Here, writes Burns, Bentham (a) asserts the 'fiduciary character' of supreme power; (b) recognizes that under non-autocratic rule sovereign power should be divided into executive and legislative power; and (c) recognizes 'a power anterior to that of the sovereign' which could 'invest determinate persons with the supreme power itself'.[20] These notions reappear when Bentham makes the important shift in the *Code* to place sovereignty in the people. Nevertheless, perhaps the change in doctrine is more important than the continuity. Burns sees the change between the early *Introduction* and the later *Code* as threefold: (a) sovereignty becomes no longer a power to legislate; (b) it is no longer a power to execute and administer the laws; and (c) the concept of limitation by convention or law disappears from the argument, 'for what limits could be relevant to a Benthamic people pursuing by majority rule and representative institutions the greatest happiness of the greatest number?'[21] The first two changes are obvious. The sovereign people possess neither legislative nor executive power. However, that Bentham thought that the sovereign people possessed unlimited power is far from clear. Burns tends to dismiss the functional limitations on the sovereign people (e.g. that their power is limited to electing and dismissing various

---

[20] J. H. Burns, 'Bentham on Sovereignty: An Exploration', *Bentham and Legal Theory*, ed. M. James, Belfast, [1974], pp. 138-9, reprinted from the *Northern Ireland Legal Quarterly* xxiv (1973). See *An Introduction to the Principles of Morals and Legislation*, XVI. 54n. (*CW*), p. 263.

[21] Burns, 'Bentham on Sovereignty', in James, op. cit., p. 149.

authorities) as not involving a direct procedural limitation.[22] Presumably, the sovereign people, using the limited powers to appoint and dismiss, can act via the majority and in pursuit of the greatest happiness without any limitation. Burns's analysis ignores the fact that these 'functional' limitations on the soveriegn people are created by virtue of the other authorities in the state: legislature, judiciary, and administration. Although the sovereign people in a limited sense direct these other authorities in appointing and/or dismissing them, they in turn limit the activities of the people. Put simply, the sovereign people obey as well as direct the government. Furthermore, the sovereign constitutive authority in its electoral capacity consists of citizens only, people, who, by virtue of the constitution (and Election Code) and being mature, male and literate, have the right to vote. The very notion of a constitutive authority based on qualifications for citizenship and acting according to a constitution implies limitations. It is true that the other authorities in the state are designed to be more responsive to the sovereign people than was the case in the United States. But this is not to conceive of an unlimited sovereign power in the people in Bentham's plan.

   Finally, Bentham's proposals for popular sovereignty in the *Code* are prescriptive, and it does not follow from his prescriptions that the supreme power in society cannot in fact be limited by express convention. Bentham would hold that governments thus limited are still sovereign governments.[23] Indeed, Bentham himself provides for the adaptation of the *Code* to a federal structure which might limit in important ways the exercise of popular sovereignty.[24]

IV

One of Bentham's most interesting contributions to a theory of sovereignty is his argument in justification of popular sovereignty. This material was written as 'Rationale' for the

[22] Ibid.
[23] See *A Comment on the Commentaries and A Fragment on Government*, IV. 34-5 (*CW*), p. 489.
[24] Ch. VI, § 3, Art. 5 (*CW*), p. 47.

brief assertion of popular sovereignty quoted above but was eventually dropped from the published *Code*. His editor, Richard Doane, used some of the manuscripts in his 'Book I' in the Bowring version, but his selection and arrangement of the manuscripts resulted in a confused and inadequate discussion.[25] In the manuscripts Bentham sets out to argue that the people have a greater aptitude for sovereign power than any other person or group, and especially a monarch. This argument, nearly obscured in the Doane version, is presented in a series of manuscripts written in August 1824.[26]

Bentham approaches the justification of popular sovereignty through his conception of moral aptitude, but his notion must not be confused with traditional ideas of morality and virtue. By moral aptitude he means specifically the desire to secure 'to the greatest number, the maximum of happiness'.[27] In this sense, he believes that the people are morally apt (or are not deficient) for the exercise of sovereignty. In the 1824 manuscript he proposes to 'prove' this assertion, and he first sets out the people's case and then the monarch's. What Bentham means by 'proof' in this context is not clear, but he adopts the language of 'desires' and 'interests' and attempts to develop an argument using these notions. It is worth emphasizing that Bentham does not use the argument here, which is often imputed to utilitarians, that each man is the best judge of his own interests and therefore is best placed to decide who should be his rulers and when one set of rulers should be dismissed and replaced with another. The argument supporting the aptitude of the people is different. The people's case consists of two main arguments. Firstly, each person desires his own happiness and endeavours to secure this at the expense of that of everyone else. But as each man tries to achieve this end, he runs into the opposition of everyone, and his own endeavours are without success. However, in so far as the pursuit of his own happiness coincides with that of others, or does not thwart theirs, the endeavour of each assists that of all:

---

[25] See Bowring, ix. 96-8.
[26] UC xxxvii, 387-412 (22-4 August 1824), xxxviii, 216-19 (25 August 1824).
[27] UC xxxviii, 216.

In the language of interest, each has a particular interest; all have a
common interest: what is by all believed to be the common interest
of all, is endeav[our] ed to be promoted by all. [E]ach particular
interest is opposed by those and those only, by whom it is regarded
as adverse to their own.[28]

It is tempting to invoke in this context Rousseau's distinction
between the 'general will' and the 'will of all' but Bentham's
distinction is not like that of Rousseau.[29] Bentham accepts
that on all occasions the individual would wish to advance
his own interests *at the expense of* those of others, and this
premiss becomes important in his later critique of the moral
aptitude of the monarch. Thus, each individual must have
some reason or incentive to advance only those interests
which coincide with the common interest. The first incentive
is that by and large the individual, following his own interest
at the expense of others, will encounter the opposition of
others and will not be successful. The second is that in con-
forming to the common interest he will gain more not only
by his immediate success, but he will also gain by participating in the aggregate happiness of society. Furthermore,
Bentham's argument is advanced from within his definition
of sovereignty. The people are not making legislative decisions, reaching some higher consensus, or expressing a general
will. Their task is simply to choose their governors and
remove them if they are not satisfied with them. The role is
a limited one and must be understood in terms of the relationship between agents or representatives and the people. This
takes us to his second main argument that in the pursuit of
the ends of subsistence, abundance, security, and equality
no individual can find a representative who depends on the
votes of a number of electors but will satisfy the desires
of that individual at the expense of every other individual he
represents. Indeed, the representative will find that his
success will depend on advancing those common interests
of a majority of his constituents where the interests of each
individual do not thwart those of others.

The main objection to these arguments is that they depend
excessively on the interests of the solitary individual as

[28] UC xxxviii, 217.

[29] See J. J. Rousseau, *The Social Contract*, trans. M. Cranston, (Penguin ed.),
1968, Bk II, ch. 3, pp. 72-3.

opposed to those of the group or party. But it must be remembered that Bentham is not giving an account of the origins of society or the basis of political obligation as we find in Hobbes, Locke, Hume, or Rousseau. He is presenting a more limited argument in justification of granting to an educated, settled electorate the power to choose and remove its governors. In thinking and in acting, this electorate may well emphasize group and party loyalties, but in their use of the secret ballot and representative system, and in some of their perceptions of their interests in security and subsistence, for example, they may also express themselves as individuals. In expressing themselves as individuals, they are called upon to make some fairly simple calculations about securing interests in relation to a choice of governors. Bentham can rightly insist that individuals, as individuals, possess the capacity to make these calculations from an individual perspective.

Bentham only claims that the sovereign people better serve the greatest happiness of the greatest number than would a monarch as sovereign. His argument against the monarch is that he has the power and is in the position to sacrifice the happiness of everyone to his own or to those who in turn would augment his happiness. He develops a number of arguments, but once having admitted that each man serves his own interest at the expense of all others, it remains only to show that the monarch, above all, is in the position to do this to the greatest extent. And if moral aptitude consists of endeavouring to secure the greatest happiness of the greatest number, then a monarch must fail in this respect. The people, with incentives to advance the common interest through a representative system, would be more likely to succeed.

Bentham develops his argument a stage further by showing that the representatives in a democracy will be more likely to become morally apt because they need to secure the votes of a majority of electors. The agents of a monarch, however, will be successful only as they sacrifice the greatest happiness to serve the monarch.[30] Thus, the moral aptitude of the people stimulates the moral aptitude of the representatives and vice versa.

[30] UC xxxvii, 406-7.

The significance of Bentham's argument might be made more explicit by comparing it with the well-known argument of Rousseau.[31] For Bentham, the individual can perceive unaided the gains which he can make by advancing interests which he shares in common with the 'greatest number'. Although he accepts that law and punishment may be required to join duty with interest, that is to say, to require individuals to follow what is in the common interest, it is not at the level of the exercise of sovereign power that legal sanctions are required. Thus he avoids the idea of a sovereign power which itself compels the individual to pursue the common interest. Sovereignty is divorced from the notion of a supreme coercive force in society, and in this sense, Bentham avoids all of the ambiguity and confusion associated with Rousseau's notion of being 'forced to be free'. He also avoids the very notion of a supreme coercive force and replaces it with a more plausible empirical conception of power distributed among various institutions (judiciary, legislature, police, etc.).

Another important comparison might be made with James Mill. He, of course, recognizes the importance of the representative system as a great security for good government in the hands of the people. But, at least in the *Essay on Government*, he fails to grasp Bentham's insight, that the representative system itself may be used to justify placing sovereign power in the hands of the people. Besides making rulers accountable to the ruled, it can make the ruled an able chooser of rulers. Bentham is thus able to use the representative system to justify an extensive popular sovereignty, a step which both James Mill and John Stuart Mill hesitate to take.

Having established that the people have the moral aptitude to exercise sovereign power, Bentham then turns to argue that they possess the intellectual aptitude. He admits that the people do not possess the intellectual aptitude for governing, but only for choosing their rulers. He argues that by consultation among themselves as to who are competent judges of intellectual aptitude, those who feel unable to make a choice of governors will for the most part defer for advice to those who are able to do so.[32] He cites the success of the

[31] See Rousseau, Bk. I, ch. 7, pp. 62-4.
[32] UC xxxvii, 408.

United States as evidence that this way of choosing governors will produce no worse governors than any other, especially in comparison with monarchy. In turning to the intellectual aptitude of monarchs, Bentham first argues that intellectual aptitude must be related to moral aptitude.[33] Knowledge and judgment are beneficial according to the purposes to which they are applied, beneficial if applied to the advancement of the greatest happiness of the greatest number, pernicious if applied to the happiness of the individual at the expense of the greatest number. The monarch, who seeks only his own happiness at the expense of the greatest number, will fail with respect to the exercise of appropriate moral aptitude. Bentham's main argument is that the cultivation of intellectual aptitude requires great exertion and self-denial and that the monarch has little or no incentive to exertion. And where accident has combined supreme power and intellectual ability, as in the cases of Napoleon and Frederick the Great, their achievements have been dissipated by the separation of their intellectual ability from moral aptitude, for example, in their embarkation on wars of ambition. But for the most part monarchs have not been noted for intellectual achievement, and, even more, have been noted for widespread incompetence and insanity. Bentham never tires of setting forth a survey of the state of European monarchy in his day.

The final step in Bentham's argument in the 1824 manuscript is to establish that the people's representatives possess sufficient intellectual aptitude.[34] Bentham in part repeats what he says about the moral aptitude of representatives, that those of the people would be more likely to use their intellects in the service of the greatest number than those of the monarch. In addition, by his ignorance and indolence, the monarch lacks the incentive and intelligence to choose able advisors and agents which further diminishes the likelihood of their possessing intellectual ability.

---

[33] UC xxxvii, 409.

[34] UC xxxvii, 411. Note that Bentham does not complete the argument by dealing with active aptitude, but his argument would not differ in form from that advanced regarding intellectual aptitude.

One interesting part of this argument, which Bentham does not develop, is that the people will naturally defer to those among themselves who are able to advise on the best choice of governors. He seems to have faith in the ordinary man that he will seek the best advice before casting his vote, or at least that he will be disposed to do so unless corrupted by sinister interests. This is a limited deference, confined to the choice of governors, but Bentham seems to suggest that a similar deference to intellectual aptitude will take place generally in society in the importance he gives to the press and public opinion in the day to day operations of government. We should note of course that he does not advocate deference to *governors*, but rather the contrary; he advocates the maximum distrust of governors by the governed. His acknowledgement of a pattern of deference within the electorate is combined with a confirmation of his view that supreme power should be placed in the people. Unlike J. S. Mill, he can recognize the importance of deference without questioning the aptitude of the people to exercise sovereign power.[35]

We have seen how Bentham has taken the problem of sovereignty from the context of the related problems of order, obligation, and law in society and has transformed it into the foundation for the establishment of the best form of government, a constitutional democracy. The important question regarding sovereignty is where it ought to be located in a society, if that society is to be well governed. Popular sovereignty by no means ensures that the society will be well governed, but Bentham argues that without popular sovereignty it will never achieve this goal. Nevertheless, there must also be some protection for the individual against the abuse of power by government. Popular sovereignty may be based on the individual's perception of his interests, but other concepts and practices are necessary if these individual interests are to be secure.

[35] This theme is discussed at length in chapter X below.

Chapter IV

Constitutional Rights and Securities

Bentham's critique of rights and especially his comment on the doctrine of natural rights as 'nonsense upon stilts' is perhaps the best known part of his political thought.[1] By arguing that rights must follow rather than precede the establishment of government and law, Bentham finds no role for supposed rights which arise anterior to civil society and government. Furthermore, his theory of fictions leads him to distrust terms like 'obligation', 'right', and 'duty' as he attempts in his writings (though not always successfully) to distinguish these from what he calls 'real entities'. H. L. A. Hart also calls attention to Bentham's 'nervousness' about the very idea of rights as possibly exciting 'a peculiarly strong suspicion that the doctrine of utility was not an adequate expression of men's moral ideas and political ideals.'[2]

In the *Constitutional Code*, Bentham deals with the concept of rights briefly.[3] Rights are fictitious entities called by lawyers 'things incorporeal'. They may be understood only in relation to obligations and in this context there are two sorts of rights: the first he calls 'natural' or 'naked' which are constituted by the absence of an obligation to forbear doing something; the second are 'sanctional' or 'exclusive' and are created by an obligation on one's neighbour to forbear doing something. As for 'moral rights', he adds in a footnote: 'A thick cloud envelopes the discourse, under it endless confusion reigns—wherever they are confounded with *legal* rights'.[4] When Bentham speaks of rights in the *Code*, they are legal rights established by the *Code*. For example, the members of the Continuation Committee have the right to argue and initiate legislation but not the right to vote in the legislative assembly; members of the legislature

---

[1] 'Anarchical Fallacies' (Bowring, ii. 501).
[2] H. L. A. Hart, *Bentham* (Lecture on a Master Mind), from the *Proceedings of the British Academy*, xlviii (1960), 312.
[3] Ch. IX, §4, Arts. 7-9 and n (*CW*), pp. 187-8 and n.
[4] Ibid., Art. 9n (*CW*), p. 188n.

have the right to propose motions.[5] Only one instance in the *Code* has been found where Bentham, probably unintentionally, seems to acknowledge the existence of a universal human right. In writing of the Public Opinion Tribunal, he declares:

> To every person, elector, inhabitant or foreigner,—to every individual of the human species, belongs the right of exercising, in relation to the condition of every department of this government, and the conduct of every functionary thereto belonging, the *statistic, executive*, and *melioration suggestive* functions above-mentioned.[6]

This might be considered a legal right in so far as it imposes on the government the obligation to forbear meddling in the activities of the legally established Public Opinion Tribunal. But as most members of the human species are not under the direct jurisdiction of any one particular state, one wonders whether the rights possessed by these people are in the end moral rather than legal. Nevertheless, Bentham does not place much emphasis on rights as such in the *Code* or, for that matter, in his other writings, and he is especially opposed to a constitutional 'Bill of Rights' as existed in the United States. He eventually replaces the doctrine of constitutional rights with his own doctrine of securities for appropriate aptitude. But before considering the notion of securities, we shall first examine his objections to constitutional rights.

I

In 'Securities Against Misrule' Bentham sets forth a number of arguments to show the deficiencies of bills and declarations of rights. He objects to the language and rhetoric of rights and argues that a clear view of what is being sought is not presented. He believes that this can be expressed more simply as security against bad government or even more briefly as 'security against misrule'. When the language of rights is employed, Bentham (in what becomes a common metaphor) sees 'a cloud, and that of a black hue, [which] overshadows the whole field'.[7] He presumably means that various rights, e.g. to life, liberty, property, a fair trial, etc.,

---

[5] Ch. VI, § 24, Art. 3 (*CW*), p. 68; § 29, Art. 7 (*CW*), p. 116.
[6] Ch. V, § 6, Art. 1 (*CW*), p. 39.
[7] Bowring, viii. 557.

do not specify what is really at stake, namely, that govern-ment should be prevented from abusing its powers. The notion of 'securities against misrule' directs attention to this basic point. Bentham also emphasizes the rhetoric of con-flict and confrontation embedded in the language of rights:

> The attitude you take is restless, hostile, and uneasy. You show that you are in discontent, but you show no clear grounds for your dis-content. What you give intimation of—though even to this no ex-plicit expression is given, is—that some rights of yours have been violated, and that a determination has been formed by you not to sit still and see them violated any longer.[8]

Bentham also finds serious difficulties with the enforcement of constitutional rights. If the claim of rights is not a legal one, it is impossible, he argues, to establish that there actually is a right, and the claimant is left to argue his case until 'exhausted with vociferation and rage'.[9] If the claim of rights is a legal claim, it is easy for unscrupulous rulers to mani-pulate the legal system so that misrule takes place without the express violation of legal rights. Thus, a bill of rights runs into difficulties of enforcement both where connected and not connected with law.

Furthermore, the doctrine of constitutional rights is applicable at one level only, where the individual runs into conflict with the state. At this level, there is no way of resolving the conflict:

> For the subjects to say to the sovereign,—This or that is our right—say or do what you will—is as much as to say, you are no longer sovereign. For the sovereign to be made to say—You have such and such a right as against me, or I have not such and such a right as against you, is as much as to say, I am no longer your sovereign.[10]

Bentham seems to be repeating here the argument made against Blackstone in the *Fragment* about the incompatibility of the doctrines of supreme sovereign power and natural rights. He is able to advance this as an argument here, because 'Securities Against Misrule' was written for a Mohammedan prince who, in fact, possessed such power. Once Bentham, in the *Code*, defines and distinguishes sovereign power on a functional basis the force of his objection might appear to

---

[8] Ibid.   [9] Ibid.   [10] Ibid.

be diminished. Nevertheless, where a law duly passed by the omnicompetent legislature is disobeyed by a citizen on the grounds that his rights are violated, the head-on conflict between the individual and the state which Bentham wishes to avoid may be inevitable.

Bentham believes that the doctrine of securities which he has evolved will avoid this sort of confrontation. He conceives of securities as functioning on a different level and in a different manner than is customary with rights. Instead of confronting the sovereign himself in 'Securities Against Misrule' he attempts to curb the sovereign's agents in the way they enforce the law. He wants the sovereign to see advantages for himself in such limits placed on his agents through the improvement in the quality of his government. Furthermore the operation of securities is intended to be indirect and should not be seen by the sovereign as antagonistic to the peculiar character of his power. 'Compared with a set of provisions, bearing expressly upon the person of the sovereign', he writes, 'opposition in this mode will be analogous to that which, in machinery, is opposed by friction, compared with that which is produced by an opposing bar.'[11] 'Securities Against Misrule' is aimed at persuading an absolute monarch to accept such practices as widespread publicity in government, a free press, and the activities of the Public Opinion Tribunal. None of these checks places a barrier before government action, but they might be seen as providing important incentives to prevent misrule.

II

Bentham's conception of securities for appropriate aptitude, which is developed in the *Code*, is more extensive than securities against misrule. Appropriate aptitude may take several forms, and Bentham usually distinguishes between moral, intellectual, and active aptitude. By moral aptitude Bentham does not mean, as we have seen in chapter III, a personal capacity for virtue in the classical Aristotelian sense, but rather a regard for the greatest happiness of the greatest number. For Bentham, moral aptitude is established in

[11] Ibid., p. 594.

society not by education and the cultivation of virtuous habits but in an external sense by preventing an individual, especially an individual who possesses political office, from acting in a way which is detrimental to the greatest happiness. Although he does not dismiss the possibility of a virtuous ruling class acting from an internal cultivation of morality, the creation of such a class is, for him, an unlikely occurrence given man's strong self-regarding character, and it is the external securities for moral aptitude to which he gives the most attention. Thus, early in the *Code* in a discussion of basic principles he postulates two rules for maximizing moral aptitude:

Rule I. The sovereign power give to those, whose interest it is that happiness be maximized. Rule II. Of the possessors of subordinate power, maximize the responsibility—namely, as towards the aforesaid possessors of the sovereign power.[12]

Bentham follows this passage with a long footnote on the use of the term 'responsibility'. Using the same metaphor as he applies to moral rights, he notes that the word comes 'to us enveloped in a thick cloud' largely because most existing governments use reward rather than punishment to secure effective compliance with the laws.[13] Although government officials often use punishment rather than reward to obtain compliance with the law by citizens, they prefer reward to punishment for themselves. Bentham argues that reward, in the form of money, power, reputation, honours, etc., is the source of evil and corruption in government. In addition, reward in the form of money can be used by the receiver to avoid responsibility so that the increase in reward may mean a decrease in responsibility. Thus, for Bentham, moral aptitude means maximizing the responsibility of rulers to the ruled by means of punishment or the threat of punishment.

For intellectual and active aptitude, Bentham sets forth three basic principles: the public examination principle where each future government official passes through the system of education and competitive examination to obtain his position; the pecuniary competition principle in which equally able candidates for office compete to take a position

---

[12] Ch. II, Art. 16 (*CW*), p. 21.
[13] Ibid., Art. 16n (*CW*), pp. 21n–23n.

at the lowest salary in order to minimize public expense; and the responsible location principle where responsibility for each subordinate official is established by one or more superordinates.[14] These principles are concerned primarily with establishing competent and efficient government with clear lines of authority at the least expense.

Within the notion of appropriate aptitude Bentham thus includes principles which range from preventing the simple abuse of power to ensuring competent government. Security against misrule is only one part of the securities for appropriate aptitude forming a branch of security for moral aptitude. It is designed to ensure that a public official acts always to advance the greatest happiness in the sense that he does not, by abusing his power, threaten the security of those over whom he exercises power. The securities for intellectual and active aptitude show especially the way Bentham includes a number of positive goals not found in a constitutional bill of rights. There is no provision (except perhaps in the minimum age requirements) in the American constitution which positively provides for good government. A right to a fair trial or to due process of law means only that those in charge of the trial possess a minimum competence, and a bill of rights can provide little protection for those who suffer at the hands of the minimally competent.

III

For Bentham's attempt to replace constitutional rights with securities for appropriate aptitude to be successful, it must provide some protection against the misuse and abuse of legislative power. We have seen in chapter III that although Bentham declares the legislature to be omnicompetent, the very existence of other authorities in the state has the consequence of placing limits on legislative power. We shall now consider how the operation of securities for appropriate aptitude affects the legislature. The securities for moral aptitude might most usefully be considered under three headings.[15] Firstly, there are securities which limit power. These include, for example, the limitation of the legislative

---

[14] Ibid., Art. 17 (*CW*), pp. 22-3.
[15] See ch. VI, § 31, Arts. 42-3 (*CW*), pp. 130-2.

term to one year, the non-re-eligibility of sitting members of
the legislature for the next two or three years (except in the
non-voting Continuation Committee), and the prohibition
of secret legislative sittings (except under certain conditions).
It is arguable that these provisions do not prevent the legislature from enacting whatever laws it wishes. Within the one-
year period of office, the legislature may enact any law. If
the legislature passes a law severely restricting, for example,
freedom of speech and the right of assembly of citizens,
there is no Supreme Court to declare such a law uncon-
stitutional and no president to veto it as is the case with the
American constitution. Nevertheless, the legislators face
the prospect of their law not surviving the annual election.
They can ensure no continuity in any law and especially
those which are obviously adverse to the greatest happiness
principle. It is true that the legislature can pass a law abolishing the limited term of office, and, indeed, the whole constitution. But in circumstances like these the legislature is
abolishing itself as the constituted legislature. And if it
simply extends the legislative term (say on grounds that more
time is needed to carry out its programme) Bentham devises
other provisions for removing the legislature from office.
The limitation of the term of office to one year and the
additional check of non-re-eligibility thus provides for as
severe a limitation on legislative power as that provided by
judicial review in the American constitution.

The second kind of security is more concerned with checking the abuse of power by individual members rather than
limiting the exercise of power. For example, arrangements
for remuneration are linked with continual attendance so
that opportunities for the member of the legislature to act
corruptly and profit from his office are limited. Similarly,
the Legislation Penal Judicatory is established to try members
of the legislature who are suspected of criminal delinquency.
On another level, arrangements are set forth preventing the
disruption of legislative sittings. These checks might be seen
as providing incentives for members of the legislature to
serve the greatest happiness. Thirdly, in the provisions of
the Legislator's Inaugural Declaration Bentham sets forth
a security which limits the kind of legislation the legislature
should adopt. The Declaration is read by the member before

an assembly of constituents just after the election.[16] In it he agrees to abide by the constitution, to remain subordinate to the constitutive authority, and to seek such ends as the greatest happiness of the greatest number. The legislator does not take an oath. Bentham had long regarded an oath as a source of mischief.[17] If an oath is used traditionally to bind a person's conscience before God, Bentham seeks a different object in placing the views of the legislator before the Public Opinion Tribunal. If the newly elected member dissents from any of the provisions of the Declaration, he is required to make this clear and append his dissenting opinion to the Declaration. If his constituents find his reservations are opposed to their interests (which are embodied in the Declaration), they can remove him from office by petition and special election. If he later deviates from the principles to which he subscribes, he can also be removed. The Legislator's Inaugural Declaration contains a full statement of principles which amount to what he calls a 'moral code' and 'a map of the field of legislation'.[18] For the latter, he goes beyond the statement of general ends to be sought by legislation to the enumeration of general policies. For example, on immigration and emigration, the legislator declares: 'in the territory of this State, I behold an asylum to all: a prison to none.'[19] Similar statements appear on the subjects of war, colonies, domestic economy, etc. Thus, the Legislator's Inaugural Declaration limits the sort of laws the legislator can enact by making him subscribe to a statement of principles.

None of these securities prevents any given legislature from passing whatever laws it wishes, even though they may be detrimental to the greatest happiness of the greatest number. Yet, we have seen how Bentham makes it very difficult for the legislature to act freely. Many of the securities for appropriate aptitude are designed to enable constituents to have grounds for judging whether or not their legislators are acting to further their interests. If the legislators do not regularly attend legislative meetings or do not follow the

---

[16] Ch. VII, § 1, Art. 1 (*CW*), pp. 133–4.
[17] See ch. VIIn (*CW*), p. 135n; *Swear Not At All*, London, 1817 (Bowring, v. 187–229).
[18] Ch. VIIn (*CW*), p. 134n.
[19] Ibid., § 8 (*CW*), p. 144.

principles of the Legislator's Inaugural Declaration, these acts may be taken as strong evidence of moral inaptitude. The securities make this inaptitude clear to the people. The ultimate sanction possessed by the people is removal from office with or without the additional security of the initiation of legal punishment for specific criminal abuses.

Several of Bentham's securities for intellectual aptitude are concerned with the provision of information to the legislature from the systems of registration and publication operating in the administration and judiciary. The legislature receives copies of all documents (including correspondence) from these other branches. It can also obtain evidence directly through the Legislation Enquiry Judicatory. The member of the legislature is thus fully informed in his work. Bentham also provides for 'correctness', 'clearness', 'comprehensiveness', 'conciseness', and 'methodicalness', both in the form of motions and in the interpretation of legislation. These qualities assist both the legislators in their deliberations and the public in its attempt to understand legislative proceedings. Among Bentham's list of securities for intellectual aptitude in the legislature is a startling innovation which he neither discusses nor justifies. He applies the whole of the education and examination system, devised originally for the civil service, to the legislature.[20] Thus, each candidate for the legislature must have undergone the course of instruction and passed the various examinations as a condition for holding office. Bentham does not spell out his proposal in the sense that he lists for the various ministers the subjects on which they are to possess expertise, but, though briefly stated, it is still intended to be taken seriously. He is also aware that his proposals place important limits on the freedom of choice of candidates by constituents but he justifies his proposal by not seeing much value in 'freedom of choice' if it means a failure to enhance aptitude in office.[21]

As for securities for active aptitude in the legislature Bentham lists two——provisions for continual sitting by the legislature throughout the year and for continual attendance by the legislator. These arrangements require greater diligence

---

[20] See ch. VI, § 31, Art. 44 (*CW*), pp. 132-3.
[21] See the more extensive discussion of this material in chapter X below.

on the part of the legislators than was common in his day. Their object is to ensure that legislation does not fail simply because (as was common) the legislative term is not sufficiently long or a quorum is not present on a particular day.

Bentham has a fairly strong case for arguing that securities for appropriate aptitude provide a wider range of securities for good government than does a constitutional bill of rights. Nevertheless, he does not provide through his securities grounds for protecting the individual directly from the exercise of legislative power. In the United States, the process which culminates in judicial review can be initiated by the individual, but Bentham's securities require a majority in society or in the constituency to see that the legislation threatens their interests. Individual remedies exist (as we shall see) for the abuse of administrative power, but there are no such remedies against legislation which is duly passed but found opposed to the interests of particular individuals. The remedies which Bentham provides require a number of people to combine to establish the security. Presumably, he thinks that a law which violates free speech and assembly will be found oppressive by a vast majority, and the legislators will be quickly removed from office. Political action based on criticism by the Public Opinion Tribunal, the removal from office of individual legislators, annual parliaments, and temporary non-re-elegibility may eventually lead to the repeal of such legislation. Nevertheless, while a measure might threaten the greatest happiness of the greatest number, it does not follow that the 'greatest number' will be inclined to challenge the legislature by the means he prescribes. The implications of his position for his account of individual liberty will be examined after we look next at his provisions for the protection of the individual from the administration.

IV

Bentham deals at length with the problem of the oppression of ordinary citizens by the state bureaucracy, and we shall find here at another level the use of securities as substitutes for individual rights. In a series of sections he explores ways of dealing with wrongs committed by inferior functionaries (subordinates) against superiors (superordinates), by superiors against inferiors, and wrongs committed by functionaries against non-functionaries who take the form of 'suitors' (those seeking an official service), 'inspectees' (those subject to government inspection), and 'evidence-holders' (those required to give information to a government body).[22] It is worth noting that he does not deal with the relationship between the private citizen and the state in special terms. He places it instead in the context of the issues of insubordination, oppression, extortion, and peculation of which it is an important part. In doing so, he reminds us that the oppression of an inferior functionary by his superior is just as important as the oppression of a private citizen by the state. Nevertheless, we shall concentrate here on Bentham's discussion of the oppression of citizens (called 'non-functionaries') by the state.

Bentham provides a number of examples where oppression might occur. Where a suitor is seeking a government service, a functionary may refuse or omit to perform it or he may inflict needless suffering on him by causing delay, vexation, or expense. The functionary may treat him with disrespect or contempt or the suitor may find himself suffering other wrongs rather than submitting to these forms of suffering.[23] An inspectee is liable to suffer the same wrongs, and, in addition, Bentham calls attention to needless suffering caused by the process of inspection, such as in disclosing industrial secrets which would render a firm bankrupt.[24] An evidence-holder may be subject to a variety of oppressive acts. He may be forced to travel long distances to give evidence without receiving any compensation; he may be required to provide lengthy written answers to an unduly long series of questions; he may be subjected to a long search, inspection, and examination and forced to bring or send at his own expense items of evidence over long distances. Numerous other burdens may be placed on him as requirements to furnish evidence without any public compensation.[25]

In dealing with remedies against oppression, Bentham first

---

[22] Ch. IX, §§ 20-3 (*CW*), pp. 383-417. I shall concentrate on the material on the oppression of non-functionaries by functionaries in § 21.

[23] Ch. IX, § 21, Art. 5 (*CW*), p. 391.

[24] Ibid., Art. 6 (*CW*), pp. 391-2.

[25] Ibid. Art. 7 (*CW*), p. 392.

distinguishes between 'generally applying' and 'specially applying' remedies.[26] Generally applying remedies are those which apply to any act of oppression by any person, whether or not he is a member of the government, and these remedies may be found in the penal code. Specially applying remedies are those which operate only where oppressors are government functionaries and the authority which provides the remedy is not a judicial authority unless one is brought in to aid an administrative authority. He further distinguishes specially applying remedies into those which are either directly applying or indirectly applying.[27] Directly applying remedies consist of remedies obtained through the administrative hierarchy. If a functionary subordinate to a minister is an alleged oppressor, the injured party can take his case either to an ordinary judicatory or to the minister who sits as a judge immediate, with right of appeal on both sides to an appellate judge.[28] The minister would have the power of providing satisfaction in whatever form appropriate to the oppressed and the power of dismissing, suspending, or transferring the oppressor, depending on the gravity of the offence.[29] The minister would also be able to call on the assistance of the judge immediate in the district to help him obtain evidence, to avoid the suspicion of favouritism, or to increase the publicity of the preceedings.[30] Where the alleged oppressor is a minister, the judge is the prime minister and where the alleged oppressor is the prime minister, the Legislation Penal Judicatory may be invoked.[31]

The indirectly applying remedies against oppression are those which do not use legal measures and courts but depend largely on the Public Opinion Tribunal such as widespread publicity and carefully gathered evidence. Bentham's list of these remedies reminds one of the securities for appropriate aptitude which we have just discussed.

One remedy is the use of 'rules of deportment' for government functionaries.[32] Bentham first introduced rules of deportment in a previous section where he applied them to non-functionaries to provide clear rules for behaviour before

---

[26] Ibid., Art. 9 (*CW*), pp. 392–3.
[27] Ibid., Art. 10 (*CW*), p. 393.
[28] Ibid., Arts. 11–12 (*CW*), pp. 393–4.
[29] Ibid., Arts. 13–14 (*CW*), p. 394.
[30] Ibid., Arts. 15–16.
[31] Ibid., Arts. 18–19 (*CW*), p. 395.
[32] Ibid., Art. 20 (*CW*), pp. 395–6.

government officials.[33] He seems to have developed the idea from codes of good manners which were part of English military law.[34] In each government office rules of deportment for both functionaries and non-functionaries are prominently displayed as a remedy against oppression. His other suggestions are more familiar. Full publicity for all meetings between functionaries and non-functionaries is provided except where secrecy can be justified (as in the case of informers). He provides in great detail for a series of cubicles which allow for public and secret meetings with government officials.[35] The public meetings are so arranged that others waiting to see the official provide a critical audience which can witness any act of oppression. A record of all proceedings is made and so are arrangements for the clearness, correctness, and completeness of evidence. He also provides for an Incidental Complaint Book in every office so that any charge can be entered at the time of the alleged offence. Finally, he wishes to substitute a system of administrative procedure (based on judicial procedure) for the arbitrary procedures currently in practice in most states. With these remedies, directly and indirectly applying, Bentham believes that he has provided important securities to obviate oppression of citizens by government officials. He would also argue that the remedies against oppression make a bill of rights redundant.

V

Bentham's doctrine of securities contains an important contribution to a theory of constitutional democracy which has been generally overlooked. While his critique of rights has been widely discussed, few scholars have taken the trouble to see how Bentham replaces constitutional rights in his later writings on democracy. We have found in his treatment of securities a more flexible and comprehensive

[33] Ch. IX, § 20, Arts. 16–20 (*CW*), pp. 387–8.
[34] Ch. IX, § 21, Art. 28 (*CW*), p. 398. Bentham does not state the provisions of the rules as he believes that a constitutional document is not the appropriate place to do so, and each set of rules should depend more on the customs and manners of the particular society which adopts the constitution. See Art. 32 (*CW*), p. 400.
[35] Ch. IX, § 26, Arts. 21–35 (*CW*), pp. 445–51.

doctrine than can be found in a theory of constitutional rights.

Although the notion of securities for appropriate aptitude appears only in his later writings, Bentham dwells throughout his life on the importance of security as the primary end of government.[36] Indeed, the idea of security, as we shall see at several points in this book, is so important for him that his conception of happiness cannot be understood without taking security into account.[37] But security is a protean term. Bentham himself at numerous points links security with liberty.[38] Some of his critics, however, see his emphasis on security as revealing his real interest in order and social control rather than liberty.[39] The connection between security and liberty arises from his recognition that liberty has two important uses in relation to law and government. In the first place (gaining the approval of Isaiah Berlin who sees this as a major part of 'negative' liberty) Bentham insists that law should be conceived almost always as limiting liberty.[40] In a characteristic passage, he writes:

Liberty is neither more nor less than the absence of coercion. This is the genuine, original and proper sense of the word liberty. The idea of it is an idea purely negative. It is not anything that is produced by law.[41]

Liberty then for Bentham is the absence of restraint and constraint, but he does not at this point, as might an anarchist, celebrate the virtues of liberty in a society without law. Instead he holds strictly to this sense of the term to point out its misuse in other contexts. Those who argue

---

[36] Cf. 'Principles of the Civil Code' (Bowring, i. 307-8) and *Leading Principles of a Constitutional Code* (Bowring, ii. 269-72).

[37] 'It has been shown that the happiness of the individuals, of whom a community is composed, that is their pleasures *and their security*, is the end and the sole end which the legislator ought to have in view', *An Introduction to the Principles of Morals and Legislation*, III. 1 (*CW*), p. 34. The italics have been added.

[38] See, for example, *A Table of the Springs of Action* London, 1817 (Bowring, i. 210); 'Anarchical Fallacies' (Bowring, ii. 520 ff.); *Rationale of Judicial Evidence* London, 1827 (Bowring, vii. 522); *Letters to Count Toreno, on the Proposed Penal Code* London, 1822 (Bowring, viii. 509-10).

[39] See C. Bahmueller, *The National Charity Company*, Berkeley, 1981, pp. 154-6; D. Long, *Bentham on Liberty*, Toronto, 1977, pp. 215 ff.

[40] I. Berlin, *Four Essays on Liberty*, Oxford, 1969, p. 148 and n. See also p. xlixn.

[41] UC lxix, 44, as quoted by D. Long, op. cit., p. 74.

that certain laws and practices are violations of liberty and therefore evil and to be condemned are reminded by him that virtually every law entails a violation of liberty in imposing obligations on individuals.[42] Even Adam Smith is criticized for disapproving of some laws as violating 'natural liberty' when virtually all laws do so.[43] Furthermore, liberty in this sense is considered by Bentham as a mixed blessing. It can be used for evil as well as good, by murderers, thieves, and bullies as well as by saints to achieve their ends. Bentham also uses this conception of liberty to criticize in 'Anarchical Fallacies' the notion of a legal right to liberty as enshrined in the French Declaration of Rights of 1791: 'What these instructors as well as governors of mankind appear not to know, is, that all rights are made at the expense of liberty— all laws by which rights are created or confirmed. No right without a correspondent obligation.'[44] And in creating obligations, even in creating obligations to respect liberty, liberty is curtailed so that for Bentham a legal right to liberty entails the violation of liberty.

Thus, in Bentham's view to a great extent (though there are exceptions) liberty and law are antithetical terms, and as the law is devised to protect the individual and his property, it accomplishes these ends through the sacrifice of liberty. Nevertheless, the law does not neglect liberty, and by imposing obligations on some it can create liberty for others. Most of what are called civil liberties are formed in this way. Bentham recognizes that liberty has this second sense, but he distrusts the way that other writers and supporters of liberty fail to see that the creation of civil liberty requires the sacrifice of 'natural' liberty. For this reason he prefers to speak of liberty in this second way as 'security'. In his *Letters to Count Toreno on the Proposed Penal Code*, he writes:

As to the word *liberty*, it is a word, the import of which is of so loose a texture, that, in studied discourses on political subjects, I am not (I must confess) very fond of employing it, or of seeing it employed: *security* is a word, in which, in most cases, I find an advantageous

[42] 'Principles of the Civil Code' (Bowring, i. 301); 'Principles of Penal Law' (Bowring, i. 411); 'Anarchical Fallacies' (Bowring, ii. 502 ff.)
[43] 'A General View of a Complete Code of Laws' (Bowring, iii. 185 and n).
[44] Bowring, ii. 503.

substitute for it: *security* against misdeeds by individuals at large: *security* against misdeeds by public functionaries: *security* against misdeeds by foreign adversaries—as the case may be.[45]

In *A Table of the Springs of Action* he speaks of '*constitutional liberty*, or rather (to speak more distinctly) *security*'.[46] In the *Rationale of Judicial Evidence*, he writes:

What means *liberty*? What can be concluded from a proposition, one of the terms of which is so vague? What my own meaning is, I know; and I hope the reader knows it too. *Security* is the political blessing I have in view: security as against malefactors, on one hand—security against the instruments of government, on the other.[47]

From these remarks it is clear why Bentham does not include liberty, like security, subsistence, abundance, and equality, as one of the major ends to be realized in legislation. The first sense of liberty is largely extinguished by legislation. To say that legislation should aim at preserving liberty is to say that there should be little or no legislation. But without basic criminal legislation and laws regarding property and contracts, the strong may oppress the weak and the dishonest may triumph over the honest. This 'natural' liberty might very well produce a condition of life for many which is 'nasty, brutish and short'. Thus, preserving 'natural' liberty cannot be an end of legislation. The second sense of liberty, which is compatible with legislation, is for Bentham confusing and open to abuse and is replaced in his theory by the term 'security'. In this form, it clearly does constitute one of the main aims of legislation, and, indeed, is given pride of place in his system. In 'Anarchical Fallacies' he argues that instead of providing for rights to liberty, property, security, and resistance to oppression in the Declaration of Rights, liberty and property might have been considered branches of security.[48] He defines personal liberty elsewhere as 'security against a certain species of injury which affects the person.' Political liberty, another branch of security, 'is security against the injustice of the members of the Government.'[49] If Bentham's frequent references to security are taken as references to what we generally depict as civil or

---

[45] Bowring, viii. 509–10.   [46] Bowring, i. 210.
[47] Bowring, vii. 522.   [48] Bowring, ii. 503.
[49] 'Principles of the Civil Code' (Bowring, i. 302).

constitutional liberty, then liberty (as security) is at the heart of his system.

The difficulty with this identification of security and liberty is that security can be used in a general sense to include states and practices which in themselves may be antithetical to liberty. Material security, like health and knowledge, may be a condition for liberty, suggests Berlin, but to provide for increasing security is not the same thing as expanding liberty.[50] Bahmueller has recently argued that Bentham aims at security at the expense of liberty in attempting to overcome contingency in his detailed social arrangements and in the elements of compulsion in Panopticon.[51] Nevertheless, Bentham's conception of security is fairly precise, which might be expected from the way he turns to 'security' as a more definite term from the vaguer, more rhetorical 'liberty'. To understand his position we might return to the two definitions of a right set forth earlier which parallel his two conceptions of liberty. A 'natural' right exists where there is no obligation to forbear doing something. In the absence of any obligation, the individual is free to act as he pleases. This kind of right parallels the first sense of liberty. The second conception of a right is one which is created by an obligation placed on someone not to do something. For example, the law of property may be seen as placing obligations on individuals not to trespass and the penal code imposes obligations not to steal and kill. These obligations in turn create rights to non-interference from others, namely that they will not trespass, steal, and kill. This second conception of a right is clearly associated with Bentham's second conception of liberty. If rights in the second sense establish a sphere of non-interference for the individual, they also recognize a state of security for him in his person and possessions. But is this negative conception of a sphere of non-interference what Bentham means by security? We have already seen that the definitions of personal and political liberty as branches of security are stated as principles of non-interference, as 'security against' interference by others and by government.

The present author knows of no discussion by Bentham

---

[50] Berlin, pp. liv–lv.   [51] Bahmueller, pp. 154–5.

which presents security as something other than the imposition of obligations on some not to interfere in the lives of others. Admittedly, these obligations can be considerable, as the government acts, for example, to prevent invasion, crime, disease, and calamity. Bentham's reforming zeal and attention to detail have led his critics to see in some of his measures which enhance security a gross interference with individual liberty and dignity. If a government sets out methodically to prevent crime without any limits on its measures to maximize security, the constant surveillance necessary to achieve this end might create conditions which would make life secure though rigidly organized. Even though the measures are rational and justifiable (and thus do not represent an abuse of government power), they may still seem destructive of dignity. In depicting the paupers of Bentham's Panopticon for the poor, Bahmueller argues that they 'were to be divested of personality and formed into a common mould, much like soldiers upon joining an army.'[52] He claims that Bentham would treat the pauper as 'less than a human being' deprived of 'moral autonomy' and 'human dignity.'[53] In reply to Bahmueller, Warren Roberts has argued that Bentham remains concerned with liberty and provides for the poor freedom from want and freedom from oppression by management and government.[54] The poor also have the opportunity 'to realize their potentials as moral beings.'[55] This dispute is not about the meaning of Bentham's text but about liberty. Bentham would argue that the kind of liberty Bahmueller champions must constantly be sacrificed by the very existence of legislation. The point is not to look back to an idyllic golden age of liberty, but to see how the individual may be made secure from undue interference in his own pursuit of happiness. Bentham might admit that to maximize security (and liberty) government activity must be considerable, but he would argue that it need not be arbitrary and tyrannical. A well-ordered society, based on rational principles of security, need not be a totalitarian one.

[52] Ibid., p. 210.
[53] Ibid.
[54] W. Roberts, 'Bentham's Poor Law Proposals', *The Bentham Newsletter*, iii (1979), 41-2.
[55] Ibid., p. 42.

Bentham's emphasis on security as the major end of government should not be minimized. Although the greatest happiness of the greatest number is the ultimate test for judging the value of actions and laws, Bentham believes that widespread security is the major contributor to the greatest happiness. Thus, to the argument often set forth by moral philosophers, that the greatest happiness might be achieved by the sacrifice of the individual liberty of a minority, he would reply that although this is logically possible, it is none the less highly improbable so long as security plays the role in his system that he gives to it. To threaten security, even the security of a minority, is, for Bentham, a threat to the happiness of all.

Thus far, we have dwelled primarily on individual security and liberty rather than on political liberty. To a considerable extent what applies to the former also applies to the latter. However, although the individual can challenge acts of government oppression, he cannot, as an individual, protect himself from oppressive government legislation, which requires (as we have seen) that the people act collectively to secure themselves from misrule. As there are no legal remedies to which the individual may turn to oppose oppressive legislation, he must rely on collective action through the ballot and the pressure of public opinion. This part of political liberty then is based on the opportunity for political action. The identification of political liberty with political action within a constitutional system might be said to have begun with Aristotle and seems somewhat foreign to the modern liberal tradition which emphasizes the law as the primary means to secure liberty.[56] Nevertheless, we have seen in chapter II the great importance Bentham gives to the Public Opinion Tribunal as the basis of reform. Here we see his emphasis on popular control taken a further step and linked with political liberty through his notion of securities.

Although, like Aristotle, Bentham sees political action as a basis of liberty, he differs from Aristotle in retaining the negative view of liberty which is common to the liberal tradition. For Aristotle, political action is free action as it

[56] See Aristotle, *Politics*, Bk I; H. Arendt, *The Human Condition*, Chicago, 1958; but cf. R. G. Mulgan, *Aristotle's Political Theory*, Oxford, 1977, pp. 15, 40, 150.

moves towards a positive end or good; for Bentham, there may seem to be an equally positive end in the greatest happiness principle, but this is mere appearance, as the aim of political action is security. In this case, the end is security against misrule by rulers. It is worth noting that it is the people and not the rulers who 'act'. The people must try to achieve a measure of security even in states with democratic constitutions because the temptation of those in power to manipulate and exploit the legal system remains very strong. For Aristotle, who had more faith in the cultivation of virtue amongst rulers, freedom emerges within the political action of citizen-rulers. They have power, free choice, and the means to action. For Bentham, the 'powerless' alone have the incentive to act to secure their own interests.

Bentham might claim that his conception of securities is superior to that associated with constitutional bills of rights, because it is more realistic. The individual, he would argue, cannot achieve much against the government while using the government (i.e. the judicial system) to do so. He requires an independent base and this can be constructed only through independent political organization. It is arguable that he may have underestimated the potential for independent judgement by a supreme judiciary (as has been the case with the United States Supreme Court). Nevertheless, many advances in securing human rights and liberties have been made, in spite of the existence of paper constitutional rights, through pressure exerted from world-wide public opinion. By using publicity and demanding accountability, a measure of political liberty has been achieved even in countries where political liberty is not treated favourably by rulers. Bentham would have been sympathetic to this use of public opinion and political action to secure liberty.

Although Bentham may be able to establish that the system of securities is superior to constitutional bills of rights, it may still be argued that his approach omits to appreciate an important characteristic of human, moral, or natural rights. What seems missing in Bentham is the sense that there are some things the state (any state) must *never* do at whatever cost and these limitations on state power are best conceptualized through doctrines of human rights. This criticism is often advanced against utilitarians especially in theories of human rights.[57] Nevertheless, it is doubtful whether this criticism applies to Bentham because of the role that security plays in his account of utility. At the heart of his conception of democracy is a society where the security of each individual (i.e. his life, liberty, and property) is maximized. It is maximized by limiting the possibilities of oppression either by one citizen over another or by the government over the citizen. If the proponents of human rights theory have persuaded us that securing rights is more important than satisfying wants, they might have found an ally in Bentham who argues that establishing security is the primary way to maximize happiness. Although utility may not embody all human ideals and aspirations, Bentham's theory at least covers the same ground as many theories of human rights.

[57] See, for example, R. Nozick, *Anarchy, State and Utopia*, New York, 1974. See also H. L. A. Hart, 'Between Utility and Rights', *The Idea of Freedom*, ed. A. Ryan, Oxford, 1979, pp. 80-6.

Chapter V

Power

The language of power pervades the whole of the *Constitutional Code*. '[I]n no existing Code', writes Bentham, 'is the scope given to the power of ruling functionaries so ample as in the present proposed Code.'[1] He opposes the doctrine of the separation of powers where accountability is established by the checks to power possessed by other branches of government. He believes that there is a fatal flaw in this doctrine, because an official cannot be held accountable for an action, if he does not possess sufficient power to perform it. What constitutional theorists had long seen as a way of avoiding despotism, Bentham regards as a licence to establish inefficient and corrupt government. In its place, he grants ample power to officials but carefully defines the nature and scope of this power through his accounts of functions and subordination. Together with his system of securities, he believes that he has resolved the main difficulty of both granting power and controlling it.

Bentham also examines the additional powers acquired by officials, not through their particular functions, but as a result of the enhanced reputations, remuneration, or honours associated with their offices. This latter form of power is not reducible to the functions of the offices themselves and forms the basis of considerable corruption in public life. His treatment of the theme of reward and punishment reflects his attempt to deal with this problem.

I

Through his conception of functions, Bentham attempts to direct power and, by directing it, to establish accountability. Directing power involves making the operations of government intelligible not only to the people but also to the members of the government. He believes that a comprehensive

---

[1] Ch. VI, § 31, Art. 13 (*CW*), p. 120.

statement of all of the functions of government, conceived in a way that can be grasped by any citizen, will have an inestimable impact on the difficult task of keeping track of the activities of rulers. Furthermore, through the notion of functions, he contends that power can be transformed into duty, and it is arguable that Bentham (though he does not use the term) develops an important notion of political virtue. Finally, he presents a complete inventory of the functions of constitutional democracy and through it prescribes, as a legislator, the main institutions of that political society. We shall now consider these aspects of his conception of functions.

Making the functions of government intelligible leads Bentham directly into a paradox which appears frequently in his work and from which he does not entirely escape. In order to distinguish and clarify the various operations of government, he needs to introduce a considerable technical vocabulary, which in turn tends to make his discussion of functions less intelligible than it otherwise might be. This is a common problem in his writing, and he does little to overcome it. Indeed, one reason why his analysis of constitutional ̄ functions has received so little attention is the difficulty of working through the technical terminology. Nevertheless, he pays great attention to his choice of terms for the functions of government. For example, in choosing the terms 'locate' and 'dislocate' for the functions concerned with appointment and dismissal, in an unpublished manuscript he justifies his choice as follows:

[*to locate*] Conjugates are or, without difficulty may be—*locator, location, located, locatee, locative, locable, locability*: negative opposites *dislocate, dislocator, dislocation, dislocated, dislocatee, dislocative, dislocable, dislocability*. A synonym is *to place*; which has, or may be thought to have for its conjugates *placing, placement, placed, placeable*: for its opposites, corresponding to *displace, displacement, displaced, displaceable*. But *to place* and its conjugates, are words that have no place in the Latin-sprung part of the language: *placing* denotes the act, but not the result of the act: *placement* has scarce as yet any place in the language: so likewise *placeable*. These conjugates flow not so easily from the English source, as do the others from the Latin. In chirurgical language, *dislocate* with its conjugates, presents an apposite image.

Of the English words commonly employed on this occasion, no one is altogether adequate. *Nomination* is but *initiative*: the commencement of a compleat location: *appointment* is indeed sometimes employed to denote *compleat location*, but sometimes likewise no more than the *consummative* operation, after the inchoative or say *initiative* has been performed by some other hand. Of compleat location, the operation may be fractionalized amongst an indefinite multitude of authorities: authorities, some individual, some corporate, acting in as many different modes or forms: in this or that one may be the original nomination: in others the confirmative choice: *choice* may be applied to both entities. Election is applied to the act of a multitude: nomination and appointment to that of an individual.

To the material on 'nomination' and 'appointment', he adds the following note:

Nominate, and appoint, are both of them most inconveniently barren of conjugates. Nominate has in common use *nominee*, but no *nominor* or *nominator* etc. It has *nominative*: but only in the confined grammatical sense. Opposites, namely disnominate etc. would not be suitable to the import of it. Appoint has, in the positive sense, no other conjugate than appointment: in the negative sense it has none. Disappoint, disappointment, may be termed pseudo-conjugates—false or deceptive conjugates: correspondent in name, not correspondent in import.[2]

If his object is simply to provide labels with a large number of conjugates for as many functions as he can distinguish, his effort, though perhaps of historical interest, would not detain us here.. However, he moves a good deal beyond the idiosyncratic choice of terms by attempting to reduce the uniqueness of government offices by seeing a number of functions as being common to all offices of government.[3] For example, he postulates four main functions which are concerned with persons within the administration: locative, self-suppletive (used in appointing substitutes), directive, and dislocative.[4] Although a number of other functions appear as categories under these four main functions, he intends that

---

[2] UC xxxvii, 91-2 (18 May 1823). The manuscript was written for the 'Expositive' section of the *Code* which was eventually abandoned by Bentham. Some slight editorial emendations have been necessary, such as making the italics somewhat more consistent. The manuscript is in the hand of two copyists with revisions by Bentham. Presumably, the punctuation and italics would have been revised at a later stage.

[3] This is the significance of ch. IX, §4 (*CW*), pp. 186-202, which deals with functions generally in administration.

[4] Ibid., Art. 44 (*CW*), p. 196.

all operations within the administration concerned with people should be grouped under these headings. In reducing diverse government activities to these few functions, he believes that he is rendering government operations simpler and more comprehensible. He is also able to set forth related functions and securities in a clearer manner. It might be argued, however, that this terminology involves the use of the same terms for essentially different activities. For example, Bentham has the electorate exercise the locative function in choosing members of the legislature; the legislature, in choosing the prime minister, and the ministers, in appointing officials in the administration. But this use of 'locative' obscures the difference between electing officials in the first examples and appointing them in the last. One can easily distinguish between an 'elective' function exercised by the electorate and the legislature, and an 'appointive' function exercised by ministers. Thus, to gain some advantages from a simple system of functions, he sacrifices to an extent the recognition of some differences in government operations. Presumably, he would not consider this a negative feature, as he would argue that nothing is gained by making a basic distinction between elected and appointed officials. The various powers they possess are common to both and can be understood no matter how they come to office. By using the single term, he is able to emphasize this aspect of government office.

Nevertheless, his scheme of functions can lead to false or misleading analogies. For example, he asserts that the procurative function is exercised in relation to things in the same way as the locative function is exercised with respect to persons.[5] It is obvious that the analogy cannot be taken very far. The promotion of persons, for example, has no counterpart in things. Things can be used, esteemed, but not usually promoted, dismissed, or punished. And to say that the purchase or hire of things is like the appointment of persons to office is so misleading as to leave Bentham open to the charge (of which he is innocent) of treating persons like things. What he has in mind in linking the two functions is ensuring that similar high standards apply to two main

---

[5] Ibid., Art. 45 (*CW*), pp. 196-7.

functions of government, the appointment of persons and the acquisition of things. By asserting that there are some parallels between them, he attempts to achieve this end.

In spite of these difficulties, his scheme of functions is an impressive achievement.[6] With the simplification of functions common to all officials, he can establish general securities applicable to all, and accountability can thus be enhanced. Of course, particular officials perform other functions peculiar to their offices, and he includes these as well as the general ones. Nevertheless, it is in matters like appointment and dismissal and the acquisition of goods on a large scale that corruption and oppression are most serious, and it is here that his attempt to depict general functions of appointment and procurement with attendant securities is most relevant.

In assigning functions to various officials, he is also assigning duties for them to perform. These are usually legal duties, but some might be called moral duties in the sense that they are secured only by the critical eye of the Public Opinion Tribunal and not by legal sanctions. He does not assume that it takes a good man to perform the functions of good government. These various duties do not depend on a theory of virtue. Bentham's self-regarding man is disposed to perform his duties by his calculation of the advantages and disadvantages for himself in doing (or not doing) so. What makes him calculate that it is advantageous for him to perform his duties depends not on the inner cultivation of virtue but

---

[6] There must be several hundred different functions which Bentham distinguishes at all levels of government. At times he runs into difficulty. For example, the executive function which is exercised by the prime minister and should be exercised by ministers is omitted from the list of ministers' functions. Cf. ch. IX, §4 (*CW*), pp. 186-202 and ch. VIII, §2, Art. 1 (*CW*), p. 149. Nor does the executive function exercised by the prime minister resemble the executive function exercised by the Public Opinion Tribunal, although both have the same name. Cf. ch. VIII, §2, Art. 1 (*CW*), p. 149, and ch. V, §5. Art. 3 (*CW*), p. 37. Bentham tends to omit functions from the general list in ch. IX, §4 which are then assigned to ministers in other sections. This is the case with the initiative and suppletive functions. See ch. IX, §17, Art. 21 (*CW*), p. 342, §19, Art. 16 (*CW*), pp. 371-2, and §5, Art. 4 (*CW*), p. 203, §25, Art. 26 (*CW*), p. 426. Finally, one wonders if Bentham realizes that he includes both an application function (exercised in the preparation of the Legislation Enquiry Report) and, later, an applicative function exercised by ministers with regard to the organization and use of things. See ch. VI, §27, Art. 39 (*CW*), pp. 102-3, and ch. IX, §4, Arts. 49, 70 (*CW*), pp. 197, 202.

rather on the system of functions and securities. Let us take, for example, the melioration-suggestive function which all officials are obliged to exercise.[7] Each official is under a duty to seek out deficiencies in the political system and suggest improvements. But many officials may feel that it is too much trouble to become active contributors to Bentham's version of the 'suggestion-box' in spite of the fact that an active reforming bureaucracy may better produce the greatest happiness of the greatest number. For the individual, the pain of exertion involved in suggesting improvements to the system, together with pains felt from the resentment of colleagues to proposed improvements which may diminish their comfort and wealth, may even deter the official from exercising this function. That he will do so, and do so gladly, requires either that the pleasures he receives outweigh these pains or that he is threatened with even worse pains (suspension, dismissal, etc.) for failing to exercise it. The pleasures might be those which accompany a monetary reward for a good suggestion (of which Bentham generally disapproves), or those rewards, including promotion, associated with a good reputation for being a hard-working official. Whether it is the prospect of greater pleasures, the fear of worse pains, or a combination of the two which inclines the official to perform the function, this inclination is developed and maintained by both the securities (as we have seen) and the system of functions. The system of functions directs power to the greatest happiness and imposes duties on officials to advance it. Officials may be dismissed for the abuse of power, but they cannot be good officials unless their power is well directed. The system of functions is intended to direct power towards good ends and might be considered a system of political virtue. Virtue in this sense consists in obeying and carrying out rules and practices which are defined through the functions, and is not too different from Aristotle's conception of general justice which consists in obedience to law.[8] By obeying the rules and performing the assigned functions, Bentham's officials might be said to cultivate virtue as their own interests begin to coincide with what is in the general interest. But the cultivation of virtue depends

[7] Ch. IX, §4, Art. 61 (*CW*), p. 200.
[8] Aristotle, *Nicomachean Ethics*, V. 1129a34.

primarily on the development of the system of functions. The task of the constitutional legislator thus becomes as important, if not more important, than that of the educator or priest in developing virtue in society. In this sense, Bentham's approach recalls the emphasis placed on the legislator in Plato and Aristotle.

Bentham's account of functions throughout the *Code* is prescriptive in character. He does not deny that in actual governments different functions are performed. He is saying that this number and combination of functions are conditions for successful democratic government, and he clearly spells out why this is the case. He would claim not only that these functions (as opposed to others) are necessary conditions but also that the use of functions itself is a necessary condition. Through the use of functions, he believes that the operations of government become intelligible. And in making governmental operations intelligible, he argues that the first step is taken towards making those who perform them accountable. One aspect of this process deserves emphasis. Bentham establishes a close conceptual link between 'function' and 'functionary'. Functions are always assigned to specific functionaries and not generally to institutions. He does not say that the state has the function to maintain order but rather that the army and the preventive service ministers do. This emphasis on definable individuals performing functions is reflected in his hostility to boards and committees exercising functions, and whenever in the *Code* a committee is proposed, its functions are usually expressed in terms of those which are exercised by particular members. In his treatment of functions, therefore, Bentham introduces into his account of democratic government an emphasis on the individual which complements the individual perspective in suffrage which we have already discussed. The state is composed of definite individuals who perform specific functions. State power is transformed into the duties of these functionaries. In making this transformation, Bentham takes an important step towards the establishment of accountable government. Specific, identifiable individuals, not an anonymous state bureaucracy, can be held accountable for the implementation of legislation.

II

In his discussion of adminstration, Bentham is clearly aware that the mere assignment of functions to various officials will not in itself establish the machinery of government. Government operations are performed not by isolated functionaries but through complex administrative hierarchies. Thus, in the *Code* after his section on ministers' functions, he immediately turns to consider the problem of subordination within government.

His choice of terms, 'subordination' and 'superordination', deserves some attention. We can see here, as elsewhere, that he chooses his words with care. In the manuscript cited above he presents this exposition of 'subordination':

The relation between functionary and functionary in any number of grades one under another, is that, for the designation of which, this word is most commonly employed: but, in a more extended sense, it is, not unfrequently, employed, to designate the relations between ruler or rulers on the one part, and subjects on the other, without reference to grade in any other shape.

Conjugate to the word *subordination*, indicative of the effect of the sort of *relation* in question, is the term *subordinate*, indicative of the *individual*, between whom and another individual, the relation has place. For the designation of this other individual, the correlative term *superordinate* may by analogy be aptly, because expressively, employed. The word *superior*, commonly employed as the correlative of *subordinate*, is not adequately and correspondently determinate. It conveys not, as *subordinate* does, the idea of a system of official grades, one above another: in a word the idea of *order* is not so decidedly conveyed [by] it.[9]

The relationship between subordinate and superordinate is defined initially in terms of power (legal power) and functions. He states that five modes of power are necessary in the superordinate-subordinate relationship to which functions are related: direction (directive function), suspension (suspensive power), dislocation (dislocative function), punition (punifactive function), and suppletion (suppletive function).[10] This amounts to the power to direct, suspend, dismiss, punish, and appoint a new subordinate. To this he adds 'incidental' powers to transfer and stop promotion. Bentham is not advancing here certain powers which can be divided among various people in

---

[9] UC xxxviii, 94 (18 May 1823). Although Bentham did not invent the word 'superordination', he gave it a distinctive meaning. See *OED*.

[10] Ch. IX, § 5, Art. 4 (*CW*), p. 203.

an administration. These are the powers, he asserts, which must be possessed by anyone who is the superordinate of another. The possession of these powers determines (or 'causes') subordination to exist. His careful enumeration of these powers is intended to establish them as necessary conditions for the relationship between superordinate and subordinate.[11]

We can see that subordination for Bentham has a specific, technical meaning involving the possession of certain legal powers by the superordinate within an administrative system.[12] He also depicts subordination in terms of accountability. The subordinate has the duty, he asserts at one point, to exercise the statistic function, that is to say, to keep adequate records of money, stock, or personnel in his possession or under his care. These obligations in turn give rise to powers in the superordinate to ensure that the obligations are carried out. In this way the powers of the superordinate are related to the duties of the subordinate.[13]

Having defined subordination and the relationship between superordinate and subordinate, Bentham moves on to deal with the details of grades within various departments. In this discussion one important idea is advanced. The power which is possessed by the superordinate should not be enhanced by other factors such as honours or even remuneration. Indeed, the effect of the pecuniary competition system may well be that the superordinate is paid less than the subordinate. 'Power being, as well as money, part and parcel of the matter of reward', writes Bentham, 'of any *addition* to *power*, the effect in respect of demand for emolument, is—not addition, but subtraction.'[14] On the one hand he believes that each official must have the full powers necessary to carry out his duties and to act as a superordinate of those under his care. In this respect, he does not try to limit or divide power so as to prevent

[11] On the basis of this discussion Bentham can distinguish superordination from superiority. There are many different modes of superiority, which do not create a relationship of superordination and subordination, such as personal strength and beauty, moral and intellectual accomplishments, useful or graceful activity, skill in various pastimes, urbanity, wealth, factitious honour and dignity, the influence of 'will on will' and 'understanding on understanding'. Ibid., Art. 12 (*CW*), pp. 204-5. In these cases one person can be inferior to another, but he would not thereby become his subordinate.

[12] At times he uses these terms in a less exact sense. See ibid., Art. 7 (*CW*), p. 203.

[13] Ibid., Arts. 17-18 (*CW*), pp. 206-7.   [14] Ibid., Art. 22 (*CW*), p. 207.

the abuse of it. Indeed the system of securities presumes that the functionary has adequate power and no excuse on the grounds of insufficient power can succeed as a way of avoiding responsibility. On the other hand, he believes strongly in the corrupting character of power. We have already seen that the absence of power is a strong reason for Bentham to place sovereignty in the people.[15] Similarly, once having provided sufficient power for the exercise of the various functions, he takes great care to limit additional power which may accrue to an official by virtue of his office. Remuneration, as a form of power, is thus strictly limited, as it is potentially corrupting to the power holder and leads to the abuse of power. The well-paid official is not as able to resist corruption as some might argue; for Bentham, he has additional means to corrupt others, to buy silence, acquiescence, or agreement, or to protect himself from discovery.

In a later discussion of subordination he assigns to the legislature the task of establishing within a 'scale of subordination' the appropriate grades and functions.[16] By a scale of subordination, he means simply a chain of command where each subordinate is subject to direction from a superordinate so long as this direction is not countermanded by any superior superordinate. Within the scale of subordination the legislature decides, for example, what record books are kept by various grades in the exercise of the statistic function or whether or not particular grades should exercise the requisitive function.[17] The most interesting material is concerned with the conditions of service of functionaries (terms of appointment, remuneration, attendance, promotion, etc.). Bentham's first proposal is that with exceptions, as in the military, functionaries are appointed for life.[18] This may appear to conflict with the power of every superordinate to exercise the dislocative function. But, as he notes, his proposal simply renders the dislocative power *'judicial*, in contradistinction to *arbitrary'*.[19] No subordinate need fear arbitrary dismissal, as certain judicial or quasi-judicial procedures have

[15] See chapters II and III above.
[16] Ch. IX, § 19, Arts. 1-3 (*CW*), pp. 366-7.
[17] Ibid., Arts. 4-6 (*CW*), p. 367.
[18] Ibid., Art. 8 (*CW*), p. 368.
[19] Ibid., Art. 10.

to be followed. But the superordinate is encouraged, even required, to dismiss a subordinate where there is evidence of the non-performance of duty or the abuse of power or trust.

A second provision of interest is that there should be no increase in remuneration on grounds of length of service or age. This would most likely be prevented by the pecuniary competition system, but Bentham also flatly opposes such an increase. He believes that increased remuneration for these reasons simply increases public expense without increasing aptitude. The prospect of future remuneration is too distant to induce someone to take a position for this reason. He is especially hostile to increased remuneration on grounds of age as being highly wasteful of public money. He also notes with some insight that 'locating patrons' use pernicious notions of 'moral merit' based on age and supposed long service in public life to justify handing out increased remuneration. Bentham argues that no case can be made for saying that public service is better or worse than the private service of the individual. And even supposing that there is 'moral merit' in dedication to public service, it might be argued that the less remuneration a man takes for such service is a manifestation of his greater regard for it.[20]

A third provision is that promotion strictly speaking has no place in the administration.[21] Bentham looks upon promotion as merely another case of appointment to a vacancy and argues that no one can make a prima-facie case to be appointed to a higher position simply on the grounds that he has occupied the next lower position. Such a claim may or may not be relevant to his being appointed to the new post which should be filled by the established examination and appointment system. Furthermore, the expectation of promotion often inhibits mobility from sub-department to sub-department. Where no expectation is held, it is easier to persuade functionaries to change.

Bentham's conception of administrative organization is not very complex when compared with modern administrative theory. Even a simple distinction such as that between line and staff does not appear in the *Code*. Nor does he deal with elementary problems of co-ordination in administrative

---

[20] Ibid., Arts. 12-14 (*CW*), pp. 369-71.
[21] Ibid., Art. 28 (*CW*), pp. 376-7.

hierarchies which might have led him to take a more favourable view of the use of committees. Although he makes a
substantial contribution to understanding problems of keeping records, gathering and providing information, establishing
'open' government and basic bookkeeping within the context
of a constitutional democracy, he has no grasp of planning
or budgeting in a modern sense. He also does not deal with
informal channels of direction and influence in government
which have led modern students of politics and administration to look behind formal institutional structures to more
dynamic political relationships.

He is mostly concerned with simple chains of command.
He seeks to establish clear lines of direction and accountability and an atmosphere where corruption and intimidation
cannot take root. We tend nowadays to see administration or
bureaucracy as a threat to democracy, and Bentham would
have shared this view. But he also believes that without reducing power (and reducing only the opportunities for the
abuse of power) it is possible, through his approach to subordination, to establish accountable administration. Through
both functions and subordination, therefore, Bentham
controls and directs administrative power.

III

Bentham tries to limit the power that officials acquire by
viewing reward as an inappropriate instrument for most
activities of government. He does not deny that reward
plays an important role in government. Various rewards
in the form of offices, reputation, money, and honours
serve as the inducements which lead people to shoulder
the burdens of public office. Nevertheless, unless strictly
controlled, these rewards become additional sources of
power, not related to the functions of government, not
controlled directly by securities, and hence the prime matter
of corruption.

The theme of reward and punishment is introduced early
in the *Code*. Having stated the overall end as the greatest
happiness of the greatest number and the two principal
means as maximizing aptitude and minimizing expense,
Bentham turns immediately to reward and punishment which

in a curious way he includes in 'expenditure'.[22] Reward and punishment become part of the means of minimizing the expense of government. He begins his argument with definitions. 'The matter of punishment', he writes, 'is evil applied to a particular purpose.'[23] Evil consists of 'pain and loss of pleasure'.[24] 'The matter of reward', he continues, 'is the matter of good applied to a particular purpose.'[25] Good consists of 'pleasure and exemption from pain'.[26] Punishment as an evil can be used consistently with the greatest happiness principle only as an instrument of coercion which will produce on balance more good than evil, that is to say, more pleasure and exemption from pain than the actual pain of coercion. Reward, as a good, is an instrument of inducement which on balance, to be consistent with the greatest happiness principle, must produce more good (as pleasure and exemption from pain) than evil. Although it might appear that the use of reward rather than punishment would easily serve to produce good, Bentham argues that the opposite is true. As an instrument of government, reward cannot be used except where also accompanied by punishment.[27] For government to reward anyone, it must on most occasions first use the threat of coercion to raise the means of reward usually through taxation. This threat of coercion might well be more powerful and hence more evil to more people than the good produced by the reward. It follows that governments interested in the greatest happiness of the greatest number should minimize reward. But Bentham finds that the opposite often takes place. Rulers, as we have noted, prefer to use punishment when dealing with subjects but in their own affairs tend to use reward.[28] This particular disposition of rulers (indeed, of anyone) is the main source of corruption.

Bentham develops his conception of the place of reward and punishment in government by establishing that only the fear of punishment can secure responsibility in the sense of maximizing compliance with and execution of the law.

---

[22] Ch. II, Arts. 1-3 (*CW*), pp. 18-19.
[23] Ibid., Art. 4 (*CW*), p. 19.
[24] Ibid., Art. 5.   [25] Ibid., Art. 6.   [26] Ibid., Art. 7.
[27] Ibid., Arts. 9-12 (*CW*), p. 20.
[28] Ibid., Art. 13.

Although reward or the hope of reward is the instrument which leads officials to take on various obligations, only the threat of punishment, he argues, is able to secure the regular fulfilment of these obligations. At times, it appears that reward induces an official to fulfil his obligations, but in fact it is usually the threat of withdrawal of reward (punishment) which achieves this. He argues that whatever can be achieved by reward followed by the threat of its withdrawal can be achieved more directly and more cheaply by the threat of punishment. Thus, reward itself is superfluous. Furthermore, the 'matter of reward', as Bentham calls it, is usually money, and money provides the means of avoiding and evading punishment. Thus, the reward itself provides the means for preventing its withdrawal.[29]

In the text of the *Code*, Bentham himself uses the withdrawal of reward as a means of securing the performance of duty, but he cannot avoid a sarcastic comment in doing so. When he proposes the withdrawal of remuneration from legislators for non-attendance in the legislature, he notes that by comparison, the ordinary English soldier is punished as a deserter if he 'fails in his attendance' by flogging or even death. He feels that the legislator has little about which to complain.[30]

Bentham regards the attitude of rulers in using punishment for subjects and reward for themselves as tending to encourage the ruling class to think that it is not like ordinary people and that its actions, however corrupt, should be presumed to have been performed with pure motives. He takes the opposite view:

The greater a man's power, the stronger his propensity in all possible ways to abuse it. Of this fact, all history is one continued proof. Ye, who, for examples, fear to look near home,—send your regards to a safe distance. Look to the twelve Caesars: there you have distance in time: look to all oriental despots: there you may have distance in time and space.[31]

He takes up this theme in his first major discussion of securities in anticipation of the resistance to the introduction

---

[29] Ibid., Art. 16n (*CW*), pp. 21n–23n. On reward generally, see further *The Rationale of Reward* (Bowring, ii. 189–266).

[30] Ch. VI, § 20, Arts. 8–9 (*CW*), p. 51.

[31] Ch. VI, § 31, Art. 22 (*CW*), pp. 122–3.

of these restraints on rulers even within a representative democracy. In the United States, for example, he notes that the 'lawyer class' would oppose any move towards good government, as it clings to the Common Law, with 'its essential and most elaborately organized uncertainty, its factitious delay, vexation, and expense'.[32] Bentham believes that in the *Code* he provides a series of remedies for securing the dependence of rulers on the ruled in spite of the tendency of those with power to abuse it. He provides for the punishment of members of the legislature, administration, and judiciary by first having them dismissed by the electorate and once dismissed, tried by the Legislation Penal Judiciary and other judicatories.[33] He also conceives the full range of securities—some legally enforceable and others enforceable by the Public Opinion Tribunal—as ways of limiting the power of rulers to act in a tyrannical manner. But an important part of these provisions is the assumption that punishment and not reward must be the relevant instrument of good government. And if the law cannot directly punish the rulers of society, it may be possible to diminish the rewards they receive and, in the process, diminish their power and their propensity to act outside the law.

This attitude towards reward and punishment strongly influences Bentham's approach to remuneration generally in the *Code*. He contends that with greater remuneration there will be greater opulence; with increased opulence appropriate aptitude will decrease; and consequently work will decline. The functionary will have a greater opportunity to participate in more pleasurable activities than his work. He will also be able to obtain accomplices and supporters to help him transgress the law and avoid punishment. Furthermore, once having received high remuneration, he is liable to develop an exaggerated sense of his value and the amount of expense he can charge to the public on various occasions. Finally, Bentham rejects the view, as we have seen, that responsibility can be increased by remuneration.[34]

Bentham returns to this theme when he is defending the pecuniary competition system against a number of potential

[32] Ibid., Arts. 27-9 (*CW*), p. 124.
[33] Ch. VI, § 28 (*CW*), pp. 111-14.
[34] Ch. IX, § 15, Art. 4 (*CW*) p. 298.

criticisms. One of these is that the functionary who becomes indigent in obtaining his position will be more inclined to commit depredation. He admits that the functionary may seek to commit depredation due to his indigence, and he will do so if he can escape detection. But if the indigent do so, he argues, so to a greater extent will the opulent. 'The most opulent of functionaries', he writes, 'have always been the most voracious of depredators.'[35] The familiar example whch he uses to make his point is that of George III. He then gives two reasons for believing that the rich will be more likely depredators than the poor. The rich will be less suspected and less closely watched because of a natural but erroneous supposition that links wealth and probity. They will also be able to obtain accomplices and supporters to prevent detection. However, the man who might become indigent through the pecuniary competition system is unlikely to accept the job if he will not be able to earn enough to meet his expenses. Thus, he will probably not be put into the position of illegally having to make up what he has lost through the pecuniary competition system.

The very possibility of increased reward opens the door to corruption. For this reason he opposes the application of the military model of symmetry in grade, power, and emolument to civilian administration. In the military services the person with the highest grade generally has the greatest power. It does not make sense for the man commanding a few to have power over someone commanding thousands of soldiers. It has become accepted traditionally that with greater power, i.e. rank, there should be greater emolument, although this is not necessarily the case as there are examples of gratuitous service.[36] Nevertheless, Bentham can see great difficulties in changing the structure of military service. If emolument is reduced, resignation could lead to dissolution or perhaps even to revolt.[37] In the civilian sector, this danger does not apply, and there is no reason to impose the military model on civilian administration. He is critical of the reforms of civilian administration made by Catherine the Great in Russia based on the Prussian military model. Although the

[35] Ch. IX, § 17, Art. 56 (*CW*), pp. 356-8.
[36] Ch. IX, § 19, Art. 29 (*CW*), pp. 377-8.
[37] Ibid., Art. 30 (*CW*), p. 378.

reforms had given wide access to the civil service, he believes that they also provided the basis for extensive corruption with increased emolument according to rank.[38]

Bentham is suspicious of the use of reward as an instrument of government, but he favours the use of what he calls 'natural' as opposed to 'factitious' reward.[39] This may take the form of money or what he calls 'natural honour'. For pecuniary reward for ordinary service, the salary of the official should suffice. For extraordinary service to the public, the person may apply to a judicatory for financial reward. Honorary reward, based on natural honour, is somewhat different; it is the reward which the community (in the form of the Public Opinion Tribunal) renders to someone for extraordinary service:

> by means of appropriate sentiments of love and respect, entertained in relation to him, with the occasional addition, of the special good will, good offices, and services . . . naturally flowing from these sentiments.[40]

This reward may be 'judicially augmented' by a decree issued by a court and entry of the service performed in the Public Merit Register which is then publicized.[41] Bentham is opposed to all forms of what he calls 'factitious honour' or 'dignity' by which he means titles and various 'ensigns of dignity' such as coats of arms. It is typical of Bentham that he turns something so amorphous and unsubstantial as public acclaim into a significant concept in his account of reward. But he is so convinced that most governments of his day, and especially England, have misused the system of reward to establish a deep-seated corruption, that only by sweeping away the whole system of 'factitious' reward does he think that this kind of corruption will cease. In its place, he tries to demonstrate the significance of simple public acclaim.

---

[38] Ibid., Arts. 30-1 (*CW*), pp. 378-9.
[39] See ch. V, §5, Art. 5 (*CW*), p. 37.
[40] Ch. IX, §15, Art. 19 (*CW*), p. 301.
[41] Ibid., Arts. 20-8 (*CW*), pp. 301-2.

Chapter VI

Expense

We have seen that Bentham regards the minimization of expense together with the maximization of aptitude as the main means to further the greatest happiness of the greatest number.[1] So great an emphasis is placed on minimizing expense in the *Code* that one might well wonder if there is potential conflict between the economic aims and those that more directly sustain the democratic system. In this chapter we shall examine the way Bentham deals generally with expense in the *Code*. We shall then take up two more specific themes: Bentham's use of competition and especially the practice of pecuniary competition; and the role of his 'disappointment-prevention' principle as applied to the difficult task of cutting government expenditure where required by reform. Finally, the extent to which his emphasis on economy might conflict with his belief in democracy is discussed.

I

One theme, stated throughout the *Code*, is that democracy can be less expensive than monarchy and aristocracy. This belief is frequently exemplified by the contrast between the minimal expense of American government at the time with the comparatively much greater expense of English government, largely due to inflated salaries, sinecure offices, widespread corruption, patronage, use of honours and dignity, general inefficiency, and waste found in the latter. Some of Bentham's proposals call for the straightforward abolition of these various practices which were widespread at the time and some of which remain in existence today. These include titles, various public honours, second legislative chambers, sinecure offices, 'pensions of retreat', incremental salaries based on age or length of service, state pensions (including

---

[1] See ch. II, Arts. 1-2 (*CW*), pp. 18-19, and ch. IX, §15, Art. 1 (*CW*), p. 297.

pensions for widows and children) paid by public funds, state subsidies for the arts, etc. These practices present little difficulty for Bentham. They simply have no place in his conception of democratic government. Nevertheless, he recognizes that even a 'purified' democracy remains constantly prone to the evils of increased expense. In this context, he sees close connections between purely economic problems of waste and loss, and moral and political issues of corruption and oppression. In the Legislator's Inaugural Declaration, he emphasizes the connection between waste and corruption as follows: 'as waste produces corruption, so does corruption waste; till thus, by depredation, oppression, and dissipation, the body politic is exhausted, debilitated, destroyed.'[2]

As we have seen, Bentham believes that democracy is a fragile constitution which can easily be transformed into a more tyrannical form of rule. He takes great pains to secure democracy from this decline and emphasizes the importance of the problem of government expense as a constitutional problem. Here we can see his legislative genius at work. His belief that the problem of expense is a major constitutional problem is most probably unique in the history of democratic thought. And yet, few would doubt today that the problem of government expenditure in modern democracies is one of the most crucial problems and perhaps more important than other issues of constitutional reform such as proportional representation and devolution. Bentham not only appreciates this problem, but he believes that it can be resolved within the framework of his constitutional democracy.

Nearly all of Bentham's institutions are designed so that expense is minimized in their basic operations. Payment of government officials is almost entirely limited to the basic salary (reduced through pecuniary competition) with a carefully restricted provision for extra pay for extraordinary public service.[3] He provides for 'single-seated' offices (i.e. one official in each position with clear chains of command) to avoid the multiplication of overlapping offices and the use

---

[2] Ch. VII, §4 (*CW*), p. 139.
[3] On remuneration, see ch. IX, §15 (*CW*), pp. 297-310.

of expensive boards and committees to make decisions.[4] Not only is the expense of government reduced but also particular officials may be held responsible for their decisions and are thus less likely to engage in wasteful practices.

The self-suppletive function, exercised when each major functionary appoints a depute or substitute, can result in the minimization of expense on several levels.[5] The purpose of the depute is to ensure that absence of the prinicipal for any reason does not act as grounds for delaying or avoiding work, as the depute is empowered to act in place of the principal. As with single-seatedness, Bentham believes that self-suppletion will increase responsibility in office and hence decrease corruption, waste, and consequent expense. In preventing delay in the completion of public business, Bentham also believes that public money is saved. In addition, the use of a depute allows the principal to exercise his power of patronage without corruption or public expense. The depute is paid, if at all, in place of the principal and thus serves without cost to the public. He enjoys the power and reputation associated with public service, and the principal takes responsibility for his actions. We can see here how Bentham creates an institution which on several different levels contributes to the minimization of public expense. His system of pecuniary competition, where equally qualified candidates compete for appointment to a position at the least salary, is the most important direct means of reducing government expenditure on personnel.[6] We shall consider this practice at greater length in the next section where his approach to competition is examined.

Besides the expense of personnel, there is also the great expense of the purchase, use, and disposal of items employed by government in its numerous activities. These range from the stationery used in every office to the expenditure for military weapons and stores, from the care and upkeep of public buildings to the expense of building roads. Bentham

---

[4] See ch. IX, § 3 (*CW*), pp. 173-86. Bentham refers to the 'individual responsibility principle': 'Corresponding rule.—Of responsibility, in whatever shape, imposed upon a trustee, the efficiency is *diminished* by every *co-trustee* added to him.' Ch. IX, § 7, Bi§4, Art. 24 (*CW*), p. 259.

[5] See ch. VI, § 23 (*CW*), pp. 59-67; ch. VIII, § 4 (*CW*), pp. 154-6; ch. IX, § 6 (*CW*), pp. 215-17; ch. XII, § 10 (Bowring, ix. 483-6).

[6] Ch. IX, § 17 (*CW*), pp. 337-64.

sees the need for an accurate and comprehensible system of records to keep track of the millions of items owned by government. Within this system (which is described at greater length in chapter VII), he devises a series of Loss Books which are designed to keep records of the various losses to the public.[7] Besides the logical arrangement of the record books designed to keep track of money and property, he devotes considerable analytic skill to listing various subjects of loss. For example, in discussing the loss of 'things movable' he includes: (a) non-receipt of things due to accident, negligence, or deterioration; (b) non-application or uneconomical application of goods; (c) deterioration or destruction due to failure of appropriate custody, by positive act or due to a failure to make repairs; (d) storage of things in the wrong place or in an inaccessible place requiring additional labour to recover them; or storage in a way that leads to deterioration or destruction; (e) excessive or uneconomical consumption; (f) loans of goods without charge, below price, or to a borrower who fails to care for them, is insolvent, or who fails to return them; (g) loss due to accident without anyone being at fault; (h) sale below price; (i) negligent or rash disposal by a custodient functionary; (j) loss due to embezzlement, theft, fraudulent obtainment, or peculation.[8] Even where goods are disposed of by auction, adds Bentham, as is the case with unwanted military stores or contraband goods, it is possible that fraud can enter and cause loss. For example, goods can be made to appear worse than they are while information as to their real value is passed to certain buyers; or, a ring may be formed among purchasers to prevent competitive bidding.[9] In other similar lists Bentham covers such subjects as the loss of money and real property.[10] Once a system of records is established covering all goods, rational policies of procurement, inspection, and disposal can be devised.[11] Bentham pursues these themes at length, making detailed arrangements for procurement and requisition. He concentrates on the form of the documents and on

[7] Ch. IX, § 7, Bi§4 (*CW*), 250–62.
[8] Ibid., Art. 7 (*CW*), pp. 252–3.
[9] Ibid., Arts. 8–9 (*CW*), p. 253.
[10] Ibid., Arts. 6, 20 (*CW*), pp. 251–2, 256–8.
[11] See ch. IX, §§ 8–9 (*CW*), pp. 268–82.

the securities established through the scrutiny of procurement by various persons. Basic procurement is left to the legislature to delegate, and procurement proceeds by the use of a specially designed Procuration Mandate. On the basis of this document, the requisition order can be issued. Bentham is aware of the importance of using different modes of procurement to minimize expense and, for example, proposes competition between hire, purchase, and the fabrication of goods by various government agencies.

The approach to minimizing expense in procurement is based on the assumption that the individuals involved will do everything possible to profit legally and illegally from the various contracts they negotiate. Although Bentham provides for criminal penalties for misdemeanours in procurement, he is aware that most corruption in this sphere which, in the end, enhances government expense, escapes detection. Therefore, he proposes that any minister having a special relationship with another contracting party (as relative, patron, etc.) must note this in the contract but is not thereby debarred from making it.[12] On the contrary, he seems to encourage these contracts so long as the effect will be procurement of goods at the least possible expense. By noting a relationship with a relative in the contract, the minister in a sense invites greater public scrutiny, and it is most likely to be a contract beneficial to the public if he takes this risk. We have covered in this section only a few of the practices Bentham employs in the task of minimizing government expense within a representative democracy. But we can see here the scope of Bentham's concern and the variety of institutions he devises to deal with this major problem.

II

We shall now consider Bentham's belief in competition as an important instrument for reducing government expense. Bentham highly esteemed the virtues of competition throughout his life. To Burke's comment that 'the service of the public is a thing which cannot be put to auction, and struck down to those who will agree to execute it the cheapest',

---

[12] Ch. IX, § 23, Arts. 6-12 (*CW*), pp. 413-15.

Bentham replies that loans, lotteries, and various kinds of contracts had already been used in this way by government and that Burke is wrong in saying that it cannot be so.[13] Bentham points to the virtues of the more powerful and appealing term 'competition' which Burke avoids in using 'auction':

> *Competition.*—This word would not, as *auction* so well did, serve the sophist's purpose. To the word *competition* no *smirk* stands associated —no pulpit—no hammer: *competition*—a power, the virtues of which had already been so well displayed by Adam Smith, not to speak of Sir James Stewart: in *competition* he beheld that security against waste and corruption which would have been mortal to his views.[14]

Competition appears in Bentham's *Code* at a number of points, such as in bids for contracts for the provision of services, but the three most important are the elections for the legislature, the system of competitive examination for entry into the civil service, and the pecuniary competition system. In these, one main aim is the prevention of corruption, and this is connected, as we have seen, to the minimization of expense. The system of 'temporarily discontinued relocability' is designed to prevent stagnation in office and the possibility of members of the legislature being elected and re-elected for life.[15] The system of competitive examination for the civil service (and the legislature) is designed to enhance aptitude in office and thereby diminish corruption and expense.[16] The pecuniary competition system, however, is directly designed to minimize government expense by introducing competition into the cost of labour.[17] Pecuniary competition assumes the success of the examination system in bringing forward through the qualification judicatory several candidates of relatively equal merit. From this basis the competition for obtaining the office at the least amount or even paying for the privilege of holding office can take place successfully.

Bentham's pecuniary competition system, though at the

---

[13] 'Defence of Economy Against Burke' (Bowring, v. 300).
[14] Ibid., p. 301.
[15] Ch. VI, § 25 (*CW*), pp. 72-91. See below, chapter IX.
[16] Ch. IX, § 16 (*CW*), pp. 310-37.
[17] Ch. IX, § 17 (*CW*), pp. 337-64.

heart of his conception of government based on the maxim of minimizing expense, has never, so far as is known, been adopted by any state, although it is fair to say that a number of modern democracies try to control expense by keeping public sector salaries low. But Bentham's system goes much further in building in the element of competition. It may be wondered why this aspect of his system has been either universally neglected or rejected when his proposals or similar ones for a civil service based on competitive examination have been widely adopted. Bentham himself anticipates and replies to a number of objections to his plan. He first considers the objection that pecuniary competition excludes the 'unopulent' and thus violates equality.[18] In his reply, he asserts that equality must be subordinate to security and cannot be regarded as an end which can be pursued without regard to other ends. He also contends that the unopulent can have more lucrative employment in the private sector and then take public office so that the bar is not an absolute one. Thus, in Bentham's eyes, the offices remain open to all in spite of pecuniary competition. Besides the argument that the man who pays for the office will have a greater relish for it, his best argument, based on general utility, is that pecuniary competition, in reducing government expense, reduces the burden of taxation. To reject pecuniary competition, he argues, is to impose a tax on rich and poor alike.

An argument which Bentham might have used is that pecuniary competition, like the system of competitive examination, is based on a principle of equality of opportunity. In all systems of equal opportunity, there are inequalities of initial conditions and outcomes, but both are coupled to equal opportunity (i.e. fair competition) within the system. Competitive examination provides equal opportunities based on an inequality of talents; pecuniary competition provides equal opportunity based on a starting-point of unequal wealth. The latter, inequality of wealth, can be remedied more easily than the former so that pecuniary competition would seem to be more open than competitive examination. Nevertheless, the practice of competitive examination has been widely adopted, but pecuniary competition has not.

---

[18] Ibid., Art. 53 (*CW*), pp. 352–4.

In Bentham's view, the able and ambitious, though poor, can easily become wealthy in the private sphere to secure success in pecuniary competition.

Bentham then deals with the objection that his system introduces venality, the sale of offices, and hence corruption.[19] This objection is of considerable importance due to the widespread practice of the sale of offices. He replies that it would be a confusion of ideas to see this practice in pecuniary competition. Under no circumstances are people at large able to purchase an office. All that takes place is the reduction of the salary of an office. Furthermore, the individual does not gain anything with his bid to take an office at a reduced salary. The benefit is purely one for the general public. To obviate the association of corruption with venality, Bentham argues that corruption is minimized by the system in so far as the man making the appointment has very little patronage at his disposal with those eligible competing to take office at the least lucrative salary. Finally, if someone believes that in spite of pecuniary competition, he stands to make a good deal from a particular office, the very fact that he is willing to pay highly for the office will alert the public to the possibility of corrupt action.

After considering another objection, that liberality is excluded by pecuniary competition, by arguing that there is no virtue in the lavish spending of public money, Bentham turns to the final objection that depredation is sharpened by indigence.[20] As we have seen in the discussion of reward, he believes that the wealthy and not the poor are the greatest depredators and can best protect themselves from detection and punishment. He also believes that it is unlikely for a person to bid for an office if he is left without funds to meet his expenses. Hence, a poor and hungry candidate would most probably hesitate to bid too little and few would risk punishment for corruption by attempting to cover losses from illegal profits from office.

Bentham's arguments in reply to objections to pecuniary competition, though of interest, fail to anticipate the widespread indifference to his proposals. Unlike competitive examination it appears to favour the rich over the poor and

[19] Ibid., Art. 54 (*CW*), pp. 354-5.
[20] Ibid., Arts. 55-6 (*CW*), pp. 355-8.

would be distrusted by radical reformers. But resistance to this one form of competition may reflect another thesis of Bentham—that government forms a class apart with its own interests. A ruling class would not be sympathetic to the loss of wealth and power associated with pecuniary competition.

III

Throughout his discussions of the various problems involved in reducing government expense, Bentham seems well aware of the political obstacles to cutting public expenditure. The reduction of public expenditure places economy in direct conflict with political power. Those who must implement the economies often have both the interest and power to resist them. In a practical sense, rulers will implement reforms such as the ones outlined in this chapter usually only to preserve their own power when faced with a worse evil such as the threat of revolution. In democracies, it may be easier to gain acceptance for reforms because rulers can be more easily dismissed, but even here there will be opposition.

Bentham also appreciates that cutting government expense is an action involving the infliction of pain on those most involved. In his later writings, he devises a principle which minimizes the force of this immediate reduction in happiness so that the pains of suffering cuts in government expenditure are not stronger than the pleasures of relief from government taxation. He calls the principle the 'disappointment-prevention' principle and regards it as an important 'branch' of the greatest happiness principle.[21] According to Bentham, the disappointment-prevention principle also forms the basis of both the civil and penal branches of the law of property.[22] Without it, the notion of vested rights would not have any force.[23] Between someone in possession of a piece of property and a usurper it might be argued that each would take equal pleasure in possessing it, and a calculation of pleasures and pains would not uphold the rights of the person in lawful possession. The disappointment-prevention principle would

---

[21] 'Bentham on Humphreys' Property Code', *Westminster Review*, vi (1826); (Bowring, v. 413-14).

[22] *Official Aptitude Maximized; Expense Minimized* (Bowring, v. 266).

[23] 'Bentham on Humphreys' Property Code' (Bowring, v. 414).

bring into the calculation the pain of disappointment suffered by someone losing possession of a vested right in the property. When the prevention of this pain is added to the calculation, the greatest happiness requires that the person remains in lawful possession or receives compensation for the disappointment which arises from his loss. Bentham defines this pain of disappointment and its relation to law as follows:

When from any cause—human agency or any other—a mass of the matter of wealth, or of the matter of prosperity in any other shape, is made to go out of an individual's possession or expectancy without his consent, the pain produced in his breast by contemplation of its non-existence, or say by the loss of it, call *the pain of disappointment*: he being disappointed at the thought of the good which, it having been in his possession or expectancy, he has thus lost.

Among the objects of law in every community, is the affording security against this pain in this shape.[24]

In one example, he applies the disappointment-prevention principle to legal reform and tries to deal with opposition to reform on grounds of loss of employment and remuneration.[25] He believes that full compensation should be given for any such loss, indeed, rather more compensation than less, and his reasons are of great interest. He notes that the greater the benefit to the whole community, the greater is the compensation that can be afforded. He then argues that one must take into consideration evils of two orders which flow from uncompensated loss: the evil suffered by the party in question; and the 'alarm produceable on the part of other individuals of other classes regarding themselves as exposed to be eventually detrimented by reform, real or supposed, set on foot by the same constituted authorities, or their successors.'[26] In addition, there is the danger that the action producing uncompensated loss might set a precedent for future action. Bentham also presents a prudential argument suggesting that compensation will reduce opposition to reform and ease the way to its institution. Finally, he adds a proviso regarding expense, that compensation should be made with as little expense as possible, and if compensation can be made without expense, it should be done in this way. An example he provides is that if a new institution replaces one in existence, effort is made to employ those who lose their jobs in the new positions with minimum compensation to cover any loss of salary. Bentham admits that not all pains suffered in reforms can be compensated, as, for example, the pain of humiliation when someone is removed from a position of pre-eminence in a particular sphere. For this reason, he expects that there will always be strong opposition to reform.

Bentham recognizes both the importance and the difficulty of applying the disappointment-prevention principle in attempting to introduce reforms which will minimize expense. In the preface to *Official Aptitude Maximized; Expense Minimized* he sets forth a number of rules and observations to guide the reformer in his difficult task.[27] So long as there are sources of expenditure which can be stopped without causing disappointment to *fixed* expectations, he argues that these should be stopped before those which do cause disappointment. He then draws a distinction between fixed and floating expectations. Fixed expectations correspond to the technical notion of vested interests. An example of a floating expectation which he provides is that 'every solicitor, who sends a son of his to one of the inns of court, *expects* to see that same son on the chancery bench with the seals before him.'[28] He believes that this important distinction can be drawn and that cutting back on expenditure affecting floating expectations will not create disappointment like that affecting fixed expectations. He also argues that if a sum for retrenchment is given, the cuts should be carried out so as to affect the fewest number of people. For example, if in a department where £10,000 must be saved and there are ten clerks earning £1000 each per year and one chief receiving £10,000 and none of the men are engaged in work that is useful, it is the chief who should lose his job rather than the clerks. The result is the creation of less disappointment. Finally, Bentham emphasizes that when reform requires the abolition of offices where there are fixed expectations about continuance, there is no immediate benefit to the community due to the compensation that needs to

---

[27] Bowring, v. 266-7.
[28] Ibid., p. 266.

be paid. He uses the analogy of a weight being moved from one side of a ship to another which does not result in the burden on the ship being diminished.

It is somewhat curious that Bentham evolved the disappointment-prevention principle so late in his life.[29] It appears in the first volume of the *Constitutional Code*, most of which was in print in 1827, only in material added in 1830.[30] Of the other works in which it appears, the earliest printed is *A Commentary on Mr. Humphreys' Real Property Code*, first published in the *Westminster Review* in 1826. Here, Bentham uses the principle to explain the basis of the law of property. It is only in the 1830 texts of *Official Aptitude Maximized*, the Equity Dispatch Court material of 1830 onwards, and the unfinished 'Pannomial Fragments' of the same period that the extension of the principle to the problem of reform takes place.[31] It is also at this time that Bentham begins to look more closely at the greatest happiness principle and attempts to deal with deficiencies in it.[32]

The disappointment-prevention principle might be said to form, for Bentham, under the overall authority of the greatest happiness principle, a principle of justice. He notes at one point that it presents a clearer and more determinate idea to the mind than is presented by such 'nonsensical' expressions as 'contrary to the first principles of justice' or 'contrary to every principle of justice'.[33] Unlike Rawls's theory of justice where each individual, shrouded in ignorance and calculating his possible gains and losses, agrees to certain principles of justice guaranteeing freedom and equality, Bentham takes each individual in his concrete condition and makes the calculation of his potential disappointment through

---

[29] D. Long argues that it is simply Bentham's older conception of security, and especially security of expectations , with a new name. See 'Bentham on Property' *Theories of Property, Aristotle to the Present*, ed. A. Parel and T. Flanagan, Waterloo, Ontario, 1979, p. 242. See also Bahmueller, *The National Charity Company*, pp. 87-8, 203. Although it is obviously related to security, the disappointment-prevention principle receives a new emphasis and application in Bentham's later writings.

[30] See ch. IX, § 17, Art. 39 (*CW*), p. 345.

[31] 'Bentham on Humphreys' Property Code' (Bowring, v. 413-4). See Bowring, v. 266-7; iii. 325-7; iii. 226-7.

[32] It is at this time that the debate takes place over the character of the greatest happiness principle between Macaulay in the *Edinburgh Review* and the *Westminster Review*. See chapters IX and XI below.

[33] 'Equity Dispatch Court Bill' (Bowring, iii. 388n).

loss an important part of any overall calculation of the benefits of government policy.[34] If Rawls's theory looks forward to a new regime based on the principles on which rational man would agree, Bentham is more concerned with the reform of existing regimes. The disappointment-prevention principle is by its nature applicable to reform, but not to revolution. It adds an important dimension to the greatest happiness principle, which, on its own, might be used to justify any action so long as it benefits the majority in society. It forms an important link between the greatest happiness principle and the 'sub-ends' security, subsistence, abundance, and equality. It especially gives added meaning to security and emphasizes the importance Bentham gives elsewhere to security as the major end of government.

In these fragments on the disappointment-prevention principle which emerge briefly in the later writings, Bentham does not make clear the emphasis to be placed on the principle within the greatest happiness principle. Is the pain of disappointment one among many pains, of no greater importance than the others, to be weighed with various pleasures in the calculation of the greatest happiness? To view the principle in this light, however, is to ignore its close link with security and Bentham's claim that the principle should function as the basis of the civil law in providing security of property. If, for Bentham, happiness in its basic sense means the establishment of security (as opposed to the simple satisfaction of wants), the disappointment-prevention principle, in providing security of property, would seem to operate as a necessary condition for happiness. Without the operation of this principle, security of property, an important constituent of security generally, cannot, for Bentham, exist. And if there is no security there cannot be much happiness. Bentham's emphasis on this principle, like his emphasis on security, would seem to form the basis for protecting rights to property generally in society. If a policy might advance the happiness of the majority by the confiscation of the property of a minority, Bentham would most probably invoke the disappointment-prevention principle to show that the threat to security is so great not only

---

[34] J. Rawls, *A Theory of Justice*, Oxford, 1972, pp. 54 ff.

to those who suffer from the confiscation but to everyone
in society (as they may suffer in the future) that the greatest
happiness requires that no property be confiscated or
otherwise taken without full compensation. Thus, the
disappointment-prevention principle in this example seems
to determine the balance of pains and pleasures in the calculation of the greatest happiness. Furthermore, there is
no conflict for Bentham between the disappointment-
prevention and the greatest happiness principles. It is possible that his conception of the relationship between happiness
and security, as expressed in the disappointment-prevention
principle, enables him to avoid the need to resolve the
problem raised by later philosophers of the potential conflict
between the principle of utility and that of justice.

IV

Let us now return to the question posed at the beginning
of this chapter concerning the possible conflict between an
emphasis on economy and efficiency on the one hand and
democracy on the other. In spite of Bentham's republican
principles and the shrill attack on monarchy and aristocracy
which runs throughout the *Code* he felt confident in recom-
mending the work to several European monarchs.[35] Some of
the material which he thought would appeal to reigning
monarchs dealt with reducing government expenditure. But
if this is the case, we might ask if these aims are either
necessarily related to democracy or, indeed, possibly in
conflict with it. Efficient government is not the same as
democratic government and may even be purchased at its
expense.

There is in Bentham's approach to expense what might be
called a democratic dimension. In the first place, he takes
as a main premiss the view (as we saw in the case of reward)
that most government expenditure involves a burden or
tax on the people. Thus, to justify a policy involving
public expenditure it is necessary to show that its benefits
are greater than the burdens imposed on the people. This

---

[35] See Bentham to King Ludwig I of Bavaria, 20 December 1827, Bowring, x.
579; Bentham to King William I of the Netherlands, 6 February 1827, BL Add.
MS 33,546, fo. 126.

calculation is, for Bentham, difficult to establish. Taxation (especially direct taxation of basic commodities) affects most members of society. Bentham assumes that where burdens are placed on the many for the sake of benefits for a few, however great those benefits may be, the principle of the greatest happiness of the greatest number may be violated.[36] If burdens are widely distributed, benefits may have to be distributed in line with burdens to provide for the greatest happiness. Only policies which establish basic security and subsistence for everyone in society will easily achieve this goal.

An example of unjustifiable public expenditure is, for Bentham, public expenditure to promote the arts and sciences. The member of the legislature promises in the Legislator's Inaugural Declaration:

As little, under any such notion as that of affording *honour* to the nation, *dignity* to its functionaries, encouragement to piety, to learning, to arts, to sciences, and in particular to fine arts, or merely curious sciences, or literary pursuits,—as little, under any such delusive pretence, will I concur in laying burthens on the comparatively indigent many, for the amusement of the comparatively opulent few: at their own expense will I leave them to pursue the gratification of their own tastes. [37]

In discussing the causes of loss in the section on Loss Books, Bentham lists (in a sarcastic vein) as a source of loss, the expenditure of public money on the fine arts or on rare books 'for the accommodation or amusement of the comparatively *opulent few*, at the expense of all, including, in prodigiously greater number, the *unopulent many*, who are incapable of participating in the benefit.'[38] At another point, he criticizes the public functionary who is praised for his liberality with public money. When exercised at a man's own expense, liberality is a virtue; but when cultivated at public expense, a vice.[39] Bentham's attitude is not one of a philistine. He encourages the private cultivation of the arts and sciences and private generosity. But such expenditure by public bodies is a tax on the poor for something from which they receive little benefit.

Bentham's opposition to public spending on the arts will seem anachronistic today, as it is widely accepted that governments have an important role to play in their promotion. The debate nowadays is over the extent to which the government should subsidize the arts which can be enjoyed only by a few. Bentham, however, looks first, not to the benefit but to the burden. Many policies in a civilized state can be defended in terms of bringing some benefit to society generally. Nevertheless, he believes that to place a burden (through taxation) on an identifiable group of people, there should be, in return, a benefit conferred upon them.

Another example of unjustifiable expenditure is the support of a purely offensive war. The legislator recites the following in the Legislator's Inaugural Declaration:

All profit, by conquest in every shape, I acknowledge to be no other than robbery: robbery, having murder for its instrument; both operating upon the largest possible scale: robbery, committed by the ruling few in the conquering nation, on the subject many in both nations: robbery, of which, by the expense of armament, the people of the conquering nation are the first victims: robbery and murder, the guilt of which, as much exceeds the guilt of the crimes commonly called by those names, as the quantity of suffering produced in one case exceeds the quantity produced in the other. [40]

Besides the sense of moral indignation which pervades Bentham's condemnation of conquest, it is worth stressing the element of calculation in these remarks. Conquest, for Bentham, is carried out by the ruling few in one country at the expense of the subject many in both countries. The people generally in the conquering nation must suffer the burdens of paying for armaments as well as suffering injury and death in battle. These burdens are not in Bentham's view outweighed by the benefits that are received by the spoils of war. The burden of a purely defensive war is more acceptable as being worth the benefit of basic security.

Between the extremes of easily justifiable and non-justifiable expense falls the majority of instances which are more difficult to resolve. Consider the example of salaries for civil servants. Bentham assumes that government and hence civil servants are necessary for basic order and security. But the money which civil servants receive entails placing

---

[40] Ch. VII, § 8 (*CW*), pp. 142-3.

a heavy burden on the people to benefit a few. Thus, expenditure such as this is placed under the most careful scrutiny. Practices aimed at increasing efficiency and accountability and reducing expense are advanced, as we have seen, in rich profusion. The object might be considered democratic, i.e. to reduce the burden on the people the payment of such salaries entails. In this realm of practices which are considered necessary but whose immediate benefit belongs to a few, Bentham's skill as a legislator emerges most fully as he attempts to reduce this burden without reducing the quality of government.

As a second part of the democratic dimension, Bentham does not favour efficiency at the expense of the people. He recognizes that by cutting down on the number of government offices in the various subdistricts, considerable savings might be made on the costs of salaries, offices, and official residences. But to do so in many cases it is necessary to shift the burden of expense from the government to the people who are then required to make longer journeys to conduct government business. 'In the case of the vast majority', he writes, 'expense in time is expense in money.'[41] This group, he contends, unlike the idle rich, must use its time constructively and suffers inordinately when faced with distant government offices. In a similar vein he sees delay in government acting as a tax on the people. Referring to judicial proceedings, he asserts that 'every particle of needless delay and vexation,—introduced or left by the Legislator or the Judge, in the proceedings,—produces the afflictive and prohibitive effect of a tax, without the profit of it.'[42] Bentham tries to calculate the costs of delay caused by inefficient government services to the public generally when assessing the merits of particular practices. He often combines discussions of delay and vexation with expense so that the words 'delay, vexation and expense' become a familiar phrase in the *Code*.[43] Thus even efficient practices must be organized so that their efficiency does not depend on a mere shift of expense from the expense of government

---

[41] Ch. I, Art. 6 inst. diss. (*CW*), p. 18.
[42] Ch. VII, § 6 (*CW*), p. 141.
[43] See, for example, ch. VI, § 27, Arts. 17-18, 28; § 31, Art. 29 (*CW*), pp. 97-8, 100-1, 124.

operations to the expense, expressed in delay and vexation, of the people.

Thirdly, in justifying the expense of government operations, Bentham takes into consideration the good produced by a practice in enhancing democracy itself. Consider, for example, the cost of providing publicity throughout government. The cost might be considered as a tax on the people for the sake of paying salaries to government officials, marginally justifiable in terms of providing information for the people. It might also be argued that the supposed benefits of publicity are not enjoyed and utilized by the vast majority of the people but mostly by a few who take an interest in various aspects of government for personal or professional reasons. Nevertheless, Bentham is clearly aware that without widespread publicity, the Public Opinion Tribunal, an essential ingredient in the democracy, cannot function. The maintenance of this key institution is taken into account in calculating the benefits and costs of publicity. Bentham sets forth two rules: maximize publicity and maximize frugality.[44] At times, both can be achieved as with the use of the manifold writing system which enables copies of documents to be made and circulated without the cost of printing.[45] At other times, however, the principles might conflict, but in assessing the principle of frugality, he places great emphasis on weighing in the balance the benefits of publicity to democratic institutions. Where these benefits are enhanced, the burden of expense in providing publicity may be justified.

In these instances, Bentham attempts to cut and minimize expense without losing sight of the importance of maintaining the democratic system itself. Ruling monarchs might find in his *Code* useful suggestions for economy. But there is little doubt that his main commitment is to democracy rather than simply to efficiency or frugality.

---

[44] Ch. VIII, § 11, Art. 3 (*CW*), p. 163.
[45] Ch. VIII, § 10, Art. 1n (*CW*), pp. 160n-1n. The note is omitted in the Bowring version as it appears elsewhere at Bowring, v. 406n. See also the more extensive discussion of publicity in chapter VII below.

Chapter VII

Political Communication

In the chapter on the Public Opinion Tribunal and at numerous other points thus far, we have seen the great emphasis which Bentham places on the scrutiny of the government by the people. The Public Opinion Tribunal operates to an extent like the inspection principle of Panopticon.[1] It attempts to serve as the all-seeing eye, casting its critical reforming gaze over the full spectrum of governmental (indeed public) activity.[2] Nevertheless, the public eye does not always see clearly and, in Bentham's view, a range of problems of political communication contribute to a partial blindness. This condition is partly due to inefficiency in the arrangements for gathering and reporting the right information to the right people. It is also due to the interest of the government (including democratic government) in withholding information about its failures, maladministration, and abuses of power. Finally, there are wider problems of the use of language which also contribute to an inability of the public to see clearly and directly the major problems of government.

Bentham's analysis of a series of problems of communication forms an important part of his theory of government and especially an essential supplement to his treatment of the role of the Public Opinion Tribunal. In this chapter we shall examine these under three broad headings. Firstly, we shall take up the problem of the inspection of government by the people and the importance of publicity. Secondly, we shall consider the organization of the gathering, recording,

---

[1] See *Panopticon; or, The Inspection House* (Bowring, iv. 37-172).

[2] See Gertrude Himmelfarb, 'The Haunted House of Jeremy Bentham', *Victorian Minds*, London, 1968, pp. 32-81, esp. 75-6 where she attempts to link Panopticon and the political radicalism of the *Constitutional Code*. However, she is mistaken in seeing the omnicompetent legislature as the connecting link instead of the Public Opinion Tribunal. For further criticisms of her interpretation of Panopticon and Bentham's political radicalism, see L. J. Hume, 'Revisionism in Bentham Studies', *The Bentham Newsletter*, i (1978), 11-13. See also S. Wolin, *Politics and Vision*, Boston, 1960, p. 348 where he mistakenly assumes that the Public Opinion Tribunal is used to direct society itself by reducing social non-conformity.

and dissemination of information both within and outside government. Finally, we shall discuss Bentham's approach to the use of language in government.

I

We have already noted the importance Bentham attaches to publicity as a major security for good government. Publicity is an important part of political communication and is linked by Bentham with inspection and public criticism. In one sense, successful inspection need not require widespread publicity. A superior functionary inspects the work of his junior and decides to promote or dismiss him. But as soon as wider considerations are taken into account, the connection becomes obvious. The criteria for one man's promotion or dismissal should be related to those of others in similar situations for a modicum of justice and continuity to be established. Warnings of bad practices and examples of good ones have to be disseminated throughout government hierarchies, and where no formal system of publicity exists, informal channels quickly develop. In a democratic government where there is scrutiny of rulers by the ruled the link beween inspection and publicity is stronger and more obvious: democratic inspection must in its nature be public and being public needs publicity.

Without publicity criticism of government officials must be severely restricted. Bentham places both public criticism and publicity at the heart of his approach to democratic government. In discussing the possible defamation of politicians and civil servants, he writes characteristically, 'The military functionary is paid for being shot at. The civil functionary is paid for being spoken and written at.'[3] He clearly intends in the *Code* that restrictions on public criticism should be minimized and that full publicity be given to such criticism. Indeed, one way of characterizing a tyrannical regime for Bentham is that it is one which is exempt from public criticism and publicity.

As Bentham believes that control of government by the governed depends on publicity, he declares in the *Code* that

---

[3] Ch. V, §6, Art. 2 (*CW*), p. 40.

publicity should be maximized in all government departments and offices.[4] He then distinguishes between a general
good and a particular good produced by publicity. The
general good is depicted as 'the efficiency it gives to the force
of the law, and to that of the Public Opinion Tribunal: to
wit, in the character of an instrument of security for appropriate aptitude on the part of all public functionaries.'[5] The
particular good is the benefit realized by particular individuals
by virtue of their receiving the desired information. In this
section we are mainly concerned with publicity as an instrument of security.

Bentham is well aware that limits have to be placed on
the rule of maximizing publicity. The first limit is that
dictated by the need also to maximize frugality in government. He proposes a rough calculation of costs and benefits
with regard to the expense of publicity. Nevertheless, he
clearly does not want publicity for important government
measures withheld on grounds of expense. While he recognizes limits dictated by expense, he looks to other means to
reduce it. For example, he recommends, as we have seen, the
manifold writing system invented by Ralph Wedgwood
(1766-1837) and enthusiastically adopted by Bentham by
which copies of documents are made by writing on ink-
soaked silk cloths (in the same manner as carbon copies are
made today) as a way of gaining publicity by providing extra
exact copies of government papers at little expense when
compared with copying by hand or printing.[6] Here is a way
of maximizing both publicity and frugality.

A second limitation on publicity arises where the evil of
publicity outweighs the benefit produced by it. Bentham
provides a number of examples such as publicity given to
secret votes at elections, military strategy and defence plans,
information about the police, information helpful to hostile
or rival governments, or information about diseases which
may be thought 'disreputable'.[7] These examples of exceptions,
especially those concerned with national security, may be
thought to cover a wide area and may be used to justify

---

[4] Ch. VIII, § 11, Art. 2 (*CW*), p. 162.
[5] Ibid., Art. 4 (*CW*), p. 163.
[6] Ch. VIII, § 10, Arts. 1-6 (*CW*), pp. 159-62.
[7] Ch. VIII, § 11, Art. 6 (*CW*), pp. 163-4.

virtually any restriction on publicity. Bentham may have been aware of the wide scope of his exceptions to full publicity, as he proceeds to add some further conditions which limit them.[8] These further conditions are concerned with both the duration of the secrecy and the number of persons who are excluded from the information. Most importantly, he emphasizes that the burden is on the advocate of secrecy to justify his case and not on the proponent of publicity. To support this emphasis, he proposes that the prime minister each year makes a report which lists the areas where demands for secrecy are no longer necessary as well as those which should be continued. He also provides for a legislative committee to prepare a similar report as a way of checking the report of the prime minister.[9]

Although the theme of maximizing publicity runs throughout the *Code* and is developed differently in different contexts, one striking development, perhaps reminiscent of Panopticon, is the way Bentham deals with the theme of publicity in relation to architecture.[10] Although publicity may not be the sole end that architectural arrangements are supposed to advance (others are the avoidance of delay, vexation, and expense), it is one of the most important.[11] In making arrangements for publicity and secrecy, Bentham proposes that factors such as 'occasions', 'persons', 'places', 'times', 'points of time', and 'lengths of time' are taken into account.[12]

The only detailed example in the section on architecture which deals with publicity is that of 'waiting boxes' for members of the public who have business to conduct with a minister or other governmental official.[13] Bentham designs in considerable detail (though without providing illustrations) arrangements for public and private chambers before which the minister and his clerks sit. The private waiting-boxes allow for secret unobserved meetings between the minister and persons such as informers whose identities must remain secret. But the bulk of the meetings are public, and the

[8] Ibid., Arts. 14–15 (*CW*), pp. 166–7.
[9] Ibid., Arts. 15–17 (*CW*), p. 167.
[10] Ch. IX, § 26 (*CW*), pp. 438–57.
[11] Ibid., Art. 4 (*CW*), pp. 438–9.
[12] Ibid., Art. 5 (*CW*), p. 439.
[13] Ibid., Arts. 21–31 (*CW*), pp. 445–9.

waiting-boxes are so arranged that those waiting to see the minister become observers of the business which passes between the minister and those ahead in the queue. This arrangement which is efficiently and carefully designed builds the element of publicity into the very structure of the building without sacrificing the need for occasional secrecy and without costing more than any other arrangement. Bentham approaches his ideal of maximizing publicity through this detailed exposition of waiting-boxes. It might be noted that unlike Panopticon where the people in the centre are observing those in the cells, here the people in the waiting-boxes are observing the public figures in the centre—and, of course, those in the waiting-boxes are free to come and go.

Thus far, we have emphasized the use of publicity as a security for the people against the government. Bentham also uses publicity to prevent oppression within government hierarchies. For example, full publicity must be given to all cases of dismissal, transfer, promotion, etc. within the government.[14] Publicity is listed as one of the major 'indirect' (non-judicial) remedies against oppression both within government and between government officials and various private citizens who have business to transact with the government.[15] Bentham sees publicity, as opposed to conflict of interest legislation, as the best remedy against partiality in awarding contracts for government purchases.[16] It is also considered useful in preventing the embezzlement of funds and fraud in the receipt and disbursement of money.[17]

Perhaps less interesting, though no less important, is Bentham's approach to the whole problem of gathering, recording, and publishing information. His ideas evolved gradually as he was writing the *Code*. In his chapter on the legislature he seems to rely on his earlier work on evidence, but later, when dealing with the administration, he develops more fully a conception of information.[18] He notes that his discussion of information should have appeared earlier in the chapter on the legislature 'but the views of the author

[14] Ch. IX, § 21, Art. 70 (*CW*), p. 408.
[15] Ibid., Arts. 10, 20 (*CW*), pp. 393, 395-6.
[16] Ch. IX, § 23, Arts. 6-7, 16 (*CW*), pp. 413, 416-17.
[17] Ibid., Art. 13 (*CW*), pp. 415-16.
[18] Cf. ch. VI, § 27 (*CW*), pp. 91-111, and ch. IX, § 10 (*CW*), pp. 283-90.

had not at that time received the correspondent extension'.[19] In this later material, he settles on three basic categories of information, each of which presents problems of procedure and organization: (a) that which is furnished spontaneously to other functionaries and to the legislature; (b) that which is obtained regularly and constantly by the registration and publication systems; and (c) that which is elicited.[20] Bentham then requires that (with exceptions determined by the legislature) information of all 'occurrences' (a technical term he employs) relevant to the various administrative offices must be furnished both to the prime minister and to the legislature.[21] As an occurrence can include virtually any fact about a person or thing, Bentham first opens the scope of information very wide and then places the burden largely on the legislature to make exceptions to the general rule. The legislature, among other things, considers the burden and expense of gathering and keeping this information and determines what information should not be transmitted unless explicitly requested.[22] The ministers, however, receive full information from subordinates in their sub-departments, and the legislature, in addition, establishes which superior offices within the various sub-departments should receive information.[23]

As is commonly the case, Bentham chooses as the contrasting practice the example of England. He notes that no comprehensive system for furnishing information from the administration to the legislature exists. No written information is furnished to either House unless there is a resolution passed and an order made with the consent of the monarch. Although these resolutions are not usually refused by the monarch when made by a member of the administration, Bentham notes that they are often refused when made by someone connected with a party not in office. The consequences of this state of affairs, he argues, are especially

---

[19] Ch. IX, § 10, Art. 9n (*CW*), p. 285n.

[20] Ibid., Arts. 9–10 (*CW*), p. 285.

[21] Ibid., Art. 11. See also ch. IX, § 4, Art. 12 (*CW*), p. 189: '*Occurrences*— to this denomination will be found referrible all *fictitious entities*, considered as presenting themselves to human notice: that is to say, in each instance, the matter of fact consisting in their so presenting themselves.'

[22] Ch. IX, § 10, Art. 12 (*CW*), pp. 285–6.

[23] Ibid., Arts. 13–14 (*CW*), p. 286.

pernicious. As no information is made available without its consent, it is difficult, if not impossible, to gather sufficient information to criticize or censure the party in power. Even where the ruling party does not oppose the provision of information, it is largely a matter of accident that this material is actually possessed by the House. There is no general system for supplying uncontroversial information, and consequently any number of evils which might have been prevented continue because of a lack of appropriate information. Although the House of Commons receives some information in the process of formulating legislation, the House of Lords often lacks even this. The two Houses act on different grounds because, among other things, of this difference in information. Finally, due to the limited, partial information which is available, effective legal punishment or punishment by the Public Opinion Tribunal is impossible.[24]

Of the three categories of information, the one which presents the greatest difficulties is the elicitation of information. Bentham introduces his discussion of the information-elicitative function in a somewhat curious way:

Art. 1. Exceptions excepted,—to every functionary belongs the information-elicitative function, exerciseable at the hands of every other person, functionary or non-functionary, in so far as the receipt of the information in question is necessary or useful.[25]

One would expect that the information-elicitative function would consist simply of the power to elicit evidence, but, as we can see, Bentham first establishes the function within a series of obligations. Although the passage is not very clear, he seems to say that the function consists of the obligation of government officials to supply information when needed by both officials and non-officials. He also notes that within the government there is no need to distinguish between simply receiving information and 'extracting' it, because each government official stands, under the registration and publication systems, obliged to furnish whatever information is required.[26] But where the person required to give information

---

[24] Ibid., Arts. 22–3 (*CW*), pp. 288–9.
[25] Ch. IX, § 11, Art. 1 (*CW*), p. 290. The exceptions are those required for secrecy.
[26] Ibid., Art. 3 (*CW*), pp. 290–1.

is not a government official, the situation becomes more complex, and here the difference between a spontaneous furnisher of information and an unwilling provider who must be questioned is of the greatest importance. For the latter, Bentham refers to prevailing judicial procedures for such interrogations and notes that happily in administration the need to obtain information from unwilling persons is not very great. The minister of each sub-department is given the power to 'extract' evidence, and the legislature decides which subordinate officials should have similar powers.[27] He also proposes giving to the legislature the power to determine which members of the army and navy (and under what conditions) should have the power to obtain information from 'persons at large' in order to secure the defence of the country.[28] The legislature determines in addition, what information the people are obliged to furnish spontaneously, as, for example, information regarding a calamity to the police or regarding invasion to the army.[29]

Bentham realizes that the compulsory 'extraction' of information may be open to abuse. He refers to the sections on insubordination, oppression, and extortion for the securities which would prevent both the disturbance of the proceedings and the oppression of the person possessing the information.[30] He makes one specific reservation, precluding inquiry into matters of religion, on the grounds that religious opinions should not be subjects of legislation and administration.[31] And where people are obliged to furnish information spontaneously he seeks to ensure that they clearly know their obligations.

Thus far, we have concentrated on the role of the administration in gathering information. The legislature also plays an important role in this process both as a major repository of information from the administration, and as the body which determines what information will be received. However, the legislature not only receives information

---

[27] Ibid., Art. 6 (*CW*), p. 291.
[28] Ibid., Art. 9 (*CW*), p. 292.
[29] Ibid., Arts. 12-14 (*CW*), pp. 292-3. Bentham cites the English example of the charge of misprision where there is a failure to report an instance of treason.
[30] Ibid., Art. 7 (*CW*), p. 291.
[31] Ibid., Art. 11 (*CW*), p. 292.

but also, through the Legislation Inquiry Judicatory, gathers its own. The purpose of the Legislation Inquiry Judicatory is strictly limited to gathering information in preparation for enacting a new law, and it is in this sense different from an ordinary judicatory. It is a unique organ of the legislature, and a major problem for Bentham is how to organize it in relation to the main body. Although it is desirable that preparatory work should be performed by the same hands which enact the legislation, for obvious reasons of time, it would be rare for the legislature as a whole to elicit evidence. On most occasions, a committee consisting of one or more persons (usually an odd number) would do the work. A member of the committee is called a 'Legislation Elicitor'.[32] A Legislation Elicitor need not be a member of the legislature: he may be a judge or a judge depute. If a deputy is an Elicitor, none of the committee meetings can take place when the legislature is in session conducting business.[33] Bentham thus avoids the problem of empty legislative chambers due to committee work by allowing (even encouraging) others besides deputies to fill the posts. Not all of the evidence (indeed, probably a small amount) necessary for the preparation of legislation has to be obtained from unwilling witnesses. Much evidence will have been already elicited for other purposes and preserved. Bentham's term for this material is 'preappointed evidence' which may be found already gathered through the registration system or at the local level by the local registrars.[34]

He assigns to the Legislation Inquiry Judicatory all of the powers which would be possessed by a judicature and any additional powers, like eliciting information abroad from government agents, which may be necessary for legislation.[35] Furthermore, some of the constraints on the 'extraction' of evidence, occasioned by cost or time, which would apply in a single court case, do not apply to the 'extraction' of evidence for a legislative purpose. Bentham notes that in one

[32] Ch. VI, § 27, Art. 24 (*CW*), pp. 99–100. Bentham considers several alternative names, including 'Legislational Inquest man'. He notes that 'Inquisitor' would be a good choice 'but for the odious idea so indissolubly associated with it.'
[33] Ibid., Arts. 26–7 (*CW*), p. 100.
[34] Ibid., Arts. 7–9 (*CW*), pp. 94–5.
[35] Ibid., Art. 15 (*CW*), p. 97.

sense a court, in being able to confront witnesses and draw inferences from silence or even hesitation, is better able to obtain the appropriate evidence than is a legislative body which does not require too much evidence of this sort. Nevertheless, at times this evidence, which Bentham calls 'negative' evidence, is often crucial to decisions, and he provides for oral examinations in order to explain or expand written evidence.[36]

As with the administration, Bentham finds the contrasting case in English practice. However, he is not without praise for the committees of the House of Commons especially when contrasted with the English judiciary. He notes especially the way the House of Commons has moved forward towards reform in alliance with 'the great majority of the people'.[37] However, the House of Commons is considered deficient in its powers for eliciting evidence in several respects. It does not possess even the powers of a judge in requiring attendance and in securing truthful responses, because the power of the House of Commons, unlike a court, is limited to the duration of the parliament, at best seven years, but often considerably less. By evading a summons and avoiding apprehension a witness might successfully avoid testifying. Furthermore, for false evidence the House of Commons can only imprison the perjuror for the length of the parliament, while the judge can inflict very severe penalties for perjury. Bentham is also critical of Royal Commissions which, he notes, lack the powers of judges and even the power possessed by the House of Commons to secure attendance and truthful replies to questions. Bentham seems to suggest that a Royal Commission is used when those in power desire to avoid an inquiry by the House of Commons.[38]

Besides the elicitation of information and evidence, Bentham provides for the preparation and distribution of various documents in his account of the Registration System.

---

[36] Ibid., Arts. 16, 19-21 (*CW*), pp. 97, 98-9. 'For, seldom can the sufficiency of the securities afforded against deception,—whether by evidence, or *for want* of evidence,—be maximized, without the benefit of instant answers or silence in return to questions arising instantly out of preceding answers or silence, and the interpretation thereupon capable of being afforded—by tone, countenance, gesture, and deportment' (Art. 21, *CW*, p. 99).

[37] Ibid., Art. 46 (*CW*), p. 105. See Arts. 39-49 (*CW*), pp. 102-7.

[38] See especially ibid., Art. 55 (*CW*), p. 110.

As we have seen, he depends largely on manifold writing which obtains cheap and exact copies of documents. To 'prevent the useful from being drowned in the mass of useless matter', Bentham also provides for the legislature to arrange for the periodic destruction of useless documents.[39] To further the aim of gathering information Bentham creates the office of the Local Registrar, who, in each of the smallest bits of territory, performs a number of important functions in gathering pre-appointed evidence.[40] He gathers information which nowadays would be contained in the census. In addition, he records births, deaths, marriages, divorces, children reaching maturity, 'lapses into insanity', and 'restorations to sanity'.[41] He records contracts, transfers of property and receives evidence as requested by the legislature or a sub-legislature. He is the custodian of maps of properties within his locality and is the general custodian of documents. This official, then, is the basic receiver of information within the state. Within the judicial system, there are officials who perform similar functions with regard to the receipt and custody of evidence.[42]

III

The culmination of Bentham's concern with the receipt, custody, and distribution of information in the *Code* appears in the chapter on the statistic function.[43] Here he attempts to construct for the administration a comprehensive system of records of all the personnel and materials with which government is concerned. Bentham's approach to this theme reflects one important premiss which he uses throughout the *Code*, that the mere gathering of information, however important and relevant, is not sufficient for providing information for good government. The way in which the information is recorded and kept is just as important, because the original information can become a useless mass and its impenetrability can prevent appropriate action. Bentham

---

[39] Ch. VIII, § 10, Art. 7 (*CW*), p. 162.
[40] Bowring, ix. 625-36.
[41] Ibid., p. 627.
[42] Ibid., pp. 579-85.
[43] Ch. IX, § 7 (*CW*), pp. 218-68.

seeks to acquire all the information of government on the one hand and, in addition, to organize it in a manner which will enable it to be used easily.

Keeping full and accurate records had long been an important concern of Bentham and a similar emphasis may be found as early as the Panopticon writings.[44] Bentham thinks that the exercise of the statistic function is so important that, as we have seen, he nearly accords to its exercise the status of a universal moral right.[45] The statistic function is exercised:

in so far as indication is afforded of facts, of a nature to operate, as grounds for judgment, of approbation or disapprobation, in relation to any public institution, ordinance, arrangement, proceeding or measure, past, present, or supposed future contingent, or to any mode of conduct, on the part of any person, functionary or non-functionary, by which the interests of the public at large may be affected. [46]

These words depict the statistic function as exercised by the Public Opinion Tribunal and reveal its full scope. Virtually all information relevant to the public interest should be recorded. Members of the government, and especially members of the administration, however, have more than a moral right to record appropriate information. They have a legal duty to do so and Bentham proceeds to design the various books and journals to ensure that they carry out their duty in a clear and comprehensive manner.

The task that Bentham has set himself is extremely complex. Before plunging into the minutiae of the different books and the heads for various entries, he dwells on basic principles. He begins by noting that there is no absolute distinction between useful and useless information. What some people think is trivial will be seen by others as necessary.[47] He tends to favour gathering more information than less and relying on clear and coherent presentation to minimize any threat posed by the supply of too much useless information.

In stating the ends that the exercise of the statistic function is supposed to serve, Bentham emphasizes that the main task of a system of records is to provide a view of information

---

[44] See L. J. Hume, 'Jeremy Bentham on Industrial Management', *The Yorkshire Bulletin of Economic and Social Research*, xxii (1970) 5, 11-12.

[45] See chapter IV above.

[46] Ch. V, §5, Art. 1 (*CW*), p. 36.

[47] Ch. IX, §7, Bi§1, Art. 1 (*CW*), p. 218.

regarding the past which will enable citizens and politicians to make adequate provision for the future. He admits that all governments, even the worst, keep some kind of records and use the past in this way. His system is designed to improve the quality of the information and increase the quantity without increasing expense to any extent. A subsidiary end is that of preventing loss in various government sub-departments and having the correct information so as to prevent loss in the future.[48] As for the subject-matters which provide the raw material for the exercise of the statistic function, he provides an analytical sketch in the earlier section on functions.[49] The distinctions are familiar ones: real and fictitious entities, persons and things, movables and immovables, occurrences, states, interior and exterior occurrences, important and unimportant occurrences, relevant and irrelevant occurrences etc. Bentham's task here is to design the registers to record the important facts about these various entities and occurrences. One important considera-tion is that of 'relative time', that is to say, the time of 'entry' of an item or person into a particular office, the 'continuance' of it or him in the use or service of the office, and finally the 'exit', if and when it occurs. During 'con-tinuance' in use, different entities will be used in different ways and record books have to be designed to reflect these different uses. Some things continue to be used for long periods and others as, for example, food, money, ammuni-tion, etc., are only used by their 'exit'.[50]

In turning to the Register Books, which are Bentham's main concern, he begins by distinguishing between Service Books which record the operations of particular offices and Loss Books. The Service Books are divided into two sorts: Outset Books (which are inventories) and Journal Books (which are diaries). The Outset Books are of two kinds: (a) the Original Outset Book contains the basic inventory of a sub-department when the registration system is intro-duced; and (b) the Periodical Outset Books record inventories at specific intervals of time. All of the books—Original Out-set, Periodical Outset, Journal, and Loss—are divided into

---

[48] Ibid., Arts. 3-5 (*CW*), pp. 219-20.
[49] See ch. IX, § 4, Arts. 1-43 (*CW*), pp. 186-96.
[50] Ch. IX, § 7, Bi § 1, Arts. 7-8 (*CW*), p. 220.

four Specific Books: (1) Personal, (2) Immovable, (3) Movable, (4) Money. In addition, the Journal Book contains a fifth division: Occurrence Book. These divisions correspond to the distinctions made earlier in the various subject-matters of government. Furthermore, for each of the four or five Specific Books, there are three Generic Books concerned with (1) Entrance, (2) Continuance, and (3) Exit.[51] Thus, the Original Outset Book, which is the basic inventory at the start of the system, is divided into four books. These record respectively the personnel, the immovable objects like buildings, land etc., the movable objects such as materials, desks etc., and money.[52]

Before examining the various books in considerable detail, Bentham pauses to justify the utility of his arrangement.[53] As for the Service Books (Original Outset, Periodical Outset, and Journal Books), he asserts the following:

(1) On any particular day the stock in hand is readily apparent for the next few days, and this can be used to estimate ordinary supply and demand for the future.

(2) Instances of extraordinary supply and demand in the past can be recognized and provision made for similar situations in the future.

(3) Data is provided for comparisons (and improvements) in the fabrication, purchase, and hire of stock with regard to cheapness, quality, economical use of materials, and prices paid for materials.

(4) Similarly, with the sale of stock, comparisons can be made which would lead to increased profit.

(5) With regard to the storage of articles, future demand in general can be estimated, and deficiency or oversupply of materials at particular places can be prevented.

(6) Generally, redundancy in supply can be detected and oversupply stopped.

(7) Misconduct by staff based on negligence or rashness can be detected as well as fraud or the non-performance of contracts.

[51] Ibid., Arts. 11-12 (*CW*), p. 221.

[52] It does not seem that the Entrance, Continuance, and Exit Books are used in relation to the Original Outset Book, as it records the basic inventory. These books are used especially with the Journal and Loss Books which record the day-to-day activities of sub-departments.

[53] See, ibid., Arts. 17-22 (*CW*), pp. 222-5.

(8) Instances of 'extra merit' requiring extra remuneration can also be determined.[54]

The above list should provide a fair sample of what Bentham thinks his system of Service Books can achieve. It will be worth adding to these his list of the uses of Loss Books:

(1) By pointing to the nature, causes, and authors of particular instances of loss, similar losses in the future can be prevented.
(2) By calling attention to loss over specific periods, 'preventive attention' can be increased where there has been an increase in loss.
(3) The attention of inspecting superordinates can be called to loss by the negligence or delinquency of their own subordinates or by non-functionaries under their control.
(4) Bad bargains with non-functionaries with respect to purchase, hire, sale, or leasing can be prevented.
(5) Efforts made to prevent loss can be recognized and rewarded, thus stimulating officials to try to minimize loss, and furnishing information for the Public Opinion Tribunal to censure those responsible for it.[55]

After Bentham depicts the exercise of the statistic function in general terms, he devotes much of the remainder of the lengthy and complex section to the presentation and justification of the entries required in the various books. Although much of this material is somewhat tedious, it is in this detail of organization that Bentham's contribution lies. If various malpractices are to be prevented and the most efficient use of resources promoted, the journal books must record the appropriate information to enable these ends to be furthered. This makes the categories formed by the entry headings of crucial importance to the success of the scheme. It is true of course that the appropriate information may be provided but no action taken as a result. Bentham is aware of this problem and attempts to deal with this deficiency in 'active aptitude' in other securities in the *Code*. Furthermore, in this section, he occasionally goes beyond setting out the organization of the various books to discuss their application. For example, he issues a 'precautionary rule' regarding the stowage of goods sent a long distance in requiring that all related materials are sent together.[56] A footnote reveals the basis of his concern. In the American War of Independence, there were examples of arms sent across the ocean with the cannons in one ship, the cannon-balls in a second, and the powder in a third with disastrous consequences when one ship was sunk.

IV

There is a close connection between the task of keeping records and a series of problems which arise concerning the language of records. Bentham frequently issues a series of injunctions about 'desirable properties' in evidence, motions, written reports, etc. which include clearness, conciseness, correctness, comprehensiveness, appositiveness, impartiality, and non-redundancy.[57] In one instance, when expounding some of the virtues of these characteristics to be embodied in evidence he explains his terms as follows:

clearness, that is to say, exemptness, as well from *ambiguity* as from *obscurity*: *impartiality*, that is to say, comprehensiveness, or say exemption from deficiency, as well as from incorrectness, in so far as those imperfections would respectively be productive of undue assistance to either side; all-comprehensiveness, for the sake of sufficiency of information and avoidance of deceptiousness, on the part of the effect: to wit, the effect produced on men's judgments by the whole body of the evidence: non-redundance, for the sake of *clearness*, and for saving of useless delay, vexation and expense, on the part of all persons interested.[58]

The properties become ends to be embodied in written documents by various devices of drafting and organizing, and these in turn become securities for intellectual aptitude.[59] A clearly drafted piece of evidence or legislation allows the people involved to grasp what is at stake on an issue and the Public Opinion Tribunal to exercise its influence. Thus, when

---

[56] Ibid., Bi § 2, Art. 25 and n (*CW*), p. 237 and n.
[57] See, for example, ch. VI, § 27, Arts. 18, 39, 44; § 31, Art. 44 (*CW*), pp. 98, 102-3, 104, 132-3.
[58] Ch. VI, § 27, Art. 18 (*CW*), p. 98.
[59] Ch. VI, § 31, Art. 44 (*CW*), pp. 132-3.

the newly elected member of the legislature reads the Legislator's Inaugural Declaration, in promising to make the laws known to all, he also promises to present legislation 'in a form as clear, correct, complete, concise, and compact as possible' so that the laws can be known directly and, in addition, serve as a subject for study in schools.[60] These all-pervasive desirable characteristics of government documents and evidence reappear in his discussion of the use of abbreviations in the exercise of the statistic function.[61] Bentham is cautious in his approach to abbreviations and is as aware of their potential misuse as he is of their utility. He notes that on the one hand a work embodying the extensive use of abbreviations gains in conciseness, but on the other hand it may very well lose clarity, especially if readers are unfamiliar with them. He sets out a series of rules to guide the use of abbreviations so that these difficulties might be overcome. Firstly, only analogous abbreviations should be used, such as initial letters, so that the connection can easily be made between the abbreviation and the term being abbreviated. Secondly, every book using abbreviations must have a list of abbreviations at the beginning. Thirdly, abbreviations in writings for the general public should be readily familiar, and their use should not diminish the role of the Public Opinion Tribunal. Finally, functionaries themselves should not be free to use in their various offices abbreviations of their own invention to avoid the influence of the Public Opinion Tribunal. Bentham gives the task of overseeing the use of abbreviations to the legislature which decides which sub-departments should use them and what abbreviations should be used.

In spite of his thorough grasp of such problems in communication as are raised by the use of abbreviations or unclear language generally, Bentham seems unaware of one problem which is frequently encountered nowadays—the use of technical language as a barrier to general understanding. It might be argued that his own use of a highly technical terminology, for all its exactness, has rendered many of his books nearly unreadable. And surely, technical language is a greater barrier to public understanding than its close cousin,

[60] Ch. VII, § 5 (*CW*), pp. 140-1.
[61] Ch. IX, § 7, Bi § 6, Arts. 1-5 (*CW*), pp. 263-7.

inexact or defective abbreviation. Bentham may fall into a trap, because he seeks refuge in technical language from the storms and pitfalls of ordinary, rhetorical, 'delusive' language. For example, talk about natural rights is regarded by Bentham as obscure, misleading, and ultimately useless rhetoric, and he replaces this, as we have seen (chapter IV), with the more precise though stipulated notion of securities for appropriate aptitude. But the latter is surrounded by a different sort of obscurity. Bentham's terminology is beyond the reach of ordinary speech. It is protected from contamination by rhetoric; any number of people would fight and die for 'liberty' or their 'rights', but who would struggle for 'securities for appropriate aptitude'? Being beyond the grasp of ordinary opinion, Bentham's technical terms are also difficult to comprehend and use so that his much esteemed Public Opinion Tribunal would most likely fail to grasp many of the provisions of the *Constitutional Code*. A positive, creative tension between ordinary speech and stipulated terms is not strong in Bentham due to his aversion to the rhetorical dimension of ordinary speech.

Bentham's opposition to rhetorical political language is based on his belief that words like 'honour', 'glory', 'dignity', etc. are delusive words 'employed by rulers, for the purpose of engaging subject citizens to consent, or submit, to be led, for the purpose of depredation, to the commission of murder upon the largest scale.'[62] This belief is of crucial importance to him, as he needs it to account for the fact that people willingly ignore their true interests. What keeps the English people from throwing off the burdens their corrupt and oppressive government places on them is not force, because Bentham readily admits that the English government is not based on force. Consent is obtained by a combination of delusion and corruption.[63] In the Legislator's Inaugural Declaration Bentham has the legislator promise that he will be sincere and never use delusion or deception to frame legislative ordinances or in debate. He promises to give to his writings and speeches 'the greatest degree of *transparency*, and thence of simplicity, possible'.[64] But Bentham cannot simplify and

[62] Ch. VII, § 8 (*CW*), p. 143.
[63] Ch. IX, § 17, conc. inst., Art. 1n (*CW*), p. 362n.
[64] Ch. VII, § 13 (*CW*), p. 146.

clarify ordinary speech to achieve the ends he seeks. He has to purge ordinary language of any number of delusive qualities, and in doing so, he continually creates (often inventively) a technical language. In spite of many successes with the introduction of new words, there is no doubt that he was unaware of the disadvantages of this new vocabulary in creating a new form of delusion which his system of communication was ill-adapted to overcome.

Chapter VIII

The Institutions of Democratic Government

We have now examined a number of Bentham's main concepts and some of the proposed institutions and practices he devises to implement them. But there are many important parts of the *Code* which have barely been mentioned. In this chapter, we shall survey all of the main institutions of Bentham's democracy. The material on the electorate, legislature, and administration, on which we have tended to concentrate, will be presented more as a review with emphasis placed on material not raised in earlier chapters. Much greater attention will be given to parts of the *Code* on which we have not yet dwelled such as the military, judiciary, and local government.

I

The state is formally divided into districts, subdistricts, bis-subdistricts and, if necessary, tris-subdistricts.[1] Bentham proposes using a single divisor to create the various divisions. Using the divisor of 20, he notes that there would be 20 districts, 400 subdistricts, 8000 bis-subdistricts and 160,000 tris-subdistricts. The smallest unit he envisages is the tris-subdistrict. Nevertheless, he is not dogmatic in his proposal. The divisor may be changed depending on the territory of the state and the size of the population. In a very small state such as a Swiss Canton there may only be one division or perhaps none at all. Even where there is no division, Bentham would still prescribe a representative system, as its virtues do not depend on the size of the state.

The first division into districts creates the electoral districts for the legislature. From each district one member is elected on a 'first past the post' basis. Within each district is a sub-legislature, and the subdistricts form the electoral units from which the members of the various sub-legislatures are chosen.

[1] For Bentham's discussion of the main divisions in the territory of the state, see ch. I, Arts. 1-6 inst. diss. (*CW*), pp. 12-18.

Furthermore, each district is called a judicial district and hence there are as many judicial districts as there are sub-legislatures. In each judicial district is an appellate judicatory; in each subdistrict (or other division), the various immediate judicatories. The smallest unit of territory is under the authority of the local headman.

Bentham himself favoured a simple form of government as opposed to a federal structure, but he was aware that the most important representative democracy, the United States, was in fact a federal system. He was thus willing to see a government which adopted the *Code* adapt it to a federal system by giving the appropriate powers to the sub-legislatures.[2] Nevertheless, he also presents a number of arguments against a federal system and in favour of a simple one.[3]

II

Bentham separates the main institutions of the state into four supreme authorities: (1) constitutive (electorate), (2) legislative, (3) administrative, and (4) judiciary. For each authority, there is a department and within each department there may be a number of sub-departments. For example, the administrative department contains thirteen sub-departments, each headed by a minister. Furthermore the sub-legislatures form sub-departments of the legislative department.[4]

We shall first examine the constitutive authority in the state, which Bentham depicts in terms of the electorate and the Public Opinion Tribunal. We have already concentrated considerable attention on the Public Opinion Tribunal (see chapter II). Here we shall emphasize the electorate and present a basic review of the qualifications for suffrage. In both the Election Code and the *Constitutional Code* Bentham favours what he calls 'virtual universality' of suffrage.[5] Although he bows to popular prejudice in excluding women

---

[2] Bowring, ix. 643-4. See also ch. VI, §3, Art. 5 (*CW*), p. 47.
[3] Ibid., pp. 644-7.
[4] Ch. IV, Arts. 1-14 (*CW*), pp. 26-8.
[5] The Election Code (*Bentham's Radical Reform Bill*) was incorporated into the *Constitutional Code* at ch. VI, §§ 4-17 (*CW*), p. 48. As for the difficulties in doing so, see the Introduction to the *Constitutional Code*, vol. I (*CW*), pp. xxv-xxvi. See also Bowring, iii. 559-60.

from suffrage, he notes that the proposal for female suffrage is not absurd.[6] Children are also excluded, and the voting age is set at twenty-one.[7] The potential voter must have been an occupier of a household within the Election District for a suggested period of four weeks. This is certified by three voters who have been resident in the district for a suggested period of twenty-six weeks. The three 'vote-makers' also certify his age and his literacy. He must be able to read the 'vote-making certificate', lines from the act of parliament which authorizes the certificate, some passages from the New Testament, and he must sign a declaration promising honesty and secrecy in suffrage.[8] Bentham does not propose to exclude criminals or the insane from voting. If they are locked away, they will be practically prevented from doing so. But for those not confined in prison, he notes:

> But the most mischievous among criminals, adjudged and denominated such after legal conviction, could not set his foot in either House, without finding himself in company with men in numbers—not to say in a vast majority—more mischievous than himself: men, whose principal differences from himself, consist in impunity derived from situation and confederacy—in impunity added to greater mischievousness: men, whose mischievousness was acting on the largest scale, while his was acting on a petty scale. Exclude criminals? *How* will you exclude criminals?[9]

Bentham perhaps prudently omits to extrapolate on the insane but his overall argument is that the effect of excluding people such as these is minimal in terms of the total electorate. More significant, perhaps, are the requirements of literacy and the qualification of 'householdership'. The former is not, for Bentham, a true exclusion as he believes that most adults can acquire literacy in two or three months of study during the period of rest from work.[10] The householders must be able to pay rent and some taxes as well as be resident for a brief but fixed period. This excludes the military unless they are also householders, foreigners, and

---

[6] Bowring, iii. 567n. See also the recent debate over Bentham's 'feminism' between T. Ball and L. Boralevi in *The Bentham Newsletter*, iv (1980), 25–48.

[7] Bowring, iii. 565. Bentham is not dogmatic about the voting age, as may be seen in his critique of James Mill, see chapter IX below.

[8] Ibid., pp. 564–7.   [9] Ibid., p. 559.   [10] Ibid., p. 560.

.

bankrupts, but Bentham does not use the qualification to exclude the poor.[11]

The main powers of the electorate are, firstly, to elect members to the legislature and to the various sub-legislatures. Secondly, they are given rather more 'dislocative' power, that is to say, power to dismiss by petition and vote a wide range of officials. These include the members of the legislature, prime minister, ministers, justice minister, all judges and judicial officers, all deputes, local headmen and local registrars, members of sub-legislatures, district prime ministers and ministers.[12] This extensive power to remove all of the main officials from office by a petition of one-fourth of the relevant electorate and then a majority vote places a relatively centralized government under community authority. In addition to the power of dismissal, Bentham provides for the power to charge the person dismissed with various offences which he will have to defend in court. This is done at the same time as the vote for dismissal is taken.[13]

III

In the Election Code, Bentham places few restrictions on eligibility for election to the legislature.[14] A person becomes eligible when at least six 'recommenders' (but no more than twelve) who have been resident in the election district for at least a year certify that he is a suitable person for office. In addition, payment must be made of a sum of money for defraying the expenses of the election. Bentham suggests £120 which would have been a considerable sum at the time, and it is not a returnable deposit. The candidate does not seem to have to be a resident of the district.[15]

The legislature consists of one chamber, elected for one year, although Bentham allows for a slightly longer period if time is needed to reach the legislature from districts located at a distance.[16] The elected member can sit in the legislature

---

[11] Ibid., pp. 559-60.   [12] Ch. V, § 2, Arts. 3-6 (*CW*), pp. 30-2.
[13] Ch. V, § 3, Arts. 4-10 (*CW*), pp. 33-5.   [14] See Bowring, iii. 566-7.
[15] In the *Code*, Bentham adds, though he does not discuss, the important qualification that eligible candidates must have passed successfully through the system of instruction and examination which he devises for the civil service. See ch. VI, § 31, Art. 44 (*CW*), p. 132. See also chapter X below.
[16] Ch. VI, § 22 (*CW*), pp. 57-9; § 31, Art. 42 (*CW*), pp. 130-1.

for one term only. Under Bentham's 'temporary non-relocability system', each member is barred from re-election for several years until there is a pool of former experienced members from which to choose new legislators.[17] Bentham seeks to guarantee full choice between at least two candidates who stand on an equal footing. In order to maintain continuity from one legislative session to the next, Bentham provides for a Continuation Committee of approximately 7-21 members who may be re-elected indefinitely. The members sit in the legislature to advise and propose motions, but do not possess the power to vote.[18]

The legislature meets throughout the year with every seventh day declared a day of rest. No other holidays are given and in case of emergency, the legislature can sit on rest days.[19] Strict rules for recording attendance and for making remuneration dependent on attendance are set forth.[20] In order that each legislative seat is filled continually, even when the member is ill, or unavoidably absent, the member is required to appoint a substitute or depute who takes his place.[21] Anyone eligible as a deputy is eligible as a depute. By the use of the depute and the requirement of full attendance, Bentham hopes to assign full responsibility for voting and debate in the assembly to the various deputies. As for voting, Bentham gives full power to the majority actually present in the legislature. He also provides remedies against attempts to exclude deputies from attending the legislative sessions.[22] As for grounds for removal from office, these include dismissal by the electorate (by petition and special election), a finding of criminal delinquency by the Legislation Penal Judicatory which is designed to try deputies and other high officials, insanity, and the acceptance of other offices in the state or in foreign states.[23]

---

[17] Ch. VI, § 25 (*CW*), pp. 72-91. Of course, choice is not confined to former members.

[18] Ch. VI, § 24 (*CW*), pp. 67-72. Bentham's theory of representation is discussed further in chapters IX and X below.

[19] Ch. VI, § 18, Art. 1 (*CW*), pp. 48-9.

[20] Ch. VI, §§ 19-20 (*CW*), pp. 49-56.

[21] Ch. VI, § 23 (*CW*), pp. 59-67.

[22] Ch. VI, § 26 (*CW*), p. 92.

[23] Ch. VI, § 30, Art. 1 (*CW*), p. 117.

IV

The prime minister is elected by the legislature and serves for a suggested term of four years. Like members of the legislature, he is not eligible for re-election until there are several former prime ministers from whom to choose.[24] The legislature decides who may be eligible for the post, but Bentham in addition excludes 'all Monarchs, and every person, connected by any known tie of consanguinity, or affinity, with any Monarch', and, in addition, imposes a residential qualification.[25]

As the chief executive officer, the prime minister must give 'execution and effect' to the ordinances of the legislature. With the assistance of the various ministers who head the sub-departments, he directs the business of the administration. He appoints, promotes, and can dismiss any of the ministers. He can also suspend or dismiss any civil servant, although the appointment of functionaries inferior to ministers is made by the ministers themselves. The prime minister is also commander-in-chief of the army and navy.[26]

Unlike the British prime minister, the prime minister has no seat in the legislature and normally communicates with it by letter. He may be invited or compelled to attend the legislature on some extraordinary occasion. He has a general duty to inform the legislature about the state of the nation and a special duty to do so about matters within his sole control such as negotiations with foreign countries or about practices in the administration in need of urgent reform. He must also inform the legislature generally about matters for possible legislation as well as initiate new amendments or ordinances on specific subjects.[27] Like members of the legislature he may be dismissed for a number of specific reasons. He can be dismissed either by the legislature or by the people (presumably by petition and then a special vote).[28]

[24] Ch. VIII, §5, Arts. 1-2 (*CW*), p. 156.
[25] Ch. VIII, §7, Arts. 2-3 (*CW*), p. 157.
[26] Ch. VIII, §2, Arts. 1-14 (*CW*), pp. 149-51.
[27] Ch. VIII, §3 (*CW*), pp. 152-4.
[28] Ch. VIII, §9 (*CW*), p. 159.

V

Bentham deals with the various ministers and their subordinates in two separate chapters. In the first, a lengthy
chapter of numerous themes and sections, he discusses
the whole administration under the heading of 'ministers
collectively'.[29] In the second chapter, entitled 'ministers
severally', he is concerned with expounding the particular
functions of the various ministers and their sub-departments.[30]
The ministers of the administrative sub-departments are
appointed by the prime minister for life.[31] Bentham believes
that knowledge and judgement associated with the detailed
operations of administration will be enhanced over a long
period of service. Nevertheless, Bentham also provides
for easy dismissal by the prime minister, legislature, or
electorate.[32]
Unlike the prime minister, each minister has a seat in the
legislature. Subject to the rules of the legislature, the minister
participates in debate, proposes legislation, and responds to
questions put to him by members of the legislature and other
ministers, but he does not possess the right to vote.[33] Under
the prime minister the thirteen ministers and sub-departments
are: (1) election, (2) legislation, (3) army, (4) navy, (5) preventive service, (6) interior communication, (7) indigence
relief, (8) education, (9) domain, (10) health, (11) foreign
relation, (12) trade and (13) finance. In each of the sub-
departments there is one minister (and depute) only, and one
functionary (and depute) in each office in the chain of
command. Bentham opposes boards and commissions, where
it is impossible to assign responsibility for decisions to any
one person. By declaring all administrative offices to be
'single-seated', he attempts to assign this responsibility.[34]
Bentham's statement of the functions possessed and exercised by ministers is lengthy and complex.[35] Briefly, with
regard to subordinate personnel, the minister has the power

[29] Ch. IX (*CW*), pp. 170–457.
[30] Ch. XI (Bowring, ix. 428–53).
[31] Ch. IX, § 13, Art. 1 (*CW*), p. 295.
[32] Ch. IX, § 18, Arts. 4–6 (*CW*), p. 365.
[33] Ch. IX, § 24, Arts. 1–2 (*CW*), p. 417.
[34] Ch. IX, § 2, Art. 1; § 3, Art. 1 (*CW*), pp. 171–2, 173.
[35] Ch. IX, § 4 (*CW*), pp. 186–202.

to appoint, direct, dismiss, and ensure the appointment of deputies. With regard to the things and money over which he has authority, he has the power of procurement and disposal as well as custodial and inspective powers. He is to keep and publish records of all government business and of the people and things under his control, and to make appropriate reports when called upon to do so. These general powers and duties (which are presented here in a highly abbreviated form) are possessed by all ministers, and, in addition, a number of specific powers and duties are given to each, according to his position.

Once the constitution is established, each minister and many subordinates must pass through the system of instruction and examination to qualify for appointment. Before gaining admission to an office, the candidate must first be placed on the Locable List.[36] To gain entry to the Locable List the candidate must receive appropriate instruction and satisfy the Qualification Judicatory, but this alone does not mean that the candidate will necessarily be appointed. Pecuniary competition follows, where candidates on the Locable List bid to obtain the various posts at a reduced salary or offer to pay to possess them.[37] For positions requiring trust, candidates also indicate what sum of money or property they are willing to provide as 'pecuniary security'.[38]

The prime minister appoints the ministers, and the ministers appoint their subordinates. With regard to the latter, the appointments made by the ministers must be confirmed by the prime minister. The appointment is considered confirmed if the prime minister does not respond to the receipt of the 'location instrument' after so many days either by appointing someone else or by suspending the appointment made by the minister.[39] The minister is not required to appoint only the highest ranked person on the Locable List or the person with the most successful bid in pecuniary competition. He is free to choose anyone he wishes on the list. Nevertheless, if having taken into account the ranking tables and the pecuniary bidding, he does not choose the highest ranked person

---

[36] Ch. IX, § 16, Art. 16 (*CW*), p. 316.
[37] Ch. IX, § 17 (*CW*), pp. 337-64.
[38] Ibid., Art. 6 (*CW*), p. 338.
[39] Ibid., Art. 31 (*CW*), pp. 343-4.

bidding at the lowest price, he must give reasons on the locat-ing instrument for his preference.[40]

Like the ministers, the subordinate officials are also appointed for life, though they are also fairly easily dis-missed by the minister, prime minister, or the legislature.[41] Bentham recognizes exceptions to this provision of employ-ment for life in the military, among workers (like artisans) taken on for a temporary period and other members of various sub-departments where a specific period of time is more appropriate for their employment.[42]

Bentham deals with the functions of individual ministers with an unusual brevity, although, as Everett has pointed out, many of the discussions, such as those of the legislation, preventive service, and indigence relief ministers, can easily be amplified by reference to Bentham's voluminous writings on these themes.[43] The duties of the election minister are connected with the operation of the Election Code in filling seats in the legislature. It is not clear, though perhaps it is assumed, that he also supervises the elections when ministers, the prime minister, and judges are subject to dismissal from office.[44]

The legislation minister works in subordination to the legislature. His major concern is with amendments to and alterations in the *pannomion*. Of his office, Bentham writes:

> The office of the Legislation Minister will thus, by the very nature of the case, become, though without the name and show of a school, a school of legislation. Into this school, young men destined for public employment, might be admitted, at about the same age as in England, France and other countries, they are admitted into the office, (for the purpose of being instructed in the business,) of an attorney-at-law. [45]

As there will be similar offices in each of the sub-legislatures, Bentham foresees 'so many *schools of legislation*, accessible to all, who, by self-regarding interest, or public spirit, shall, at any time, feel themselves prompted to seek entrance.'[46] The minister has numerous other duties such as looking after

[40] Ibid., Art. 9 (*CW*), p. 339.
[41] Ch. IX, §19, Art. 8; §18, Arts. 4-5 (*CW*), pp. 368, 365.
[42] Ch. IX, §19, Art. 9 (*CW*), p. 368.
[43] C. W. Everett, 'The Constitutional Code of Jeremy Bentham', *Jeremy Bentham Bicentenary Celebrations*, London, 1948, pp. 14 ff.
[44] Bowring, ix. 428.   [45] Ibid., p. 435.   [46] Ibid.

legislative buildings, accommodation, and archives. He is responsible for an annual report on the *pannomion* concerning laws which have expired or are about to expire; he arranges the printing and distribution of the *pannomion*; he reports on legislation to the sub-legislatures and watches over the activities of these subordinate bodies in order to report to the legislature; he proposes reforms of the form of the law and also reports recommendations regarding the rules of legislative assemblies;[47] he receives proposed amendments to the law from the judiciary which, if not rejected by the legislature and if in the appropriate form, are adopted.[48] All proposed amendments to the *pannomion* are printed in the government newspaper by the legislation minister who also arranges the periodical publication of the Amendment Calendar.[49]

The preventive service minister functions to prevent and mitigate delinquency and calamity. He must deal with such calamities as earthquakes, collapse of buildings, floods, fires, epidemics, diseases generally, unhealthy employment, shortage of food, and famine.[50] Bentham stresses the use of the military forces in conjunction with the preventive service. The prime minister can attach various portions of the defensive force to the preventive service as is deemed necessary.[51] Bentham does not dwell much on the role of the preventive service in preventing crime and apprehending criminals, but this is clearly one of its main functions.[52] The preventive service is an interesting combination of police, fire, health, and safety services.

The interior communication minister executes legislation concerning all modes of transport and the machinery of transport within the state. He is concerned with roads, lakes, rivers, canals, bridges, tunnels, aqueducts, toll-houses, the post, carriages, telegraph stations, inns, vehicles, and beasts of conveyance.[53] Bentham deals very briefly with the indigence relief and the domain ministers. The indigence relief minister administers the law concerning the relief of poverty.[54] The domain minister gives 'execution and effect'

---

[47] Ibid., p. 429.   [48] Ibid., p. 435.   [49] Ibid., p. 436.
[50] Ibid., p. 439. It is worth noting that Bentham provides for overcoming scarcity in essential supplies where 'freedom of trade is inadequate to the purpose'.
[51] Ibid., p. 440.   [52] Ibid., pp. 440-1.   [53] Ibid., p. 441.   [54] Ibid.

to the law regarding any immovable object (land, buildings, etc.) which is at the disposal of the government for the benefit of the community but which does not fall under the authority of another minister.[55]

The education minister presides over the system of instruction and examination for the civil service. He also arranges for the inspection of all educational institutions in the state, keeps records on them, and suggests improvements. Bentham seems especially concerned with educational institutions which require particular religious views, and the education minister and his subordinates keep records of institutions where people are required to hold particular opinions about morals, religion, or government. Where the educational institutions belong to the various sub-legislatures, Bentham limits the power of the education minister to enforce uniformity in education contrary to the wishes of the sub-legislatures.[56] Finally, the minister is to consider, in light of population pressure, the establishment of colonies with orphan children on vacant land either in new states or within the same state.[57]

The health minister, working in conjunction with the preventive service minister, enforces laws concerned with the preservation of national health.[58] Besides supervising subordinates in his own sub-department, he appoints and dismisses medical personnel in the military service and the indigence relief sub-department. He supervises hospitals, lazarettos, and laboratories. He is responsible for inspecting the state of health in prisons, 'madhouses', buildings under the control of the indigence relief and education sub-departments, and shops and storehouses used for keeping drugs and medical instruments.[59] To these functions Bentham adds eight more: (a) authoritatively-eliminative function, where, subject to an appeal to a judge, medicines which have deteriorated and have become unfit for use are destroyed; (b) water-supply-securing function, where in towns designated by the prime minister, the quantity, quality, and distribution of water supplies are examined; (c) malaria-obviating function where the minister reviews all potential sources of malaria, i.e. lands, mines, sewers, drains, public places, etc.; (d)

[55] Ibid., p. 443.   [56] Ibid., p. 441-2.   [57] Ibid., p. 443.
[58] Ibid.   [59] Ibid., pp. 443-4.

health-regarding-evidence-elicitative-and-recordative function, where reports regarding mortality and disease are received from local registrars in the exercise of their functions and also from hospitals and other institutions under the control of other ministries; (e) appropriate custoditive function where the minister is in charge of all medical museums possessed by the government; (f) aptitude-securing function, where he supervises the examination of those who aspire to civil service posts which involve the practice of medicine; (g) professional confederacy-checking function where he reports to the constitutive authority about medical associations, rates of pay, hours of service, etc., where the public interest is at stake; and (h) appropriate-publication function, where he gives, subject to limits of expense, full publicity to all matters of interest regarding health.[60]

The foreign relation minister is required to give 'execution and effect' to all laws and other government arrangements concerning relations between the government and other governments or citizens of other governments.[61] His department is responsible for negotiations with foreign governments and for providing hospitality to foreign diplomats and agents. In conjunction with the navy, he supervises the appointment of commanders and the purchase and repair of ships used in conveying agents abroad. He is responsible for keeping records about, for example, the observance of treaties. Finally, he reports to the legislature each year about the state of foreign relations, showing, for example, how commerce is affected by various treaties, laws, and other arrangements.[62]

The trade minister, working closely with the finance minister, records developments in trade and suggests possible legislation to the prime minister and the legislature.[63] For the most part Bentham envisages the minister functioning in a free trade economy. Nevertheless, he notes that even here a number of difficulties may arise which will require government intervention. For example, the trade minister is to examine the effects of taxation and the money supply on the price of commodities, prevent frauds by suggesting appropriate legislation in spheres such as the control of

[60] Ibid., pp. 444-5.   [61] Ibid., pp. 445-6.
[62] Ibid., p. 447.   [63] Ibid., pp. 447-8.

weights and measures, regulate temporary monopolies to protect inventions and new processes, and provide information about how profits in trade might be increased.

The finance minister is in charge of all of the finances of the state.[64] He establishes and operates the mint. He makes annual reports to the legislature on the country's finances including full accounts and estimates. A major function he performs is that of ensuring that those who possess and use public money do so without deriving any private benefit or without receiving any benefit at the expense of the public.

Bentham deals briefly with the army and navy ministers, because he devotes a whole chapter to the defensive force. The ministers enforce their respective codes (Army Code and Navy Code) and, in addition, are required to carry out the temporary orders of the prime minister when he is acting as commander-in-chief.[65] The powers of the army minister differ somewhat when dealing with the professional army where he possesses full powers of appointment and dismissal and with the radical force (consisting of unpaid volunteers) where the emphasis is placed more on supplies and various other arrangements.[66] The navy minister is in charge not only of naval personnel, but also of ships, harbours, beacons, buoys, dockyards, etc. He also possesses powers as given by the legislators to regulate private vessels and to take possession of them without the consent of their owners in case of military necessity.[67]

Where there are conflicts of authority among various subdepartments, Bentham empowers the prime minister to draw up lines of demarcation or to require various ministers to co-operate in an action.[68] He also recognizes that many conflicts will arise over who is to control the services of particular persons and things, and he assigns priority to those subdepartments concerned with basic security. Army, navy, preventive service, and interior communication (in so far as it aids the former) are given special priority. Bentham here reflects his emphasis on security as the main end of government. He also hopes that the arrangement of ministers in contiguous offices, close to the prime minister, and the use

[64] Ibid., pp. 448-52.   [65] Ibid., pp. 437, 438.   [66] Ibid., pp. 437-8.
[67] Ibid., pp. 438-9.   [68] Ibid., p. 452.

of 'conversation tubes' will enable the prime minister to resolve inter-subdepartmental disputes more easily.[69]

VI

Bentham's first main assumption in establishing the defensive force is that its sole object is defensive. 'Offence and aggression', he writes, 'as towards other nations, much more *conquest*, are repugnant to the essential and leading principles of the constitution delineated by the present Code.'[70] He first divides the military into two groups: the radical and the stipendiary. The radical is the 'root' of the military and consists of unpaid volunteers. The stipendiary force is composed of paid professionals. As Bentham conceives of both an army and navy in the military force, he eventually comes to four categories: radical land, stipendiary land, radical sea, and stipendiary sea forces. The radical land force is the main one and consists of all members of the community who are capable of contributing to national defence.[71] Bentham notes, however that the development of a stipendiary force represents 'considerable progress made in the career of civilisation' in so far as a few people are withdrawn from useful labour to allow all of the others to devote their attention to maximizing the means of subsistence and abundance.[72]

Due to the fact that the stipendiary force does not provide for its own subsistence, it must necessarily be small in relation to the population as a whole. Though small, the stipendiary land force is also very powerful. And being powerful, it is both a security and a danger. The army can threaten the government as well as save it.[73] Bentham's awareness of the threat to the political society posed by the very existence of a professional military force provides an interesting and important dimension to his discussion of national defence. On the one hand the stipendiary force must be sufficiently large to repel external enemies, but if too large and powerful, it poses a threat to the constitution. To resolve this difficulty, Bentham proposes two rules:

---

[69] Ibid. See also ch. IX, § 26, Arts. 16–19 and n (*CW*), pp. 441–3 and nn.
[70] Bowring, ix. 333.   [71] Ibid., p. 334.   [72] Ibid.
[73] Ibid., p. 335. Bentham denies that the navy can be as great a threat as the army, as it is more fragmented and often at a great distance from the state.

Rule 1. Minimize the stipendiary force, so far as is consistent with security against hostility from without.
Rule 2. Maximize the radical force,—to wit, so far as is consistent with the non-employment of compulsory means for the formation or maintenance of it. [74]

By minimizing the size of the stipendiary force, Bentham believes that the threat to the constitution by insubordination will be minimized. In addition, the expense of military service will be minimized as will the power and disposition of the military to engage in offensive wars. By maximizing the size of the radical force, Bentham feels that any insubordination on the part of professionals will be checked even further. However, he emphasizes that compulsion should not be used to achieve the object of a large radical force. Compulsion means enhanced suffering by those being compelled, increased expense in organizing the compulsion, and the possibility of civil war with one part of the people objecting to compulsion and the other part enforcing compulsory service with the assistance of the professional force. [75]

Bentham does not see the stipendiary force solely as a threat to democracy. Besides its role in the defence of the country, the stipendiary force will also serve under the justice and preventive service ministers to deal with the suppression and prevention of criminal delinquency on a large scale where the ordinary police force cannot deal with the problem. Bentham has no illusions about the need for the military to act in domestic politics to deal with those who threaten the constitution:

A casualty to which a democratic constitution, like any other, stands perpetually exposed, is—that of giving birth to a knot of malefactors, who, acting in manifest opposition to the ordinary official establishment of the government, constitute thereby a sort of temporary government of their own formation, . . . waging war upon the government established by law . . . yet were it not for a body of well-trained military men in readiness to act for their suppression, no limit might be assignable to the quantity of mischief which, before an end could be put to it, might be produced by them. [76]

[74] Ibid., p. 339.
[75] Ibid., pp. 339-40.
[76] Ibid., p. 335. See also p. 336 for some interesting comments about problems regarding a standing army in a confederacy.

Bentham's radical force consists entirely of unpaid volunteers who are organized especially in and around the large urban centres. Although the government provides the basic equipment for the force, this amounts to little more than basic weapons and facilities for infantry training. The reason for confining recruitment to the larger urban centres is to enable volunteers to participate on their day off from work with minimum travel and without the need to sleep away from home. This reduces expense and does not exclude the poorer man who might be willing to join up on these terms.[77] Bentham sees the radical force as an improvement on the use of the militia in both Britain and America.[78] These forces were in his view seriously defective, as they were based on compulsion and were paid. As a result, they were too expensive and there was resistance among those compelled to serve. Bentham's volunteer force, based in small geographical areas, is obviously different. Furthermore, the lowest ranks have the power to choose and dismiss their commanders and instructors by vote.[79] Any member can be dismissed by a majority vote. Neither officers nor members of the lower ranks are paid. The officers receive the dignity, prestige, and powers of their offices as compensation. Only the instructors might receive payment, but this would come from the pupils themselves.[80]

Bentham conceives of the radical land force as a citizen force trained quickly and inexpensively in basic tactics and in the use of weapons like the musket. The legislature is left to decide if more sophisticated training in such areas as cavalry and artillery is needed.[81] Even here, he believes that sums can be raised by contribution to provide for this training, although he is cautious, because it may allow the rich to have more training and more sophisticated weapons than the poor.

Bentham does not dwell on the radical sea force. Those eligible are fishermen and sailors in private vessels and their vessels make up the navy. Furthermore, although generally opposed to compulsory service, he recognizes that in the sea service, in case of necessity, it is better to draft already skilled seamen into military service.[82] Furthermore, he proposes a registration system for the radical sea force which

[77] Ibid., pp. 343-4.   [78] Ibid., p. 345.   [79] Ibid., p. 348.
[80] Ibid.   [81] Ibid.   [82] Ibid., p. 404.

will provide a complete list of ships and personnel in the private sphere available for military service.[83]

Bentham considers the professional forces in great detail, and we shall only deal here with a few characteristics of this part of the military force. He believes for the most part that voluntary enlistment should prevail, although, at times, he recognizes that compulsion may be necessary:

The state, a Representative Democracy *recently* constituted: its *finances* in a low state: *money* sufficient for procuring a military force in sufficient quantity, *not assured*; the *number needed* of the land-force stipendiaries, bearing a large ratio to the whole population of the state. In this case, the adoption of the compulsory system may be matter of necessity. In this case appears to be, as yet, in a great degree, the late Spanish Colonies.[84]

Bentham contrasts with this example that of the United States with settled finances and democracy firmly established. Here the size of the professional army in relation to the total population was small, and he believed that no compulsion was required.[85]

The stipendiary army consists of privates and officers. The privates are of only one rank; they possess no power of command and are the subordinates of the officers. They enlist voluntarily by contract or, in certain cases, are chosen for compulsory service by lot. During his service a private has remedies against oppression by superiors in the same way as members of the civil service. The officers are divided into the ordinary officers consisting of the ranks immediately superior to that of private, e.g. corporal and sergeant, and the erudites, the superior officers who pass through the examination system and pecuniary competition. The latter are, for the most part, appointed by the army minister and prime minister. Bentham proposes that before appointing erudites to the lowest ranks they might spend a year as privates.[86] As for the terms and conditions of service, he leaves to the legislature to decide such matters as enlistment ages, length of service, renewal of service, amount and forms of remuneration, and compensation in case of wounds.[87] The legislature also determines the most appropriate form of promotion, although Bentham proposes, as a basic premiss,

---

[83] Ibid., p. 406.   [84] Ibid. p. 357.   [85] Ibid.
[86] Ibid., p. 351.   [87] Ibid., pp. 353–4.

promotion on grounds of seniority in service.[88] He incorporates a number of exceptions to this general rule such as
direct promotion by the prime minister or by the prime
minister and army minister jointly as a reward for meritorious
service.

As for pecuniary competition, Bentham restricts its use
to the initial appointment of the erudite officer class and
does not use it in promotion.[89] Among the evils that he foresees with pecuniary competition in this context is that a
rich young man with the minimum aptitude might take
command from an experienced senior thus diminishing overall aptitude and violating the principle of 'contentment
maximization'.[90] It is worth noting that the contentment-
maximizing principle makes no appearance in the earlier
treatment of the civil service or in the later discussion of the
judiciary. Its use reflects Bentham's belief that the military
service should be treated differently from the non-military
service because of its obvious power and the potential threat
to the constitution. But contentment maximization is also
important because of the difficulty of maintaining effective
discipline under arduous circumstances.

Bentham appreciates the difficulties involved in promotion where discontent can easily develop. Promotion simply
by seniority of service does not resolve the problem of
advancing the most able to senior positions. As the decisions
of senior officers can have serious and lasting effects on
the rest of the military as well as on the whole of society,
the question of promotion is especially important. He carefully avoids dogmatism here and invites the legislature to
consider a series of interesting proposals. The legislature
might wish to distinguish between wartime and peacetime
service. In periods of war the demand for promotion on the
basis of extraordinary service and merit will be more important, and arrangements for promotion during periods of
war might differ from peacetime promotion. In peacetime,
Bentham proposes that officers might have experience on a
yearly basis of different grades, as, for example, first and
second lieutenants changing roles. 'By this means . . . ',
he writes, 'each functionary will acquire experience in the

[88] Ibid., pp. 358–9.   [89] Ibid., p. 362.   [90] Ibid. See also pp. 340 ff.

business of all the grades: and whatever degree of unpleasant-
ness may stand attached to a state of unremitted and immut-
able subordination, may thus be diminished.'[91] Where
promotion is based on meritorious service, he proposes that
the votes of privates and fellow officers are recorded in a
secret ballot which will be used (though not in any binding
way) by the appropriate minister and prime minister in
reaching their decisions.[92]

Although the chapter on the military is rich in proposals
for effective military organization, we shall consider only two
more themes. The first is the constitutional provision giving
the legal right to the military to take all steps necessary to
defend the country, to inflict evil on the people for the sake
of avoiding a greater evil.[93] Bentham recognizes that all
countries will act on grounds of military necessity to defend
themselves; he wishes to place this action under the authority
of law, not to prohibit it, but to regulate it. His objects are
to minimize the evil itself, to arrange for compensation, and
to prevent the abuse of power. He takes up such matters as
the requisition of food, clothing, and shelter when no funds
are available, compulsory enlistment, obtaining assistance in
building fortifications and the conveyance of materials. He
distinguishes between power exercisable with and without an
order, with the latter depending on the need for self-
preservation during war. His main object is to provide within
a legal framework an efficient means of acting on grounds
of military necessity which avoids as much as possible the
abuses associated with military actions of this kind. He
emphasizes the importance of publicity and evidence––to
establish (a) the necessity for the action and (b) the damage
as grounds for compensation.

The second theme is Bentham's consideration of non-
military employment during peaceful periods.[94] The possibility of such employment is confined to the professional
army, as the radical force already has other employment.
Bentham distinguishes between the furlough system where
soldiers obtain their own employment and an employment-
allotting system where it is provided for them. He prefers any
system which keeps the soldiers fit and prepared for their

---

[91] Ibid., p. 364.   [92] Ibid., pp. 365-6.
[93] Ibid., pp. 383-92.   [94] Ibid., pp. 415-18.

main employment of fighting and defending the country. He sees a number of uses for soldiers such as assisting the police, collecting taxes, apprehending and arresting people in accordance with judicial orders, keeping up fortifications, roads, naval works, and building roads, canals, bridges, tunnels, dikes, and embankments. Bentham clearly sees a major domestic role for the military at peace.

VII

Nearly a third of the text of the *Constitutional Code* is devoted to the judiciary and various judicial officers. Bentham's destestation of the English judicial system which he found corrupt and oppressive and his equally strong hatred of the institution of the Common Law fuelled numerous writings, and much criticism remains in the *Code* of these institutions and practices. However, his main task in the *Code* is to set forth his plan for a different judicial system. He had not completed this part of the *Code* at the time of his death, and it was reconstructed from the manuscripts by Richard Doane. But the main outline is as Bentham intended and the amount of material is considerable. We must be content to survey in the briefest way the main offices and functions he proposes for the judiciary.

Bentham proposes, as we have seen, two main judicatories (he prefers the term 'judicatory' to 'court' because of the association of the latter with monarchy).[95] The lowest is the immediate judicatory, established at the bis-subdistrict level or perhaps lower, and the higher, the appellate judicatory, is established at the district level.[96] An appeal from an immediate to an appellate judicatory is possible in every kind of suit.[97] For the same reasons that he proposes that one official serve in each administrative office, he establishes here that one judge only is to sit in each judicatory.[98]

The immediate judicatory is located within each judicial subdistrict so that any person can reach it on foot and return home (allowing six hours for judicial business) within twenty-four hours without having to incur the expense of sleeping away from home. As a rough guide, he suggests that no one

[95] Ibid., pp. 458-9. [96] Ibid., p. 468.
[97] Ibid., pp. 469-70. [98] Ibid., p. 470.

should have to travel more than twenty-four miles in a full day, although, in locating the judicatories, such factors as the condition of roads and various topographical features will have to be taken into account. Bentham emphasizes the importance of reducing the delay and expense of those requiring judicial services, and this, he believes, justifies the creation of a large number of judicatories.[99]

In the immediate judicatory, the main official is the judge whose primary function is to give 'execution and effect' by means of 'appropriate *decrees*—opinative and imperative —and the *mandates* thereto conducive' to legislative ordinances except where legislative and administrative functionaries are themselves under an obligation to do so.[100] Once the constitution is established, to be eligible for appointment as judge immediate, one must pass through the system of education and examination and then serve as a judge immediate depute for at least two years.[101] During this period the experience necessary for the principal position is gained. In addition, before appointment is secured, the prospective appointee must establish his 'irreproachableness' by refuting any accusations made against him.[102] Bentham also excludes anyone who has served as government advocate, eleemosynary advocate (advocate for the helpless), or professional lawyer and their deputes from eligibility as a judge.[103] As these persons have served in positions where partiality in advocacy has been part of their experience and psychology, they would find it difficult to exercise the impartiality required of a judge. To be eligible for appointment as an appellate judge, both two years as a depute and one year as an immediate judge must have been served.[104] Both immediate and appellate judges are appointed by the justice minister.[105] They may be dismissed by the justice minister and presumably, like all officials, by the electorate.[106]

The judge immediate is assisted by both permanent and occasional deputes. The permanent depute is appointed to office by the judge who is fully responsible for him.[107] He

[99] Ibid., pp. 473–4.   [100] Ibid., p. 465.   [101] Ibid., p. 525.
[102] Ibid., p. 527.   [103] Ibid., pp. 527–8.   [104] Ibid., p. 528.
[105] Ibid., p. 529.
[106] Ibid., p. 532; see ch. VI, § 30, Art. 1 (*CW*), p. 117.
[107] Ibid., pp. 484–5.

acts when the judge is unable to do so, is away, or the post is vacant. Bentham also sees the permanent depute as playing an important role in reducing delay when there is more judicial business than can be dealt with by the principal judge. The permanent depute is appointed for life unless or until appointed to a principal judgeship or to the office of immediate registrar.[108] He receives no financial remuneration, although Bentham notes that he does receive distinction, power and, if he has ability, reputation. He regards the depute as better off than an articled clerk of an attorney or a law student in England in having a shorter apprenticeship and more certain prospects of appointment to a paid position.

The judge immediate deputes occasional are appointed by the judge immediate for a limited period to hear one or more suits.[109] Like the permanent depute, they can assist in reducing delay in judicial business. They are also appointed if it is thought that the judge and permanent depute are not competent to hear a case or if a depute is regarded as having extra ability in a particular sphere. When used by the judge immediate to obviate delay, the depute is usually appointed for one day only to hear a number of small cases, such as those for simple assault or the payment of small debts. He may also be appointed by the judge as the choice of all the parties to a suit. Thus, it seems possible for parties to a suit to choose whom they wish to act as judge and in effect to bypass the sitting judge. In making the appointment, however, the judge immediate determines what powers the depute will exercise. Bentham also provides for referees to act in civil suits in an analogous way to the deputes occasional. In this way he builds a system of arbitration into his judicial arrangements. Financial remuneration is allowed for occasional deputes and referees so long as the amount is freely agreed by all parties. Nevertheless, the judge immediate will see that no corruption arises from the deputes occasional or referees prolonging their cases so as to receive more remuneration. As for the appointment of occasional deputes to deal with delay, the judge immediate must ensure that the appointment is a matter of last resort and that the position of the permanent depute does not

---

[108] Ibid., p. 548. [109] Ibid., pp. 550-4.

become a sinecure by virtue of the work being given to occasional deputes.

Besides the judge and his various deputes, each immediate and appellate judicatory contains a registrar. His main job is to record all evidence, written and oral, to ensure its clearness, correctness, and comprehensiveness, and to record all of the proceedings of the judicatory.[110] Bentham also sees the registrar and judge acting as 'mutual checks' on each other. If a registrar, for example, omits to provide a depute to work with a judge depute, the principal judge or his depute may appoint him. Nevertheless, the registrar is made fully responsible for the depute's actions even though he is the appointee of the judge. Bentham also notes that while the judge can have material inserted in the records kept by the registrar, he does not possess the power to change or obliterate records already established. All judicial registrars, like judges, pass through the educational system and, apparently, serve an apprenticeship as deputes. They are appointed by the justice minister but may be dismissed in the same manner as judges.[111] For most judicial officers Bentham envisages the same system of education, appointment, apprenticeship, and conditions for dismissal that applies to judges.

The government advocate represents the government in both penal and non-penal cases.[112] He is subject to the power of the judge in the same manner as all judicial officials. But he has a special role to look out for misconduct in the judicial process either by a judge or by anyone who by delay, falsehood, or vexation generally attempts to impede the course of justice. If he suspects misconduct by a judge, he should report it to an appellate judge and provide full publicity for the legislature and the Public Opinion Tribunal to criticize and even dismiss him. If the judge is accused of misconduct, the government advocate officiates at his trial, although he is himself liable to punishment as an accomplice if it turns out that the misconduct has been known to him. Bentham envisages a system of education and apprenticeship (up to five years as probationary lawyer) similar to that for other judicial officers before appointment as government advocate.

---

[110] Ibid., pp. 465, 579–85.   [111] See ibid., pp. 528, 529, 532.
[112] Ibid., pp. 465, 570–5, esp. p. 571.

The government advocate-general has authority over all of the government advocates in the nation. He appoints, suspends, dismisses, inspects, and directs their activities.[113] He directs and co-ordinates a number of connected suits by directing several government advocates to undertake proceedings. He is appointed for life by the prime minister and can be dismissed for specific reasons by the prime minister and without reasons by the legislature and electorate. The justice minister can also dismiss him if he commits a criminal offence and the prime minister cannot under these circumstances reappoint him. Bentham notes that the reason he is appointed by the prime minister is that there is a special link between the government advocate-general's and the prime minister's duties to execute and enforce the law. The government advocate-general's registrar is appointed by the justice minister from the list of immediate registrars. Although he can be dismissed by the government advocate-general, he can be reappointed on appeal by the justice minister. Bentham gives the power of appointment to the justice minister rather than to the prime minister or to the government advocate-general in order that the registrar may serve to 'check' the government advocate-general. The registrar is unable to veto or even to delay an action of the government advocate-general, but he can give full publicity to his actions. Appointment by the justice minister gives him a measure of independence from the government advocate-general and the prime minister. In addition, the justice minister, by his close proximity to the judiciary, is better placed to assess the aptitude of various appointees. Finally, the arrangement checks any sinister dimension to the patronage possessed by both the prime minister and the justice minister.

The eleemosynary advocate is another important judicial functionary whose main task is to represent and assist in court those who are incapacitated in some way or are too poor to obtain assistance for themselves.[114] We might see his position as part of a larger attempt by Bentham to enable the poor to have full access to judicial services.[115] The burden on the poor includes not only the costs of legal assistance but also the costs of transporting witnesses, compensating

---

[113] Ibid., pp. 575–7.   [114] Ibid., p. 465.   [115] See ibid., pp. 489–93.

them for their loss of time, and the costs of obtaining evidence generally. Bentham regards the condition where one has only the assistance of the Public Opinion Tribunal to enable one to redress a wrong as a tyranny. Where the poor are excluded from protection by the law or cannot establish a satisfactory legal defence because of their poverty, the result is that 'a correspondent portion, more or less considerable of the whole population of the country, is placed in a state of outlawry'.[116] He proposes to provide 'justice for the helpless' (a) by reducing the expense of judicial services; (b) by placing the burden of expense on those better able to bear it; and (c) by requiring those who must compensate the public for wrongdoing to contribute to the assistance of the poor. He initially provides funds for the helpless by creating the Equal Justice Fund.

The Equal Justice Fund is derived from several sources. The principal source consists of pecuniary penalties levied in court, especially those for offences against justice, such as lying in court. By using this money for the fund, Bentham hopes to provide for the indigent and to secure efficient and fair judicial proceedings. This source of funds will be supplemented by voluntary contributions especially for cases where the use of public money has been refused or thought inappropriate. For example, if the funds of a person who injures another are not sufficient to compensate the person injured, if the costs of obtaining evidence in a case outweigh the benefit to the person who is injured, or if the losing party in a case wishes to appeal but there is some doubt as to the strength of the appeal, the use of voluntary contributions would enable these cases to proceed. To this end an 'Equal Justice Box' is provided in every court to receive contributions. Bentham, of course, does not rely on contributions as the main source of funds and, in order to augment funds coming from fines, he proposes that the legislature instructs judges to use fines in preference to other forms of punishment. Government advocates are also instructed to watch for delinquency in the conduct of litigants and to call for punishment by judges when instances occur.

---

[116] Ibid., p. 489.

In this part of the *Code* Bentham becomes an ardent defender of the rights of the poor to receive equal justice:

In all hitherto established systems of Judicial warfare,—partly through negligence, partly by design, the relatively helpless have in the lump been left without defence: the relatively helpless, that is to say, everywhere the vast majority of the people; although in relation to Judicature, to leave a man without defence, is on the part of government to deny him justice.[117]

Bentham calls this injustice: 'established upon an all-comprehensive scale' and 'established by express law'.[118] Even in the United States, which he admires in numerous ways, the poor, he believes, are excluded from access to the courts by the design of lawyers and the wealthy classes and by the ignorance and negligence of the rest.[119] The key judicial official who provides assistance for those in need is, as we have noted, the eleemosynary advocate (or advocate of the helpless).[120] He serves in each immediate judicatory and offers assistance to all parties in suits who cannot afford legal assistance by a professional lawyer or other person of equal aptitude. Where both sides require assistance, he will appoint two deputes (chosen by lot) to the two sides. He stands in the same relation to the judge as the government advocate and serves under similar conditions. During the latter part of their probationary period professional lawyers under a judge and under the direction of the eleemosynary advocate are also empowered to assist the helpless.

Bentham defines the quasi-jury as 'an ever changing body of Assessors, convened from the body of the people at large, for the purpose of its serving, by the exercise given to its function, as a *check* applied to the power of the *permanent* judges.'[121] The quasi-jury is based on the English jury, but is so constructed as to avoid the numerous failings he believes are embedded in the jury system.[122] Furthermore, Bentham's quasi-jury differs considerably from the English jury especially as it has less direct power, though its power extends over the whole range of judicial activity.[123] A number of features of the quasi-jury are not found in the jury system. The quasi-jury is composed of two groups which Bentham calls the

---

[117] Ibid., p. 493.   [118] Ibid.   [119] Ibid.
[120] See ibid., pp. 577-9.   [121] Ibid., p. 465.
[122] Ibid., pp. 465-6.   [123] Ibid., p. 554.

select (or, more erudite) and the ordinary (or, more popular).[124] Both groups are chosen from the electoral roll, but
the former is a voluntary body which brings added intelligence to the work of the quasi-jury.[125] Although the
number serving on the quasi-jury is determined by the legislature, Bentham proposes the number of three with twice
as many ordinary quasi-jurymen as select.[126] The ordinaries,
he suggests, have as their interest, that of the greatest number
(presumably by virtue of their being ordinary citizens) and
the selects will guide the ordinaries by virtue of their aptitude.
Nevertheless, the ordinaries will be always in the majority
(by 2 to 1). The ordinaries are paid for their work at a rate
of double the lowest paid labourer.[127] This is intended to
provide subsistence for the majority of the people so that
service as a quasi-juryman will not be 'an intolerable hard-
ship'.[128] The select quasi-jurors, however, serve without
payment.[129]

   The field of service of the quasi-jury is similar to that
of the judge with whom it sits. There is a quasi-jury attached
to each immediate and appellate judicatory.[130] The principal
occasion for service by the quasi-jury is in the quasi-trial or
recapitulary examination. This follows the original trial
where the quasi-jury participates fully in exercising all the
functions of a judge except the imperative function (i.e.
issuing the decree or decision). The quasi-jurors listen to the
evidence, question the parties and witnesses, freely give their
opinions regarding the evidence, the conduct of the parties
and the judge, and make whatever criticisms they believe
appropriate. At the conclusion of the original trial, either of
the parties or the judge himself may move to reconsider all
of the evidence in a quasi-trial. The quasi-trial may be concerned with questions of law or fact and although new
evidence is not normally admitted, it is possible, should
important new evidence arise since the original trial, to
introduce it. The quasi-trial may also be used where it is
believed that there has been an incorrect decision on the part
of the judge. At the conclusion of the quasi-trial the quasi-

[124] Ibid., p. 559.   [125] Ibid., pp. 556, 563, 564.
[126] Ibid., p. 559.   [127] Ibid., p. 567.
[128] Ibid., p. 556.   [129] Ibid., p. 567.
[130] Ibid., pp. 556-7.

jurors present their opinions which cannot overrule the decree of the judge but, if necessary, are sent with his decree to the court of appeal. Obviously, no judge can ignore a considered opinion opposed to his own coming from the same court. If he does, the appeal court will deal with the problem, and if neither do so, the Public Opinion Tribunal will have been alerted sufficiently to press for the dismissal of one or more judges. Thus, although the quasi-jury does not possess the power to *rule* on the guilt and innocence of parties in a few restricted cases as does the English jury, it has wider powers to influence judicial decisions in all cases coming before the courts.

The use of the quasi-jury will lead to explicit, written decisions and explanations of decisions on the part of both the judge and quasi-jury. This will establish responsibility by both and especially the judge who is not prevented (though he is certainly deterred) from making whatever decisions he wishes. He is none the less severely constrained by the mere presence of the quasi-jury. The quasi-jury also has the power to send to the appellate judge a number of cases which otherwise might not be heard on appeal. It can call on the assistance of the government advocate or eleemosynary advocate when proposing an amendment to the original judge's decision for consideration by the appellate judge.[131]

We shall now briefly consider the organization and functions of the appellate judicatories. A case comes before an appellate judicatory when a party at the lower level alleges error or inaction.[132] With some exceptions, the appellate court does not act as an immediate judicatory. Appeals are allowed for a variety of forms of misdecision as well as for misconduct by the immediate judge. However, appeals will only be received if there has been a recapitulary examination by a quasi-jury. If the immediate judge alone pronounces the decree, and an appeal is lodged, it must first go before

---

[131] Ibid., p. 556. For further material on the quasi-jury, see 'Principles of Judicial Procedure' (Bowring, ii. 141-69). Bentham also includes several 'ministerial judicial functionaries' in his cast of judicial characters. The most important of these are the judiciary messenger (Bowring, ix. 466, 636-7) and the judiciary prehensor (Bowring, ix. 466, 637-9). Several other officers are listed at Bowring, ix. 466.

[132] Ibid., pp. 585-8.

either the same judge acting with a quasi-jury or to another judge with a quasi-jury. Where the original judge refuses to use a quasi-jury, a direct appeal may be made to the appellate judicatory. In addition, a quasi-jury sits in each appellate judicatory. Legal assistance is also available during appeals from an eleemosynary advocate attached to the appellate judicatory.

Bentham devotes a full chapter to the status and functions of professional lawyers.[133] The theme is especially important to him not only because of his well-known antipathy to the 'lawyer class' in England and the United States, alleged bastions of privilege and guardians of the despised Common Law, but also because the success of his entire judicial system depends on his creating an efficient system operating at minimum expense. Only in this way can he provide easy access to the courts for even the poorest in society. To further these ends, he insists on the abolition of various classes of attorney which complicates litigation and makes it expensive. He also excludes complex written pleadings commonly used at the time and favours a series of standard forms for much legal business. Furthermore, the lawyer does not normally act as a substitute for the principal in a case before a judge. All parties normally attend hearings and participate, and this reduces the importance of the lawyer. In addition, Bentham believes that with the replacement of 'imaginary law' (Common Law) by 'real law' (the *pannomion*), the work of the lawyer will be very much reduced. He also considers fixing prices for legal work although he does not see this as providing on its own a satisfactory way of limiting lawyers' fees. Finally, the judge can, when reviewing a demand for services by a lawyer, take into account not only the time actually expended but also whether or not there was a need for it to be expended.

To become a professional lawyer, once the constitution is established, the candidate must first pass through the education and examination system for the civil service.[134] He is then placed on the Probationary Professional Lawyers' List. He serves as a probationary lawyer for a suggested period of four years, two of which are spent as an observer in the judicial inspectors' gallery. The second two-year term

[133] Ibid., pp. 589-97.   [134] Ibid., pp. 591-2.

is spent either as an observer or as an eleemosynary advocate. Once a probationary lawyer begins working as an eleemosynary advocate or becomes a fully qualified professional lawyer, he is no longer eligible to become a judge or registrar.[135] At the conclusion of four years (roughly at the age of twenty-three) he may be appointed a government advocate or eleemosynary advocate. He will also, of course, be able to work as a private lawyer. Once he becomes a full lawyer, he is placed on the Professional Lawyers' List and is permitted to serve in any judicatory. For service in an appellate judicatory, however, previous service in an immediate judicatory is necessary. A lawyer may be removed from the list in a given judicatory by a decree of the judge, subject to appeal, after a full hearing. Upon appeal, the appellate judge may extend the disqualification to all judicatories in the state.[136]

Bentham ensures the presence of the Public Opinion Tribunal at judicial hearings by the creation of a 'committee' in the form of judicial inspectors.[137] Virtually anyone other than the litigants themselves and the judicial officials can become judicial inspectors by their presence in the gallery of a court. They may be probationary lawyers, litigants in other suits waiting for their hearings, witnesses in this or other suits waiting to be heard, friends of the litigants, or people who have come to the hearing out of curiosity or by chance. Bentham places great emphasis on a 'committee' such as this to keep track of proceedings and give publicity to any mischief which might occur. He seeks to ensure that each party to a suit has at least one friend serving as a judicial inspector. Judicial inspectors may, with the help, encouragement, and at the discretion of the judge, ask questions and comment on proceedings. But they lack the powers of giving judicial opinions and authorizing appeals which are possessed by the quasi-jury.

At the head of the entire judicial authority in the state stands the justice minister.[138] Once the constitution is established, the justice minister must have passed through the education and examination system, served two years as an immediate judge and two years as an appellate judge. Like the prime minister, he is appointed by the legislature

[135] Ibid., p. 592.   [136] Ibid., p. 596.
[137] Ibid., pp. 569-70.   [138] Ibid., pp. 597-612.

and can be dismissed for the same reasons and by the same procedure.[139] He is appointed for life but is easily dismissed by the legislature or electorate.[140] The importance of the justice minister may be established by a brief survey of some of the functions he performs.[141] He appoints, suspends, transfers, and dismisses judges and many other judicial functionaries. He is responsible for all buildings and equipment related to the judiciary such as the prisons and the courts. He makes inspection visits to the immediate judicatories to ensure they are functioning properly, to preserve conformity with the law and symmetry of decisions, to assess the aptitude of functionaries, especially with a view of promotion from immediate to appellate judgeships, and to settle differences which may have arisen between various judicial officers. He receives petitions complaining of a denial of justice and oppression arising from suits in the appellate judicatories. He exercises what Bentham calls the 'dispunitive' function in presiding over remissions of punishment. Finally, together with the legislation minister he plays an important role in conserving and maintaining the *pannomion* and the system of judicial procedure by supervising the decisions of the judges and the form they take.

One of Bentham's recurring complaints about the Common Law is that it is difficult to determine, even among experts, what the law is on a particular point. By using written codes the problem does not disappear. Judges must still interpret the law, and Bentham does not try to make judges into automatons. Instead, he uses their work to enhance the clarity and intelligibility of the provisions of the various codes. The judges work closely with the legislature in proposing amendments to the *pannomion*. Bentham develops four important functions for judges in relation to the law as a whole. The first is the judges' contested-interpretation reporting function.[142] This function is exercised where there

---

[139] Ibid., pp. 608-9, 610.
[140] Ibid., pp. 607-8.   [141] Ibid., pp. 597-607.
[142] Ibid., pp. 502-4. In this discussion of the role of judges in the development of the *pannomion*, a useful corrective is provided to the common view, as expressed, for example, by S. R. Letwin, p. 165: 'Lawmaking was for him essentially like geometry. From a leading axiom or axioms, the whole system had to be constructed.' This view may attempt to depict (though incorrectly) Bentham's approach to codification, but it ignores his conception of the development of law

is an appeal based on a point of law from the decision of an immediate judge. The appellant (with the help of his lawyer or the eleemosynary advocate) formulates his interpretation of the law. The judge also states whether or not he feels a change is necessary. These interpretations are then put into a contested interpretation report which is drawn up by the registrar who will also incorporate any other interpretations set forth by interested parties. The appellate judge will then either adopt one interpretation or set forth his own in a report which then will be sent to the justice minister. The justice minister will also prepare his own report. The report of the justice minister and copies of the other reports are sent to the office of the legislation minister and are then examined by a standing committee of the legislature, the contested interpretation committee. If the report of the justice minister is not acted upon by the committee and legislature within a certain period of time, the interpretation proposed by the justice minister is considered adopted. Furthermore, the justice minister publishes an annual report which records diversities of interpretation in various judicatories so that these can be harmonized. Although Bentham is not altogether clear, it seems that all instances of contested interpretation work their way up through the justice minister to the legislative committee. At the minimum they come to the cognizance of the justice minister who reports on differing interpretations of various parts of the *pannomion* by different judicatories. These will then be brought into harmony (though without retroactive effect) through amendments or other changes in the law.

The second function is called the judges' eventually-emendative function.[143] Where an amendment to the *pannomion* is thought desirable by a judge, this is set forth (with reasons) together with the opinions of the government advocate and eleemosynary advocate and sent in a report to the appellate judge and justice minister. If the appellate

within a legislative system already established. This discussion of judges will also correct the view of E. Stokes that for Bentham 'to permit a power of interpretation to the judiciary, or to allow it to challenge the commands of the legislator, was clearly to set up another will in defiance of the popular will.' (*The English Utilitarians and India*, Oxford, 1959, p. 72.)

[143] Ibid., pp. 504–8.

judge or justice minister veto the amendment, it fails, but if they do not (or if they approve it), it becomes law. Bentham recognizes that the justice minister together with one appellate and one immediate judge are given the power to make any change in the law they wish. Nevertheless, he does not think that this represents a threat to the legislature which remains supreme and can change the law as it pleases. These functionaries can only become powerful, argues Bentham, if there is a faction in the legislature sympathetic to their views.[144] The ultimate power remains in the legislature.

The third function is the judges' sistitive function, which is exercised where the judge halts a case in which an injustice might be done if a law is interpreted in a particular manner.[145] He issues three decrees: the first gives effect to the law as it is; the second gives effect to the law as it might be if an amendment proposed by him is adopted; the third stops the execution of either decree until the legislature decides which interpretation it believes is best. The proposed amendment is dealt with in the same manner as under the judges' eventually-emendative function.

The fourth function is the pre-interpretive function which is exercised by any person requesting through a judge an interpretation of the law on a particular point before litigation actually commences.[146] If, in doing so, the judge believes that the law should be amended, he can propose an amendment following the procedure outlined above. Bentham provides securities against frivolous applications, but he feels that great benefits can be derived by clarifying points of law before suits are begun thus reducing both the anxiety of potential litigants and even the need to bring cases at all.

Bentham believes that the exercise of these four functions is of crucial importance in preserving and improving the numerous codes that make up the *pannomion*. Had they been used in France, he observes, the 'swarms of commentaries' which had arisen in the twelve years of 'Buonaparte's Codes' would not have been needed and the people would have been less perplexed by the law.[147] Although he opposes 'judge-made law' and favours legislative supremacy, he also

144 Ibid., pp. 506-7.   145 Ibid., pp. 508-11.
146 Ibid., pp. 511-12.   147 Ibid., p. 512.

appreciates the potential knowledge and skill of judges when channelled into the improvement of the *pannomion.*

VIII

The two main officers at the local level are the local headman and local registrar. The local headman is the functionary who 'shall at all times be as near as possible to the spot'.[148] He is a unique official (different from the French *maire* or the English mayor) performing a wider range of functions than anyone except the prime minister, though, of course, in the smallest unit of territory. His authority is coextensive with the whole body of legislation which he helps to administer. Since he is the official most usefully placed to deal with local problems, he is more likely to take charge of the administration of the law at this level than the subordinates of the various ministers who are located centrally. Furthermore, the prime minister, ministers, or immediate judges can call on him to assist in the execution of laws and orders so long as their orders conform with the will of the legislature.[149] The local headman is elected in the same way as a member of the legislature having passed through the education and examination system and placed on the Locable List. His position, however, is subject to pecuniary competition. He may be removed from office by a minister, immediate judge (subject to appeal), prime minister, legislature, and the electorate of his subdistrict.[150]

Besides his general duties in assisting in the implementation of legislation, he also performs a number of other functions which Bentham describes at length. We shall mention only a few of these.[151] He convenes and presides over meetings in his territory. He commands the volunteer army and navy (if any) stationed in his territory. He takes all necessary action to minimize, control, and prevent calamity or criminal delinquency. Under the direction of the indigence relief minister he assists in the administration of the laws regarding the poor. He assists the foreign relation minister in providing hospitality for foreign agents passing through his territory. A number of his functions are related to the

---

[148] Ibid., p. 612.   [149] Ibid., p. 614.
[150] Ibid., pp. 623-4.   [151] See ibid., pp. 614-23.

judiciary and are called 'judicature-aiding functions'. Like a
judge, the local headman has the power duty to suppress
civil disturbances and is well placed to do so as head of the
radical military force in his territory. He assists the judiciary
not only in the direct assistance of a judge in carrying out his
duties but also in acting independently as an additional
source of judicial power. He is especially useful in emergencies
or where someone 'on the spot' is needed to apprehend a
potential criminal. He also assists the judiciary in arranging
the sale by auction of goods following a judicial decree.
Furthermore, he is a source of information to inhabitants.
He plays a special role in the reconciliation of disputes,
especially disputes within families, which take place within
his territory and disputes which arise during travelling, e.g.
between travellers and innkeepers and when accidents take
place. He takes charge of the body of a stranger or traveller
who dies within the territory.

The local registrar has the same local field of service as
the headman, and his duties consist of recording a wide range
of events taking place in his territory. Unlike the local headman, he is a civil servant, appointed for life by the justice
minister though dislocable by the justice minister and the
electorate in his subdistrict.[152] As we have seen (chapter
VII), the local registrar plays an important role in the whole
system of political communication by recording births,
deaths, maturity, insanity, contracts, wills, property, maps of
land, and by maintaining an office and 'document chamber'
so that access and publicity can be given to this material.[153]

According to Everett, 'the relation between the local
headman and the local registrar represents almost the only
usage by Bentham of the checks and balances principle.'[154]
This is not entirely true, as Bentham develops an analogous
relationship between judges and judicial registrars.[155] The
local registrar records the official actions of the local headman and then adds whether or not he approves of a particular
action. The registrar cannot prevent the local headman from
performing a given act. But, if the registrar writes on a
document or order 'disapproved', the headman must add
(with his signature) 'ordered notwithstanding' if he wishes

---

[152] Ibid., pp. 625-6, 635-6.   [153] Ibid., pp. 626-35.
[154] Everett, op. cit., p. 11.   [155] See Bowring, ix. 579-80, 585.

to carry out the action. The headman also inspects, criticizes, and suggests improvements to the work of the registrar. But the important check is that of the registrar on the headman, as the registrar is the experienced civil servant and can serve as the headman's 'natural Mentor'.[156] The headman, as an elected official with limited tenure of office, is usually less experienced.

IX

Although the various sub-legislatures in each district perform a wide range of duties, Bentham emphasizes that they act always in subordination to the legislature.[157] In giving effect to the arrangements of the central government, they may be directed by the prime minister or a minister, as well as by the legislature. But in these cases the sub-legislatures may appeal to the legislature if they disagree with the order thus preserving legislative supremacy. Members of the sub-legislatures are elected, serve and can be dismissed in the same way as members of the legislature. In addition, they can be removed by the legislature itself.

Besides carrying out the directives of the central government, the sub-legislatures provide buildings and other public works within the jurisdiction of the education, domain, indigence relief, and preventive service ministers. Under close scrutiny by the legislature they have the power to raise money by taxation. They elicit information, secure publicity, and hold inquiries as part of their legislative duties. In spite of the close inspection by the legislature, Bentham hopes that the sub-legislatures will make useful experiments in legislation on a limited scale which will eventually benefit the whole of society.

Each sub-legislature contains the same number of sub-ministers as there are ministers in the central government with the obvious exception of the foreign relation minister.[158] Other sub-departments might be consolidated depending on local circumstances. The sub-legislatures are allowed to develop their own radical defence forces so long as these do not conflict in any way with the national

[156] Ibid., p. 624-5.   [157] Ibid., pp. 640-3.   [158] Ibid., p. 643.

force. There may also be some judicial officers related to the sub-legislatures. On the whole, Bentham does not spell out very clearly the role of the sub-legislatures and the subordinate ministers. He partly wishes to maintain a degree of flexibility so that his *Code* might be adapted to a federal structure. He also leaves room for experiment and does not wish to restrict unduly these subordinate authorities. Nevertheless, it is difficult to see the relationship, for example, between the local headmen and the subministers of the sub-legislatures. Do they ever come into conflict? There might be disputes over the jurisdiction of the preventive service subminister and the local headman in dealing with a calamity. Nevertheless, one point is made abundantly clear, that the legislature remains supreme over all of these subordinate authorities.

X

The picture of representative democracy which emerges from this survey of the main institutions and offices is one which highlights the radical and democratic character of the state. Bentham's account of the citizen-army where the privates can dismiss the officers, his attempt to limit the power of the professional army to turn against the democratic constitution, his provisions for giving to the poor full access to all judicial services, his use of the quasi-jury to limit the abuse of power by judges, and the 'dislocative' power placed in the hands of the electorate to remove any administrative and judicial officer testify to his determination to keep government fully accountable to the people not only at periodic elections but also on numerous other occasions. Few modern democratic states provide for similar popular control.

What is less clear is the extent to which these institutions constitute either a *laissez-faire* state, an interventionist state, or an early version of the modern welfare state. It is true that Bentham's depiction of the thirteen ministers (on which most commentators have dwelled) bears little resemblance to government administration in his own day and foreshadows some of the ministries of the present (e.g. health, finance, trade, preventive service, etc.), but his discussion of the functions of these ministers is sketchy and incomplete.

Although the range of functions performed by the ministers might be seen as considerable in terms of Bentham's day, there is no clear indication of the extent of government involvement which he envisages. The reason for this is that Bentham's ministers are primarily directed to administer whatever laws are passed by the legislature. Depending on a variety of circumstances, these laws may require greater or less government involvement in the economy and society. Bentham gives no real indication in the *Code* of the specific laws regarding health, police, transport, etc., which he envisages, as these would have no place in a constitutional document. It is true, of course, that the mere fact of the existence of these ministries, directed by experts who sit in the legislature, would most likely lead to legislation in these fields, but the exact character of that legislation and the amount of government intervention intended cannot be determined *a priori.* Above all, he proposes a flexible, evolving system of accountable government and a *pannomion* which, as we have seen in the accounts of the functions of judges and the legislation minister, develops over time and according to changing circumstances.

Chapter IX

Bentham and James Mill
on Representation

The view that James Mill's *Essay on Government* contains a summary of the views of Bentham and the Benthamites is at least as old as T. B. Macaulay's critique of the *Essay* in the *Edinburgh Review* of March 1829.[1] Macaulay also believed that Bentham came to the defence of Mill in the *Westminster Review*, and it was only a public disclaimer by Bentham himself that set the record straight.[2] The Benthamites, however, did not distinguish between the views of Bentham and Mill, and Bentham published no critique of Mill's *Essay*. As a result, Mill's *Essay* has come to be regarded as a useful and brief summary of Bentham's views on representative government.[3] In this chapter we shall show how Bentham's theory of representation differs considerably from that of Mill. Furthermore, we shall consider the extent to which Macaulay's critique of Mill, which had an important impact on the development of radical theories of representative government, applies to Bentham as well as to Mill.

[1] This chapter is based on the debate which arose over Macaulay's critique of the *Essay on Government* which began in the *Edinburgh Review*, No. 97 (March 1829), xlix, pp. 159-89. Perronet Thompson replied in the Benthamite *Westminster Review*, No. 21 (July 1829), xi, pp. 254-68. Macaulay wrote two further articles in the *Edinburgh Review*, No. 98 (June 1829), xlix, pp. 273-99 and No. 99 (October 1829) 1, pp. 99-125, to which the *Westminster Review* replied twice, No. 22 (October 1829), xi, pp. 526-36 and No. 23 (January 1830), xii, pp. 246-62. Mill's *Essay on Government* has a complex history, but it first appeared in the second part of the *Supplement* to the fifth edition of the *Encyclopaedia Britannica*, vol. iv, which was published in September 1820. Mill's *Essay* and the articles from the *Edinburgh Review* and *Westminster Review* have been usefully collected in *Utilitarian Logic and Politics*, eds. J. Lively and J. Rees, Oxford, 1978 to which references here will be made. For Macaulay's association of Bentham with Mill's *Essay*, see p. 99. For the significance of the debate in the later development of utilitarian thought, see J. H. Burns, 'The Light of Reason', *James and John Stuart Mill*, ed. J. M. Robson and M. Laine, Toronto, 1976, pp. 5-6, 15-17.

[2] Lively and Rees, op. cit., pp. 153, 177-8.

[3] See, for example, A. H. Birch, *Representation*, London, 1971, p. 55: 'These ideas were expounded by Bentham in a number of writings between 1809 and 1832 and they were also set out, somewhat more clearly, in the *Essay on Government* which James Mill wrote in 1820.'

There is some evidence that Bentham in fact disagreed with Mill's position in the *Essay*. A brief manuscript has survived headed 'J. B. versus Mill' which begins: 'Written on reading Mills [sic] article Government as reprinted from Supplement to Encyclopedia Britannica . . .'[4] The manuscript is dated 23 April 1824, the year that the whole of the Supplement to the fifth edition of the *Encyclopaedia* was published. At this time, Bentham was drafting the *Constitutional Code*, and the manuscript bears the heading of chapter VI of the *Code* where he takes up the theme of representative government. Bentham does not appear to have developed the theme of the manuscript further and no reference to Mill appears in the actual text. As a critique of Mill's *Essay* the manuscript concentrates on Mill's proposals to limit the right of suffrage to those over forty and to exclude women and children. Bentham, as we have seen, favours virtual universal suffrage. Besides arguing for the importance of including youth (as sources of virtue, activity, and for civic education), he makes one important point almost in passing. He notes that the age of legal maturity is already set in most countries and refers to this age as the best starting-point for a decision on the age for eligibility for suffrage.[5] Mill had approached the problem in an *a priori* manner from notions of maturity and responsibility, while Bentham seeks to start more empirically and develop his argument from practices in existing countries. In light of Macaulay's later critique of Mill, it is worth noting that in method Bentham neatly distinguishes his own more empirical approach from that of Mill.

I

Bentham (in the *Code*), and Mill (in the *Essay*) disagree on the fundamental point of whether or not the representative system can in itself achieve an identity of interests between rulers and ruled even where elections are held on the basis of universal

---

[4] UC xxxiv, 302-3. This was reprinted in part in E. Halévy, *La Formation du Radicalisme Philosophique*, 3 vols., Paris, 1901-4, iii. 444 and fully in *Bentham's Political Thought*, ed. B. Parekh, London, 1973, pp. 311-12.

[5] In Bentham's Election Code, which, as *Bentham's Radical Reform Bill*, was in print in 1819, he suggests the voting age of twenty-one. See Bowring, iii. 565.

[6] Note that in the manuscript discussed above (see note 4) Bentham refers to the 'many excellent and unexceptionable' (Parekh, op. cit., p. 312) pages in Mill's *Essay* besides those which deal with the restrictions on suffrage. This

suffrage.[6] Bentham would agree with Macaulay when the latter asks:

Is it not clear that the representatives, as soon as they are elected, are an aristocracy, with an interest opposed to the interest of the community? Why should they not pass a law for extending the term of their power from one year to ten years, or declare themselves senators for life?[7]

Macaulay contends that Mill's only answer is that of frequent elections, and indeed, Mill states that limiting the term of office 'is the only security of which the nature of the case admits'.[8] Mill considers, as we shall see, the possibility of punishing delinquent representatives but dismisses the proposal as being impractical in stopping the abuse of power. He also believes that the good representative who is re-elected at each election should serve for as long as he lives.[9] However, like Macaulay —though from an entirely different perspective—Bentham doubts that the interests of a government elected by universal suffrage for a limited term can be assumed to be identical with the interests of the people. But unlike Macaulay, Bentham does not adopt the broader Whig view of representation of interests. In the *Code* he seeks ways of securing good government by representatives through several devices which will overcome the criticism that Macaulay makes of Mill.

While not rejecting Mill's security of frequent elections, Bentham argues that there are additional securities which will be more effective. He considers this problem in his treatment of 'relocation' to the legislature.[10] His basic provision is that no sitting member is eligible for re-election until there is a

remark might be interpreted as evidence of Bentham's agreement with Mill especially since there is no evidence of further explicit disagreement. In placing the *Code* and the *Essay* side by side, however, the differences become quite obvious. It is worth noting that Bowring takes some credit for the evolution of Bentham's ideas on representation. See ch. VI, § 25, Art. 53n (*CW*), p. 90n, and Bowring, x. 528-30. Perhaps Bentham, whose argument was not complete until 1826 or 1827, saw his ideas as moving in the same direction as those of Mill but with additional refinements.

    [7] Lively and Rees, op. cit., pp. 114-15.

    [8] Ibid., p. 76. See also J. Mill, *On the Ballot; from the Westminster Review for July 1830*, London, 3rd ed., 1830, p. 13. In Mill's essay on 'The Liberty of the Press' in *Essays . . .* , London, n.d., he qualifies his position and argues (p. 19) that 'it is doubtful whether a power in the people of choosing their own rulers without the liberty of the press, would be an advantage'. See also pp. 20-1.

    [9] Lively and Rees, op. cit., p. 77.

    [10] Ch. VI, § 25 (*CW*), pp. 72-91.

pool of former members two or three times the number of existing members of the legislature.[11] This will provide a choice of experienced men at each election. Without this clear choice he notes that 'any supposed opening, for improvement or correction of abuse, will be but illusory.'[12] This strong remark contrasts directly with Mill's assurance that frequent elections alone will secure an identity of interests between representatives and the people. Bentham, however, presents evidence of stagnation and corruption in various institutions which supposedly provide for rotation in office but in fact continue the selection of the same people.

In making a general case against continuation in office through re-election, Bentham develops two important arguments. Firstly, the deputy who wins one term of office effectively secures office virtually for life whatever his abilities as a legislator.[13] When re-election comes, he has his experience and services to plead in his favour, and his opponent, without these advantages, has little chance against him. But the incumbent may have shown very little ability or intelligence in office and this aspect of his achievement will never be weighed in the balance against him. The mere fact of his having held office will most probably allow him to continue. Secondly, by continuing to hold office, the deputy is prone to succumb to corruption both from those in superior positions (like the prime minister and justice minister) and from what Bentham calls the 'leading men among each Deputy's Electors'.[14] The matter of corruption is the familiar list of 'money, money's worth, power, (power of *patronage* included,) and reputation' besides (in monarchies but not in this constitution) '*ease* at the expense of *duty*, and *vengeance* at the expense of *justice*'.[15] What causes corruption, Bentham continues, is not so much receiving these objects but the continual expectation of receiving them. And as the deputies are corrupted by the prospect of patronage and increased reputation, so the higher officials also become corrupted by the consequent increase in their power and reduction of their responsibility in relation to the legislature.[16] The

[11] Ibid., Art. 1 (*CW*), p. 72.
[12] Ibid., Art. 4 (*CW*), pp. 72-3.
[13] Ibid., Art. 18 (*CW*), p. 76.
[14] Ibid., Art. 19.
[15] Ibid., Art. 20 (*CW*), pp. 76-7.
[16] Ibid., Art. 21 (*CW*), p. 77.

object of corruption from the 'leading men' among the electorate is to gain influence through the deputy which can be used among the deputy's colleagues. In the process, these 'leading men' also become corrupted in receiving small personal benefits, extra courtesies and flattery, and special benefits for their particular district at the expense of the general interest.[17] The deputies themselves, under the influence of all of this corruption, become salesmen of their votes and talents, especially those of speaking and management.[18]

Bentham believes that the sole justification for allowing continuity in office is that it provides for experience among the deputies. But the term 'experience', he finds, is an ambiguous one and not entirely appropriate in this context. By concentrating on providing for experienced legislators, he believes that the electorate are then deprived of a choice between experienced men. In addition, experience is an indeterminate notion. An experienced man might be either competent or incompetent, and his experience gives no clue as to which he is. Bentham prefers the term 'aptitude' to 'experience' and argues that there are other ways of securing this among deputies.[19] He devises another institution which provides experience in a way that avoids the difficulties he identifies in the continuity of elected members of the legislature. He calls this institution the continuation committee.[20]

The continuation committee is chosen by the secret ballot of members of the legislature from its members or from members of the existing committee. The task of the committee is to bring forward the plans and proceedings of the previous legislature to the present one. Although members of the committee can initiate debate and propose motions, they do not have the right to vote. Through the continuation committee the collective experience of preceding legislatures is brought forward, and experienced, able men can give the benefit of their experience to the present legislature. Bentham lists a number of advantages in using a committee such as

---

[17] Ibid., Art. 23.
[18] Ibid., Art. 25 (*CW*), p. 78.
[19] Ibid., Art. 32 (*CW*), pp. 79–80. See also ibid., Art 53n (*CW*), p. 90n.
[20] Ch. VI, § 24 (*CW*), pp. 67–72.

this, in avoiding the loss of good measures which were not enacted in the last legislature, saving time with unfinished legislation, and saving valuable information which was obtained in the previous session. But perhaps most important is the link that the continuation committee provides between legislatures that otherwise would have to be provided by the re-election of deputies. With the continuation committee, therefore, his proposal for 'temporary non-relocability' becomes more plausible.

Bentham conceives several objections to the 'temporary non-relocability' system which he poses and then answers. To the objection that freedom of choice is taken away by the non-eligibility of the sitting deputy, Bentham argues that freedom of choice has no use except as a security for appropriate aptitude. In this case freedom of choice would only enhance inaptitude in office. He then argues that the deputy will not suffer undeserved pain due to his loss of office, because he knows in advance and is prepared for his not being immediately eligible for re-election. Finally, to the objection that no one with ability will seek an office with so little power because of the brief period of service, Bentham argues that people will still be attracted to serve in the legislature. There is always the inducement of obtaining advantages for oneself and one's friends (which he admits can never be stopped). Furthermore, the seat in the legislature can be used as a stepping-stone to other seats—in the continuation committee, the sub-legislatures, and to another seat in the legislature once the non-relocability period ends.[21]

In adding up the merits of the system of temporary non-relocability (and continuation committee) as opposed to continuity in office with only the security of frequent elections, Bentham argues that while his scheme maximizes competition and holds out the prospect of able men coming into office, the other system (with re-election virtually assured) contains no motives for exertion. His system also gives new and able men a chance to win a seat as well as securing a large number of 'tried' men for the legislature. Those who are out of office become 'political watchmen' as leading members of the Public Opinion Tribunal. They can keep an eye on the

---

[21] Ch. VI, § 25, Art. 52 (*CW*), pp. 88–9.

174 Bentham and James Mill on Representation

follies and corruptions of those in office. The sub-legislatures are also provided with a supply of men of considerable aptitude who otherwise would not be willing to serve in these bodies. In turn, new members of the legislature will most probably bring to their work knowledge and judgement acquired by service in the sub-legislatures.[22]

II

Besides the securities established by 'temporary non-relocability', Bentham also develops constitutional proposals for the punishment of members of the legislature. Mill believes that punishment is not a good remedy for the abuse of power by representatives, because 'abuses of power may be carried to a great extent, without allowing the means of proving a determinate offence.' To this, he adds: 'no part of political experience is more perfect than this.'[23] Bentham is not naïve about using punishment against the omnicompetent legislature. If, for example, the legislature overspends to a considerable extent on a necessary enterprise it is doubtful that legal punishment of the members would be possible 'without preponderant evil in the shape of dissension and danger of civil war'.[24] The remedy for much of the abuse of power by the legislature is publicity and the display of displeasure by the Public Opinion Tribunal.[25] Nevertheless, there are instances where punishment is an important and efficient security, and Bentham provides for these both in the way he combines the possibility of punishment with dismissal from office by the electorate and in the institution of the Legislation Penal Judicatory.[26]

In addition to the provision for periodic elections, Bentham also grants to the electorate a specific dislocative function which is exercised to remove members of the legislature from office. This is done by a petition signed by a percentage of the electors (Bentham suggests one fourth) which requires the Election Minister to hold an election. The voting cards bear the words 'dislocate him' and 'retain him' and the

[22] Ibid., Art. 53 (CW), pp. 89-90.
[23] Lively and Rees, op. cit., p. 77.
[24] Ch. VIIn (CW), p. 134n.   [25] Ibid.
[26] Ch. V, §3, Arts. 4-10 (CW), pp. 33-5; Ch. VI, §28, (CW), pp. 111-14.

electorate choose either one course or the other. If the majority vote for dislocation, an election is called in the district in the normal manner. In addition to these voting cards, the electors are furnished with a second set worded 'accuse him' and 'absolve him' which are then employed in another vote if the first vote has led to the decision to dislocate the functionary. If the electorate decides to 'accuse him', the member will be tried before the Legislation Penal Judicatory.

This system for removal from office and eventual punishment applies to all government officials. Bentham is aware that it will apply more easily to members of the administration than to members of the legislature, especially because the trial is conducted under the auspices of the legislature itself. For this reason, he proposes that where a member of the legislature is accused, the accusers can stipulate that he is tried either that year or by one of several succeeding legislatures in order to obviate any partiality by the existing legislature.[27]

The Legislation Penal Judicatory is used to try only present and preceding members of the legislature, the prime minister, and the justice minister.[28] Other courts try lesser officials including the ministers.[29] Obviously, Bentham intends that the Legislation Penal Judicatory will be invoked only under extraordinary circumstances. The judges (three or five) are chosen by secret ballot by the legislature and all will either be members of the legislature or have no connection at all with the government.[30] If men of ability and high moral standards can be found, Bentham prefers that the judges are not members of the legislature to avoid criticisms of partiality. Remedies for false and unfounded accusations are also provided.[31]

Bentham does not place undue emphasis on the Legislation Penal Judicatory as the only solution to the problem of the abuse of power. But it is interesting that this believer in legislative omnicompetence has no place in his system for special status for legislators. It may be politically impossible

[27] Ch. V, § 3, Art. 10 (*CW*), pp. 34-5.
[28] Ch. VI, § 28, Art. 1 (*CW*), p. 111.
[29] See Ch. IX, § 21, Arts. 11-19 (*CW*), pp. 393-5.
[30] Ch. VI, § 28, Arts. 2-7 (*CW*), pp. 111-12.
[31] Ibid., Art. 14 (*CW*), p. 113.

to try a member, but once he is removed from office by the electorate, it may not be difficult then to proceed to a criminal trial.

In dealing with both the re-election and punishment of representatives, Bentham attempts to establish additional securities for making democratically elected representatives more accountable to the people. It is a theme which runs throughout the chapter on the legislature (VI) in the *Code*. We might cite two additional examples of Bentham's continual attempts to improve or define further this accountability. Firstly, he adopts the term 'deputy' rather than 'representative' in the *Code*, because he finds 'representative' 'ambiguous' and 'indeterminate'.[32] It seems that early in his career Bentham toyed with the term 'delegate' rather than 'representative'.[33] One person can 'represent' another without having been appointed by the person for that purpose, e.g. guardians for orphans and administrators of property of intestates. The English monarchy and aristocracy are also said to represent the people. With the term 'deputy' Bentham believes that no ambiguity need arise.

Secondly, while Bentham seeks to hold the deputy accountable to his constituents, he is aware that the deputy should not simply reflect the aggregate of the interests of his constituency. The deputy's aim is to act in a way which advances the general interest and not necessarily the interests of his constituents.[34] Bentham expects the deputy to exercise his independent judgement. He states that a difference of view may develop 'without detriment to moral aptitude on either side'. He adds: 'They may have good reason for dislocating him; he for exposing himself to be so dislocated.'[35]

Bentham's solution to the problem of conflict between deputy and constituents exemplifies his awareness of the difficulty of simply identifying interests of rulers and ruled. He argues that the deputy's *vote* might follow the will of the majority of his own constituents in so far as the national interest is an aggregate of particular interests. If a majority vote against a proposal thought to be in the national interest,

[32] Ch. V, § 2, Art. 3n (*CW*), pp. 30n-31n.
[33] Steintrager, *Bentham*, p. 49.
[34] Ch. VI, § 1, Art. 9 (*CW*), p. 43.
[35] Ibid.

this would be evidence that most probably it was not in the national interest.[36] To avoid insincerity on the part of the deputy, however, he might speak in support of an arrangement he thinks is in the national interest but vote according to the views of his constituents. 'By his *speech*', writes Bentham, 'his duty to the *public* is fulfilled; by his *vote*, his duty to his Constituents.'[37] In proceeding thus the deputy may persuade his constituents to support his position, or he may discover that the view of the constituents, rather than his own, is in the national interest.[38]

Bentham's view of the relationship between deputy and constituents anticipates a fair degree of creative tension between them. Although the constituents can easily dismiss the deputy, he exercises his independent judgement to interpret to them what measures he believes are in the general interest. Unlike James Mill, Bentham does not regard the relationship as one of a simple identity of interests.

III

We have argued thus far that Bentham escapes a number of the important criticisms that Macaulay makes of Mill's theory of representative government. Macaulay might argue, however, that Bentham merely compounds the difficulties he has found in Mill and having admitted that no strict identity of interests is possible, Bentham should abandon the whole theory rather than seek refuge in a series of institutional refinements. It would be easy to criticize the practicality of Bentham's proposals. Modern states tend to rely, for better or worse, on party systems to provide men of experience and aptitude for public office. Bentham does not entirely neglect political parties. He accepts that in the English system there would be contending parties 'for such parts of the plunderage as are at the disposal of the Monarch, and for all such other power as is open to competition'.[39] As these parties would need to appeal to the Public Opinion Tribunal for support, they would be under a degree of control by the

[36] Ibid., Art. 10 (*CW*), pp. 43-4.
[37] Ibid., Art. 11 (*CW*), p. 44.
[38] Ibid., Arts. 11-12.
[39] Ch. VI, § 31, Art. 37 (*CW*), p. 128.

people. But Bentham does not foresee the parties playing a major role in supplying personnel for public office. Nor does he appreciate that a party system could largely nullify the positive effects he claims for the scheme of temporary non-relocability, for example, by providing for virtual continuity in office (e.g. alternation by two men in a safe seat).

Nevertheless, on a practical level, Bentham argues that the example of the United States provides ample evidence that a representative government based on virtual universal male suffrage can function without difficulty. He often refers to the United States in this way, and it is of interest that James Mill in the *Essay* does not. It is Macaulay who brings in the example of the United States, and he uses it to argue that America, because of special conditions, provides no evidence for believing that the poor will not plunder the rich if given the vote.[40] But Bentham is in a strong position in pointing to the success of representative democracy in the United States. He can then argue that his proposals represent refinements in an already established practice, and, in addition, that he presents these within a theoretical structure which can be applied to any society. And since he does not claim that representative government establishes an identity of interests, he does not have to show that this exists in the United States.

Bentham takes an even stronger view than Mill about the poor confiscating the property of the rich under a representative system. Mill argues that the poor ('that class of the people, who are below the middle rank') will emulate the middle classes, aspire to their position and adopt their values.[41] He contends that the vast majority of the poor are guided by the opinions of the middle classes.[42] Although Bentham most probably would not have rejected Mill's remarks, he does not in the *Code* dwell on the virtues of the middle classes. His view is closer to that taken by Perronet Thompson in the *Westminster Review* defence of Mill: 'It is not the poor but the rich, that have a propensity to take the property of other people. There is no instance upon earth,

<hr/>

[40] Lively and Rees, op. cit., p. 121. Macaulay says that high wages, the low cost of the necessities of life, and the opportunity to become rich without capital with only industry and frugality make the United States a different case from Europe where the majority are very poor and vast amounts have been accumulated by a few.

[41] Ibid., p. 94.   [42] Ibid.

of the poor having combined to take away the property of the rich.'[43]

It is interesting that both Bentham and Macaulay, proceeding inductively, use the example of the United States to support opposing views on this important issue. Perhaps the weakness in Macaulay's position can best be seen in his prediction that the United States would face a similar condition in the twentieth century as then existed in Europe.[44] Although it may no longer be as easy to become rich by frugality and hard work nowadays as in Bentham's day, it is fair to say that the poor have not yet risen to confiscate the property of the rich in the United States. Indeed, it might be argued that Europe has become increasingly like the United States in this respect rather than the United States like Europe.

IV

Bentham uses the example of the United States throughout his later writings as evidence for the possibility of a number of important reforms. He differs from James Mill's approach in the *Essay* and cannot be treated, as was Mill by Macaulay, as an *a priori* thinker. Nevertheless, Bentham approaches some arguments in the same way that Mill does in relying on a number of explicit assumptions about human nature. Macaulay is highly critical of these in Mill and it is apparent that he would be equally critical of Bentham. The most important are the assumptions that men are basically self-interested and self-aggrandizing and that those with sufficient power will stop at nothing including terror to achieve what they desire. On the basis of these assumptions both Bentham and Mill argue that only a government which is controlled by the governed can be prevented from oppressing the people. Monarchy and aristocracy are thus excluded and the way is opened for the justification of representative government.

Macaulay challenges this approach with a number of counter-arguments. Is it not possible, asks Macaulay, that rulers fairly easily satisfy their desires and then derive satisfaction from protecting the community? Is it true, he continues,

[43] Ibid., pp. 136–7.   [44] Ibid., p. 121.

that this reign of terror has actually existed among monarchies?[45] He believes that any empirical investigation of Mill's belief will show that it is fallacious. Macaulay then argues that the physical desires of a ruler are like those of anyone else and require little to satisfy them. Many of the remainder of his desires are dependent upon his having a good reputation with the people. The ruler desires especially posthumous fame and fears posthumous reproach.[46] Macaulay even places these sentiments in the form of a geometrical proof (which he 'humbly' offers to Mill) and proves that 'no ruler will do any thing which may hurt the people'.[47] Macaulay's position is simply that all men desire both to injure and to benefit their neighbours and it is mistaken to base a theory of government on the assumption that men desire only to harm their neighbours.[48] Macaulay's position seems at first glance irrefutable. He even quotes at length from Mill himself to show that Mill grants the importance of pains derived from the unfavourable sentiments of mankind which is the starting point of Macaulay's 'theorem'.

Although Bentham does not dwell on this theme in the *Code*, his position is sufficiently close to that of Mill to be included in this part of Macaulay's critique. In chapter XI we shall examine Bentham's distinction between self-regard and sympathy in some detail. It will suffice here to say that although Bentham believes that men are capable of action from sympathetic motives, he argues that especially in the case of rulers, they will tend to act from self-interested motives and in a self-aggrandizing manner. Furthermore, recalling Bentham's discussion of power, rulers may be assumed to abuse the great power they possess whenever the opportunity arises. For Bentham, therefore, every ruler is a potential tyrant.

Let us assume that Bentham cannot establish his rule about the advancement of self-interest empirically or, at the

---

[45] Ibid., p. 104.   [46] Ibid., p. 105-6.
[47] Ibid., pp. 106-7; '(1) No rulers will do that which produces pain to themselves. (2) But the unfavourable sentiments of the people will give pain to them. (3) Therefore no rulers will do any thing which may excite the unfavourable sentiments of the people. (4) But the unfavourable sentiments of the people are excited by everything which hurts them. (5) Therefore no rulers will do any thing which may hurt the people.' (The numbers are not in the original.)
[48] Ibid., p. 107.

minimum, cannot finally free it from the objections of Macaulay. Nevertheless, it can be argued that Bentham's approach still has merit. He is saying that there are some basic propensities in the human condition which must be accepted or taken seriously in approaching politics. For Mill, it is the importance of terror as a basic constituent of the relationship between rulers and ruled. For Bentham, it is the self-aggrandizing character of human desire and action. If these aspects of the human condition are neglected, Bentham argues, the legislator is bound to fail in his task of providing for the greatest happiness of the greatest number. This tendency to make assumptions about the human condition which then have a bearing on politics is common in political theory since Plato. They are used to establish a basis for prescriptions about how government should be organized and cannot be refuted empirically. Bentham does not deny that men can act with sympathy for others, and no amount of examples of sympathetic action, even by rulers, would lead him to abandon his assumption about the primacy of self-regard. Even if at a given period there were no self-regarding actions, he would still say that the primacy of self-regard and the tendency towards self-aggrandizement are the main assumptions which the legislator should bear in mind in devising constitutional arrangements.

For Bentham these assumptions are as important as the greatest happiness principle and the various subordinate 'ends in view' for approaching a law or constitutional arrangement. If the greatest happiness principle is the critical standard for assessing a proposal, the assumptions about the human condition provide a naturalistic standard. Bentham does not derive his various proposals from the 'naturalistic' standard and so no naturalistic fallacy is committed. Yet, if a proposed arrangement seems to contradict the import of this standard (e.g. in assuming that rulers will rule for the sake of the greatest happiness without further checks), it will be viewed suspiciously.

Although empirical evidence cannot refute the assumptions, Bentham is willing to argue that these are the most important assumptions regarding politics and more useful than any others which may be put forward. Thus, for Macaulay merely to offer counter-examples is not sufficient. To be fair,

Macaulay goes beyond this and argues that rulers do rule for the good of their subjects if only to avoid the pain of being disliked. Bentham would none the less argue that rulers cannot be trusted to do so, and they must be controlled on the assumption that they may not continue this enlightened policy. In the end, empirical evidence plus an intuitive response leads one to accept either Macaulay or Bentham. The present author prefers the pessimism of Bentham and Mill to the cautious optimism of Macaulay.

Chapter X

Bentham's *Code* and
J. S. Mill's *Considerations*

The relationship between John Stuart Mill and both his father and Bentham is highly complex, and an account of Mill's whole philosophy can be set forth in terms of the history of his agreement with and divergence from the views of the earlier utilitarians. Yet, no attempt has been made to place Bentham's *Code* and Mill's *Considerations on Representative Government* side by side to explore their similarities and differences.[1] In the last chapter we have emphasized the differences between Bentham and James Mill on the theme of representation so that there is no longer any excuse to consider the *Essay* a brief and convenient substitute for the *Code*. We shall now examine J. S. Mill's classic work on representative government in light of Bentham's achievement in the *Code*.

I

It is not easy to assess Mill's debt to Bentham in the *Considerations*. Bentham's name is occasionally invoked (as opposed to James Mill who is not mentioned), but no work of Bentham and especially the *Code* is discussed.[2] It is well known, however, that Mill differs in his political views from the earlier radicals, and in spite of superficial agreement and a similar use of language, the differences rather than the

---

[1] On the relationship between Bentham and Mill generally, see J. M. Robson, 'John Stuart Mill and Jeremy Bentham, with some Observations on James Mill', *Essays in English Literature from the Renaissance to the Victorian Age*, eds. M. MacLure and F. W. Watt, Toronto, 1964, pp. 245-68; F. E. L. Priestley, 'Introduction' to *The Collected Works of John Stuart Mill*, ed. J. M. Robson, vol. x, Toronto, 1969, pp. vii-lxii. So much attention has been given to the general view of Bentham through Mill's eyes that similar ground will not be covered here. References to Mill's *Considerations* are to the *Collected Works of John Stuart Mill*, ed. J. M. Robson, vol. xix (*Essays on Politics and Society*), Toronto, 1977.

[2] *Considerations*, pp. 390, 441, 481, 521, 527. All of the references except one (popular dismissal of judges) are favourable.

similarities strike the reader as being more important. But let us look briefly at the similarities.

Many points of agreement between Bentham and Mill are at a fairly superficial level and may even be the starting-points for substantial disagreement. For example, Mill refers to and adopts Bentham's classification of aptitude (moral, intellectual, and active) and shares Bentham's concern with fostering active aptitude.[3] But Mill uses the concept almost exclusively to foster aptitude in the people which will then be reflected in the quality of the government. Bentham's concern is with developing aptitude amongst the rulers or potential rulers, and he has little to say in the *Code*, at any rate, of aptitude in the people. Both Bentham and Mill believe that representative government is the best form of government. But disagreement begins once Mill takes up the question of whether it is suitable for everyone.

At times Mill simply reflects his Benthamite background. Like Bentham, he emphasizes the importance of the press, especially the newspaper press (for Mill it replaces the Greek *agora*).[4] When he writes that 'to inquire into the best form of government in the abstract (as it is called) is not a chimerical, but a highly practical employment of scientific intellect', he is surely echoing the way Bentham transformed such an inquiry into both a practical and 'scientific' enterprise.[5] Mill also uses Bentham's language of 'duty and interest', and 'sinister interests', and furthers his policies—e.g. female suffrage and the rejection of boards and committees in administration.[6] At a deeper level there is considerable agreement of outlook and approach. This might be expressed best by conjecturing that had Bentham thought of it, he would have been as enthusiastic an advocate of Thomas Hare's system

---

[3] Ibid., p. 390.   [4] Ibid., p. 378.   [5] Ibid., p. 380.
[6] Ibid., pp. 391, 441, 481, 521. At a number of secondary points Bentham and Mill are in agreement: both support universal suffrage subject to a literacy qualification, though Mill adds numeracy and excludes those on relief. Both reject the doctrine of the balanced constitution, believe that the prime minister and not the legislature should appoint ministers, and that drafting legislation requires special expertise. Both favour 'single seatedness' in the administration, competitive examinations for the civil service, and the choice of the chief executive by the legislature for a fixed term. Neither supports the indirect election of officials nor takes a favourable view of colonies. Finally, both emphasize the importance of communication between localities and the central government.

of proportional representation as Mill.[7] Mill and Bentham share a belief in the importance of institutional devices like this to resolve constitutional problems.

II

The most striking difference between Bentham's *Code* and Mill's *Considerations* is in their respective attitudes towards the role of the people in a representative democracy. Unlike Bentham, Mill makes the condition of the people, their readiness and preparedness for representative government, his prime concern. The success or failure of this form of government depends most on the capacity of the people to sustain it. For Bentham, it is always the ruling class and not the people who threaten the constitution. They have the power either to make it work or to destroy it. They are prone to corruption and form the 'sinister interests' most opposed to representative democracy. As there is still a ruling class in a democracy, the government will remain subject (though securities will provide some protection) to corruption by sinister interests. As we have seen in Bentham's argument justifying popular sovereignty, the representative system itself, based on secret suffrage, is sufficient to enable the people and their representatives to identify their interests with the general interest.

Mill requires that the people somehow be 'fit' for democracy. He wants their active participation and their co-operation with the law and public authorities.[8] Bentham, on the other hand, expects such co-operation, but he approaches the problem differently. He seeks to establish a series of securities which will also act as incentives for popular support for the democratic regime. By establishing an effective but fair police force or a system of rules which prevents administrative officials from oppressing the people or a judiciary which brings wrongdoers to a speedy and fair trial, Bentham provides incentives for the people to support the regime. These incentives depend on the quality of the government

[7] See Thomas Hare, *A Treatise on the Election of Representatives: Parliamentary and Municipal*, London, 1859. See also Thompson, *John Stuart Mill and Representative Government*, pp. 102–12.

[8] See especially *Considerations*, ch. I, pp. 374–82.

so that if the government is good, the people will tend to support it. Only in this way does Bentham believe that the people will become 'fit' for democracy.

A clear example of the difference between Mill and Bentham may be seen in their discussions of the consequences of selling votes. Mill writes:

> Again, representative institutions are of little value, and may be a mere instrument of tyranny or intrigue, when the generality of electors are not sufficiently interested in their own government to give their vote, or, if they vote at all, do not bestow their suffrages on public grounds, but sell them for money, or vote at the beck of some one who has control over them, or whom for private reasons they desire to propitiate. Popular election thus practised, instead of a security against misgovernment, is but an additional wheel in its machinery.[9]

In a later chapter Mill abandons his previous support for the secret ballot in order to take the vote out of the realm of private choice and to give a man an interest in public affairs.[10] For Bentham, however, the secret ballot is an excellent security against the abuse about which Mill complains. It does not prevent anyone from selling his vote but it does prevent the buyer from knowing that the seller has voted as he said he would. This element of uncertainty is sufficient, Bentham believes, to form the basis of a security for good government. The man who sells his vote is not hindered (so long as the system works) from voting for the best person. For Bentham, the secret ballot thus acts as an incentive for a person to vote for the best man. He admits that the voter may not vote in this way. But on the other hand, he is not prevented from doing so, and this is of great importance.[11]

We can also see the difference between Bentham and Mill in the latter's use of Bentham's concept of aptitude. Throughout the *Code*, as we have seen, Bentham distinguishes between moral, intellectual, and active aptitude and seeks to establish and secure aptitude in all of these forms in the ruling class.[12] In applying the notion of aptitude to the people (and he does

---

[9] Ibid., p. 378.
[10] Ibid., ch. X, pp. 488–500. J. H. Burns, 'J. S. Mill and Democracy, 1829-61', *Political Studies* v (1957), reprinted in *Mill, A Collection of Critical Essays* (Modern Studies in Philosophy), ed. J. B. Schneewind, London, 1969, p. 319: 'undoubtedly influenced and prompted by his wife. . .'.
[11] See *Bentham's Radical Reform Bill* (Bowring, iii. 559).
[12] See the discussions of aptitude in chapters III and IV above.

not emphasize this to any extent), Bentham is mainly concerned with encouraging the individual to identify his interests
with the general interest (moral aptitude). Intellectual
aptitude consists of performing intelligently the tasks of an
elector and those of a member of the Public Opinion Tribunal.
Bentham is never in any doubt that the ordinary man, so long
as he is not oppressed or misled by those in power, possesses
appropriate aptitude or will defer to those who possess it.
The main problem of aptitude lies more with rulers than with
the people.

Mill, however, after acknowledging the source of these
categories in Bentham, applies them in a way which, so far
as is known, does not appear in Bentham.[13] For Mill is
concerned primarily with the extent to which a regime
develops or fosters intellectual aptitude in the people which
is then reflected in the character of the government. From
Bentham's point of view, Mill's belief that good government
depends on the aptitude of the people suffers from several
deficiencies. There is a vagueness about what constitutes a
sufficient aptitude in the people to support representative
government. Mill seems anxious to exclude people from representative democracy until they are morally and intel-
lectually prepared for it, on the grounds that they might be
worse off with a representative system. But how does one
know if the people possess aptitude unless they are actually
constituting the representative democracy? And, if a representative system fails, there is no reason to place the blame
on the people rather than, as Bentham does, on the ruling
élites who actually possess the power to make the system
work. Furthermore, to say, as Mill does, that one criterion of
the goodness of government is the extent to which it fosters
in the people certain qualities opens the door to a kind of
paternalism which in the *Code* Bentham avoids. Bentham
seeks the more limited aim of preventing the government
from oppressing the people so as to allow the people to
develop through a number of channels their various aptitudes,
talents, and capacities. It may be argued that to conceive of
Mill's theory as paternalistic contradicts his well-known
devotion to individual liberty. Furthermore, Mill's views

---

[13] *Considerations*, p. 390.

about the people may simply reflect his concern with education and individual development. 'It is the educative argument which dominates,' writes Alan Ryan, 'for Mill's concern is to show how the educative considerations he has already developed are to be applied to representative government.'[14] Nevertheless, it is precisely the 'educative argument' that leads Mill into some difficulty. For pupils require teachers, and if the task set is to educate a whole society for representative government, who then will be the teachers if not the existing ruling élites. Teachers need not be paternalistic but they may be so, and the relation between teacher and pupils, especially where the pupils are mature adults, is hardly a relationship between equals. There is a tension in Mill between the emphasis on education and the emphasis on participation in so far as it concerns the capacity of the people to operate a representative democracy. The former can be paternalistic but the latter tends to be egalitarian. Bentham sees the virtues of participation without confusing them with intellectual education.[15] For Bentham, the education required by the people can be acquired by self-education.[16] His theory does not divide society into teachers and pupils.[17]

To remedy these difficulties Mill tends to rely on a 'sociological' argument about when the people are ready for representative government. 'The people', according to Mill, may 'have still to learn the first lesson of civilization, that of obedience.'[18] Until they do, they are only suitable for rule by a military leader. Or, he argues, they may be extremely passive and too ready to submit to tyranny; they may have only local allegiances and require a strong central ruler to weld the nation together prior to the institution of representative government. These reflections appear throughout the *Considerations* both at the point where Mill considers whether or not a people is suitable for representative government and in later chapters on nationality and the government of dependencies. In the latter chapter, he presents some examples

[14] A. Ryan, *J. S. Mill*, London, 1975, p. 200.
[15] See Thompson, op. cit., pp. 49–50.
[16] See Bowring, iii. 560; and above, chapter III.
[17] Mill writes: 'When we desire to have a good school, we do not eliminate the teacher' (*Considerations*, p. 545).
[18] Ibid., p. 415.

of fitness and backwardness with respect to civilization and representative government. British possessions such as Canada and Australia are fit for representative government; India is not.[19]

To his credit, Bentham avoids speculations such as these which might be used to justify colonialism.[20] He appreciates the fact that many states may not be able to operate a democratic system of government, as their leaders may lack the desire, ability, and the experience to do so. He does not, however, find fault in the *Code* with the people or with their state of civilization, but rather with corruption, favouritism, and other characteristics among ruling élites. He sees the problem as a moral and constitutional problem and not one of historical evolution. Corruption can be found in any society as long as constitutional and other legal arrangements do not prevent it.

This basic difference in their approaches to the problem of the aptitude of the people leads to a number of differences between them in their proposed constitutional arrangements. In the examples which we shall now consider the differences depend exclusively on Mill's apprehensions about the aptitude of the people even where they are deemed suitable for representative government. Unlike Bentham, Mill is sympathetic to a second chamber in parliament.[21] For Mill, the second chamber is a means of counterbalancing the absolute power of the democratic assembly. He proposes a Chamber of Statesmen, made up of former top politicians, judges, professors, etc., to counteract the People's chamber. However, he does not regard the second chamber as a major issue, as he believes that the main checks to popular power must be established in the democratic assembly itself presumably through such a practice as double voting. In contrast, Bentham's persistent attack on the House of Lords

---

[19] Ibid., p. 562.

[20] Bentham's legislator regards 'all such dominion, as no better than an instrument, and device, for the accumulation of patronage and oppressive power, in the hands of the ruling few in the dominating State, at the expense, and by the sacrifice, of the interest and felicity, of the subject many, in both States.' Ch. VII, §8 (*CW*), p. 143. But see Lea Campos Boralevi, 'Bentham and the Oppressed', Ph.D. thesis, European University Institute, Florence, 1980, pp. 215-59; and D. Winch, *Classical Political Economy and Colonies*, London, 1965, pp. 25-39.

[21] Cf. *Considerations*, ch. XIII, pp. 513-19 and Bentham's 'Anti-Senatica', op. cit.

as the personification of sinister interest and on the tendency of new states to adopt a second chamber is a familiar theme in his later writings.

Mill abandons the traditional radical doctrine of parliaments of short duration which enables the people to exert greater control over their representatives.[22] Where democracy is weak, he concedes that the term might be short, but where it is strong, a longer term is best. On balance he does not find the term of seven years in England worth changing.[23] Bentham is not dogmatic about the length of the legislative term, because some variation is required due to the distance between the legislature and the various districts.[24] Nevertheless, he favours annual parliaments if possible. Both annual parliaments and temporary non-relocability are ways of limiting the opportunities for the abuse of power by members of the legislature and highly valued by Bentham as securities.

Mill opposes the payment of members of parliament. He does not do so as a matter of economy but rather to avoid making the occupation of legislator 'an object of desire to adventurers of a low class'.[25] These 'adventurers' would be 'incessantly bidding to attract or retain the suffrages of the electors, by promising all things, honest or dishonest, possible or impossible, and rivalling each other in pandering to the meanest feelings and most ignorant prejudices of the vulgarist part of the crowd.'[26] If the people want someone of outstanding ability, who lacks the independent means to support himself while in parliament, they can raise the money by public subscription.[27] Bentham, however, provides for the remuneration of members of the legislature in the *Code.*[28] There is no evidence that he was worried about attracting a 'low class' of persons by virtue of this payment. He was more interested in using remuneration to secure attendance, as the member is paid only after attending the legislative sitting for the day. He is paid by the day and is not paid if he (or his depute) does not attend even though he may be genuinely ill.[29]

---

[22] *Considerations*, ch. XI, pp. 501-3.   [23] Ibid., p. 502.
[24] See Bowring, iii. 561-2; see also ch. VI, §22 (*CW*), pp. 57-9.
[25] *Considerations*, p. 499.
[26] Ibid.   [27] Ibid., p. 500.
[28] Ch. VI, §19, Art. 1 (*CW*), p. 49.
[29] Ch. VI, §20, Arts. 1-7 (*CW*), pp. 49-51.

Both Bentham and Mill are strong advocates of universal suffrage, but Mill, like his father, is apprehensive of the implications of granting power to the people through the vote. In Mill's discussion the influence of de Tocqueville is especially strong.[30] Mill argues for plural voting in order to oppose an educated class to the ordinary people otherwise elected through universal suffrage. Bentham would reject this approach and instead places considerable emphasis on an equal suffrage.[31] Furthermore, in spite of his praise for Bentham's support for female suffrage, Mill introduces a number of qualifications not found in Bentham. For example, Mill excludes from suffrage those on parish relief.[32] Bentham argues that the poor have every interest in the good government of their country, as they are unable to pack up like the rich and move elsewhere.[33] Mill also includes numeracy as well as literacy as qualifications, while Bentham sticks to simple literacy (to be gained with a few months of study). Mill's main proposal, however, is that of plural voting to assign to education an influence which serves as a counterweight to mass voting. He is aware of the danger of granting through education an undue influence to wealth and class, but he seems willing to risk class voting to give this influence to education. Bentham does not engage in this 'tinkering' with suffrage, but believes that other ways exist to bring the influence of education and wisdom to bear on government without opposing or curtailing democratic suffrage such as through the professional civil service or a well-constructed system of laws.

III

As for the actual machinery of government, Bentham and Mill differ considerably in their analyses of the organization and functions of the various branches. To an extent these

[30] *Considerations*, ch. VIII, pp. 467-81. See the reference to de Tocqueville at p. 468.
[31] Bowring, iii. 561, 564-6.
[32] *Considerations*, p. 472. Provisions such as this have led R. J. Halliday to complain recently: 'Indeed, throughout the whole argument of *Representative Government*, very little remains of Mill's stated commitment to equality', *John Stuart Mill*, London 1976, p. 136.
[33] Bowring, iii. 560.

differences reflect even further their differing attitudes towards the role of 'the people' and their representatives in government. But elsewhere there are simply differences of opinion about how government should be organized. Both believe that the controlling power in a representative democracy should be exercised by the people through their representatives, but they differ considerably in their conceptions of the functions of the legislature. Mill stresses that the legislature should 'control' but not 'administer'.[34] In elaborating his view, he writes:

Instead of the function of governing, for which it is radically unfit, the proper office of a representative assembly is to watch and control the government: to throw the light of publicity on its acts: to compel a full exposition and justification of all of them which anyone considers questionable; to censure them if found condemnable, and, if the men who compose the government abuse their trust, or fulfil it in a manner which conflicts with the deliberate sense of the nation, to expel them from office, and either expressly or virtually appoint their successors. This is surely ample power, and security enough for the liberty of the nation.[35]

To this he adds that the legislature should be the 'Committee of Grievances' and the 'Congress of Governors' of the nation. The legislature is primarily a debating chamber. Mill's position partly reflects his view that the people and their representatives are not qualified either to govern or to legislate—both of which require specialist skills.

There is no doubt that Bentham in the *Code* intends the legislature to be more than a 'Congress of Opinions'. Besides giving power to the legislature to appoint and dismiss the heads of the administration and judiciary, he states that it should give 'not general only, but upon occasion, *individual direction* to their conduct, as well as to that of all the several functionaries respectively *subordinate* to them; eventually also to punish them, in case of non-compliance with its directions.'[36] The tasks of the administration and judiciary are conceived in terms of giving 'execution and effect' to legislative ordinances.[37] At another point he writes: 'Only by unalterable physical impotence, is the Supreme Legislature

---

[34] *Considerations*, pp. 424-5.
[35] Ibid., p. 432.
[36] Ch. IV, Art. 3 (*CW*), p. 26.
[37] Ibid., Arts. 4-5 (*CW*), pp. 26-7.

prevented from being its own Executive, or from being the sole Legislature.'[38] Bentham does not intend that the legislature should in fact take on these roles, as the executive and various sublegislatures are better able to perform them, but only that it has the power and capacity to do so if these 'subordinate' authorities in the state prove to be incompetent.[39] The role Mill gives to the legislature is one which Bentham to an extent would place in the hands of the Public Opinion Tribunal, that of watching, discussing, and criticizing the government, and giving publicity to its activities. But for Bentham the legislature is part of the government and must itself be watched by the Public Opinion Tribunal as carefully as any other branch.

Mill does not see the function of the legislature as one of making laws, and he takes the task of formulating legislation out of the hands of the legislature and places it in a specialist 'Commission of Codification'.[40] Members of this commission are appointed by the Crown for approximately five years and only removed (as with the judiciary) by parliament on grounds of personal misconduct or if they refuse to draft a law requested by parliament. The Commission neither proposes nor enacts laws, but intelligently constructs them. However, the legislation constructed cannot be amended by parliament. It can be accepted, rejected, or, sent back to the Commission to be reformulated.

Bentham might have been an enthusiastic supporter of Mill's proposal, and he would certainly have supported Mill's sentiments that 'legislation would assume its proper place as a work of skilled labour and special study and experience . . .'.[41] But as in numerous other cases Mill seems partly motivated by his fear of the low intelligence of the people and their representatives. Although Bentham favours the use of expertise in formulating legislation, he does not share Mill's preoccupation with the infirmities of the people, and it is interesting to note that his own solution to the same problem is different.[42] Indeed, the entire issue is cast differently as a

---

[38] Ch. VI, § 1, Art. 6 (*CW*), pp. 42-3.
[39] Cf. ch. VII, § 12 (*CW*), p. 145.
[40] *Considerations,* p. 430.
[41] Ibid., p. 432.
[42] Cf. Thompson, op. cit., p. 122n, who fails to appreciate Bentham's contribution.

series of related problems. Firstly, there is the problem of the form of motions and amendments to motions which arise from the floor of the legislature. Bentham devises general rules for motions, especially those which affect the form and substance of the *pannomion*.[43] Secondly, the office of the Legislation Minister performs many of the tasks which Mill gives to the Commission of Codification and brings expertise, as we have seen, to the form of legislation and to the task of preserving all of the codes which make up the *pannomion*.[44] Thirdly, the Continuation Committee, providing continuity in the legislature, brings to legislation a substantive expertise in proposing ordinances of utility.[45] Fourthly, the Legislator's Inaugural Declaration (the 'map of the field of legislation') commits members of the legislature to principles which may be enshrined in legislation.[46] Finally, Bentham is preoccupied throughout all of his writings with the task of the codification of law and with bringing expert attention to what in most states, and especially in states under the Common Law, is a hopeless confusion.[47] It is worth noting that Bentham does not propose a commission to draft a code of laws but believes that it is best done by one known draftsman, preferably a foreigner, who takes full responsibility for the substance and consistency of the code.[48]

Mill devotes only one chapter to the executive, while Bentham deals with the administration at great length in the *Code*.[49] Nevertheless, there are three differences between them that are worth noting. Relying on the example of India, Mill believes that the minister should be a politician who is then surrounded by an advisory council composed of experts.[50] Bentham's ministers are appointed for life (though easily dismissed), and they possess expertise related to their

[43] Ch. VI, § 29 (*CW*), pp. 114-17.
[44] Bowring, ix. 428-37. See the discussion in chapter VIII above.
[45] Ch. VI, § 24 (*CW*), pp. 67-72.
[46] Ch. VIIn (*CW*), p. 134.
[47] See especially *Codification Proposal* (Bowring, iv. 535-94).
[48] Ibid., pp. 554-63.
[49] *Considerations*, ch. XIV, pp. 520-33. Halliday (pp. 131-2) finds the origin of Mill's confidence in the expertise of professional administrators 'obscure' and ascribes it in part to his 'ideal toryism'. Yet a similar confidence can be found in Bentham, as Alan Ryan, (p. 207) notes: 'Mill did not relax his Benthamite concern with good management.'
[50] *Considerations*, pp. 522-3.

position by having passed through the system of instruction and examination before appointment. Secondly, Mill's chief executive has the power to dissolve the legislature and call elections, while Bentham's prime minister does not.[51] Thirdly, Mill expressly rejects Bentham's principle that judges (and other officials) can be removed from office by the people.[52] Although Bentham rejects the popular *appointment* of judges, Mill still feels that Bentham's proposal for *dismissal* by the people is close to American practice, which is 'one of the most dangerous errors yet committed by democracy'.[53]

Bentham and Mill differ considerably in their discussion of local government and federalism. Thompson states that in contrast to Bentham and under the influence of de Tocqueville, Mill stresses decentralization more than Bentham and does not affirm the superiority of 'simple' as opposed to 'federal' government.[54] Although Bentham is a strong advocate of centralized government, it is worth recalling the extensive powers granted to the local headman and the power of the people to remove any official within a particular subdistrict.[55] Furthermore, although he prefers 'simple' government (as Thompson notes), Bentham is also willing to see the *Code* adapted to a federal structure with the sublegislatures becoming the state governments.[56]

IV

One major criticism that Mill makes of Bentham's political thought is that his theory leads to the 'tyranny of the majority', that is to say, that he gives absolute power to the majority in society to impose its will, not necessarily through legislation but more especially through the 'despotism of public opinion'.[57] We shall now consider what reply Bentham might

---

[51] Ibid., p. 526.   [52] Ibid., p. 527.
[53] Ibid., p. 528.   [54] Thompson, op. cit., p. 132.
[55] See the discussion of the local headman in chapter VIII above, and Bowring, ix. 612-25.
[56] Thompson, op. cit., p. 132; ch. VI, § 3, Art. 5 (*CW*), p. 47.
[57] This criticism appears in Mill's essay on Bentham published in 1838 as a review of the Bowring edition. See J. S. Mill, 'Bentham', in *Jeremy Bentham*, ed. B. Parekh, pp. 1-40, esp. p. 29.

have to this criticism.[58] We have seen the way Bentham defines public opinion as a judicial power and conceives the press as having a crucial role in its representation. From Bentham's point of view, it is difficult to conceive of despotic public opinion. There is considerable merit in his argument that the Public Opinion Tribunal is a crucial factor in avoiding despotism. None the less, Mill would still say that when power is given to the majority a kind of despotism is likely to result, and for Mill this despotism will be directed against the individual's personality and against 'deference to superiority of cultivated intelligence'.[59] Mill criticizes Bentham for not providing for institutions to secure these ends as well as those which secure the accountability of the rulers to the ruled. Many of the practices and institutions devised by Mill in the *Considerations* are designed to establish the competent, educated minority as a counterforce (however limited) to the ascendancy of the majority in a democratic society.[60]

In his recent book on Bentham, James Steintrager takes up the problem of the 'tyranny of the majority' and provides a defence of Bentham's position. He emphasizes both that the electorate is intended by Bentham to be an informed electorate and that the legislature is independent in a 'Burkean' sense as well as 'filled with men like himself [Bentham], relatively wealthy, educated and independent of mind'.[61] Steintrager's useful argument may be developed in a number of ways, by examining Bentham's attempts to build competence into his system as a counterforce to potential majority tyranny. We can point to the aptitude system where the whole of the administration passes through a system of education and examination. These officials, as we have seen, bring competence, even expertise, to government office, and they do not owe their appointments directly to the people (although they can be removed from office by the electorate).

---

[58] The following paragraphs have appeared in an expanded form in my 'Jeremy Bentham and Democratic Theory', *The Bentham Newsletter*, iii (1979), 54–7.

[59] J. S. Mill, 'Bentham', in Parekh, op. cit., p. 31.

[60] Thompson, op. cit., pp. 89–90, argues that the 'competent minority' are given 'only slightly more political power than that to which their numbers would entitle them anyway.'

[61] Steintrager, *Bentham*, p. 107.

All government officials (with some exceptions like the army) must exercise what Bentham calls the self-suppletive function and appoint substitutes or 'deputes' who act in their places when ill or incapacitated, or who assist when the principals are overburdened with work. Bentham places considerable emphasis on the institution of deputes not only for maintaining efficient and responsible government and minimizing expense (see chapter VI) but also for bringing new and perhaps different people into government service.[62] The deputes in the administration (at least the permanent ones) must be taken from the 'Locable List' and hence have passed through the education and examination system.[63] He views these deputes as functioning as apprentices gaining experience in public office before obtaining permanent official posts. The legislative deputes are discussed in different and more interesting terms. He notes that as the seat of the legislature will be the metropolis of the state, there will be a great number of men in the capital city who will be eager to have these jobs.[64] Because many legislators will have come from the provincial districts from which they are chosen, the deputes will have a different, more metropolitan background. Bentham develops this argument by noting that a number of people otherwise excluded from office might be admitted as deputes. He lists the old and infirm who are interested in politics but would not be able to keep up with the demands of office, and the rich who, though recommended to the electorate, are 'by the indolence naturally attendant on opulence' not willing to seek office, as 'new men' whose aptitude would not be appreciated by the majority of electors.[65] Thus, in this revealing discussion of legislative deputes, Bentham has devised a means of bringing men of special promise and competence into public life who would otherwise neither offer themselves nor be chosen by the electorate.

Let us now look at the legislators themselves. It may be thought that with annual elections and the 'temporary

---

[62] Bentham provides a brief account of the evolution of the principle of 'self-supply' in his thought. See ch. VI, § 25, Art. 53n (*CW*), p. 90n.
[63] Ch. IX, § 6, Art. 8 (*CW*), p. 216.
[64] Ch. VI, § 23, Art. 15 (*CW*), p. 63.
[65] Ibid., Arts. 23–5 (*CW*), pp. 65–6.

non-relocability system' the legislature is under the firm
control of the majority of the electorate. The passage where
Bentham says that the legislator can speak in support of an
arrangement according to his own conviction but vote
against it in following the opinion of his constituents might
be interpreted as emphasizing the dependence of the legislator more than his independence.[66] This apparent dependence
of the legislator on his constituents need not, however,
preclude high competence among the legislators. And the
competence of the legislator, together with his wealth, are
important sources of independence from the electorate. We
have seen how Bentham carefully builds competence into the
adminstrative system and employs the institution of legislative deputes. But does he provide for the ability of the
legislators beyond the assumption (which Steintrager makes)
that those who run for office will be wealthy, educated, and
independent?

We have already referred in chapter IV to Bentham's
proposal to provide for the intellectual aptitude of the
members of the legislature by requiring candidates to have
passed through the same system of education and examination as devised for the civil service and judiciary. Unfortunately, Bentham puts forward this important proposal
in a brief passage which has almost escaped notice.[67] The
obvious consequences of introducing this requirement
for legislators are to restrict severely those who might be
chosen by the electorate as their representatives and to
ensure that those who are chosen possess considerable
competence. Bentham, so far as is known, does not take up
this passage at any other point in the *Code*. Nor does he
spell out what qualifications are relevant for legislators. We
might expect that so momentous a proposal, which would
completely alter the relationship between electorate and
legislature, would be discussed in some detail.

However, it does appear that Bentham was well aware
of what was at stake. Not much manuscript remains for

---

[66] Ch. VI, § 1, Arts. 10-11 (*CW*), pp. 43-4. Cf. Steintrager, op. cit., p. 108
and Bentham's own remarks at the close of the Legislator's Inaugural Declaration, ch. VII, § 14 (*CW*), p. 146.

[67] See the brief reference in T. Peardon, 'Bentham's Ideal Republic', *Jeremy
Bentham*, ed. Parekh, p. 139.

this part of the *Code*, but one surviving sheet is of special interest. It is an earlier version of Bentham's proposal and contains the following passage:

For some time after that, at which, by the conclusion of the preparation period, restriction in this shape would be rendered practicable, any application made of it, to the situation of Deputy of the people, may in some eyes be too great a liberty taken with their power of choice. But, should ever the time arrive, when those same attainments are in the possession of all subordinate functionaries, the legislature will have to consider whether it be consistent, or upon the whole justifiable, that the possession of these same elements of appropriate aptitude should in the situation of those functionaries on whose will the conduct of all others depends, be left to chance. [68]

Bentham obviously knows that his proposal represents an important limitation on the freedom of choice of the electorate. He weighs against this limitation the importance of establishing intellectual ability in the legislature especially after making arrangements for competence in other spheres of government. This proposal surpasses in scope and effect any of those made by Mill in his numerous attempts to offset a widespread suffrage with competent government. Depending on their education, the members of the legislature would not only possess competence but they would also possess independence and stand apart from the electorate they would be chosen to represent. Their independence would make them leaders; it might also make them teachers, but Bentham, unlike Mill, does not dwell on this analogy in the *Code*. Bentham's proposals, however, may well obviate Mill's charge that he allows for (and does not prevent) the 'tyranny of the majority'.

[68] UC xxxix, 46 (25 February 1826).

Chapter XI

The Greatest Happiness Principle

There is no necessary connection between utilitarianism and democracy. Many democrats have not been utilitarians and many utilitarians (including Bentham himself during a considerable portion of his life) have not been democrats. Nevertheless, the democratic principles of the *Constitutional Code* rest on a utilitarian foundation, and this study of Bentham's theory of democracy would be incomplete without an examination of it. In this chapter we shall be concerned with the meaning and significance of the greatest happiness principle as it appears in the *Code* and in related writings.

Bentham formulates the greatest happiness principle in chapter II of the *Code* as follows:

Of this constitution, the all-comprehensive object, or end in view, is, from first to last, the greatest happiness of the greatest number; namely, of the individuals, of whom the political community, or state, of which it is the constitution, is composed; strict regard being all along had to what is due to every other—as to which, see Ch. vii, *Legislator's Inaugural Declaration*.

Correspondent fundamental principle: the *greatest happiness principle*.

Correspondent all-comprehensive and all-directing rule—*Maximize happiness.*[1]

It will be useful to compare this formulation with the second major statement of the principle which appears in chapter VII as part of the Legislator's Inaugural Declaration:

---

[1] Ch. II, Art. 1 (*CW*), pp. 18-19. The major discussions of the greatest happiness principle appear in chs. II, VII, and IX, §25, Art. 1 (*CW*), pp. 18-25, 133-46, 419-20. Other references to 'ends in view' appear at ch. IX, §1, Arts. 1-2; §7, Bi§1, Arts. 2-5; §15, Art. 1 (*CW*), pp. 170, 218-20, 297. Most commentators, including David Lyons, *In the Interest of the Governed*, Oxford, 1973, whose work is discussed here at length, rely on the compilation of manuscripts in Doane's 'Book I' (Bowring, ix. 1-145) some of which were not written for the *Code* or were subsequently excluded from it. This chapter is based primarily on that part of the *Code* Bentham himself published. Thus, Lyons's brief attempt to extend his discussion from the *Introduction to the Principles of Morals and Legislation* to the *Constitutional Code* suffers, because he does not use the important discussions in Bentham's own text.

I recognize, as the *all-comprehensive*, and only right and proper end of Government, the greatest happiness of the greatest number of the members of the community: of all without exception, in so far as possible: of the greatest number, on every occasion on which the nature of the case renders it impossible by rendering it matter of necessity, to make sacrifice of a portion of the happiness of a few, to the greater happiness of the rest.[2]

In both of these accounts, Bentham states that the end of government is the greatest happiness of the greatest number. This is confirmed when he summarizes his principle in the same section of the Legislator's Inaugural Declaration as *'greatest happiness of greatest number maximized'*.[3] In his later years, however he became increasingly dissatisfied with the phrase, 'the greatest happiness of the greatest number'. Although he believed that the phrase was an improvement over the vague and somewhat general 'utility', he was troubled by several difficulties with it. He could not formulate it as the greatest happiness of all because (a) the happiness of all was often an impractical achievement and (b) the happiness of some might only be achieved at the expense of others.[4] For example, the notion of the greatest happiness of all could not incorporate deterrent punishments.[5] There is some evidence that he found the phrase cumbersome and the last part somewhat superfluous.[6] More importantly, Bentham realized that the phrase implied a disregard for the welfare of the minority in society so long as the happiness of the majority was maximized. In an unpublished manuscript, dated 3 June 1828, he expresses this fear:

So long as the greatest number—the 1001—were in the enjoyment of the greatest degree of comfort, the greatest degree of torment might be the lot of the smallest of the two numbers—the 1000! and still the principal status or the proper object of endeavour of the greatest happiness of the greatest number be actually conformed to —not contravened.[7]

---

[2] Ch. VII, § 2 (*CW*), p. 136.   [3] Ibid., (*CW*), p. 137.
[4] See Bowring, ix. 6.   [5] See UC xxxvii, 106 (15 June 1823).
[6] See R. Shackleton, 'The Greatest Happiness of the Greatest Number: the History of Bentham's Phrase', *Studies on Voltaire and the Eighteenth Century*, xc (1972), 1480-1.
[7] UC cxii, 154 (3 June 1828). The MS contains the notation 'not for 1830'. See also *Bentham's Political Thought*, ed. Parekh, pp. 309-10.

The date when Bentham abandoned the use of the phrase 'the greatest happiness of the greatest number' can now be roughly ascertained.[8] The two passages quoted from chapters II and VII above were most likely drafted in a final version at some time between 1824 and 1827. Although the *Code* was not published until 1830, these passages were in print by 1827.[9] Thus, 1827 can be the latest date of their composition and a slightly earlier one is more probable. Shackleton has noted a manuscript dated 8 June 1829 where Bentham states difficulties in the standard formulation of the greatest happiness principle; the *Westminster Review* article on the 'Greatest Happiness Principle' of July 1829, attributed to Bentham but subsequently denied, contains the revision of the 'greatest happiness of the greatest number' to more simply 'the greatest happiness'.[10] Since the *Code* passages quoted above retain the formula, 'the greatest happiness of the greatest number', at some point between 1827 and 1829 Bentham must have decided on the revision. Furthermore, in 1831 Bentham published a revised version of the Legislator's Inaugural Declaration (chapter VII of the *Code*) as a pamphlet and incorporated his new conception of the greatest happiness principle:

I recognize, as the *all-comprehensive*, and only right and proper end of Government, the greatest happiness of the members of the community in question: the greatest happiness—of all of them, without exception, in so far as possible: the greatest happiness of the greatest number of them, on every occasion on which the nature of the case renders the

---

[8] The development of Bentham's principle has been discussed recently by L. Werner, 'A Note about Bentham on Equality and about the Greatest Happiness Principle', *Journal of the History of Philosophy*, xi (1973), 237-51, which elaborates the earlier discussion of A. Goldworth, 'The Meaning of Bentham's Greatest Happiness Principle', *Journal of the History of Philosophy*, vii (1969), 315-21. Beginning with the view that 'despite the popularity of these convictions about Bentham's later opinion, the basis for holding them is pretty shaky', Werner (pp. 243-7) proceeds to show a firmer basis in the manuscripts used by Bowring for the *Deontology*. However, the account offered here will establish from texts written, published, revised, and published again by Bentham himself a clear account of the new formulation of the greatest happiness principle.

[9] See the note by Doane to the Bowring edition, ix. p. iii.

[10] Shackleton, op. cit., pp. 1480-1; see Werner, op. cit., pp. 245-7 where he provides substantiation for the claim of Perronet Thompson, the real author of the *Westminster Review* article, that Bentham did in fact revise the form of his principle. See also BL Add. MS 33,551, fo. 326. For the passage in the article which announces the change, see J. Lively and J. Rees, *Utilitarian Logic and Politics*, p. 149.

provision of an equal quantity of happiness for every one of them impossible: it being rendered so, by its being matter of necessity, to make sacrifice of a portion of the happiness of a few, to the greater happiness of the rest. [11]

In the summary of the statement he replaced '*greatest happiness of the greatest number maximized*' with the new formulation, '*greatest happiness maximized*'.[12] By comparing this material with the earlier statement in chapter VII of the *Code*, we have direct proof from texts Bentham himself wrote, revised, and published of his determination to reduce the 'all-comprehensive end' of the 'greatest happiness of the greatest number' to 'the greatest happiness'. Nevertheless, the change does not seem to have been a substantive one, but rather an attempt by Bentham to remove some of the ambiguity from the way the main principle had been formulated. As Bahmueller has noted, the phrase 'greatest happiness of the greatest number' is retained to play a secondary role in explaining how the greatest happiness principle should be implemented.[13]

II

Having clarified this historical problem, we shall now examine several aspects of his conception of the greatest happiness principle. Returning to the initial formulation in chapter II, it is clear that the principle is initially restricted in application to the individual members of the political community to which the constitution is applied. This restricted application of the principle seems at first to confirm David Lyons's thesis that the principle is intended by Bentham to be 'parochial' rather than universal.[14] That is to say, the calculation

[11] *Parliamentary Candidate's proposed Declaration of Principles: or say, A Test proposed for Parliamentary Candidates*, London, 1831, p. 7.
[12] Ibid., p. 8. See also the copy of the *Constitutional Code*, vol. i, London, 1830 in the Library of University College London (shelf mark: Bentham Collection, 2 c. 19) where Bentham has crossed out the reference in ch. VII (see above, note 3) to the '*greatest happiness of greatest number maximized*' to leave '*greatest happiness maximized*'.
[13] See Bahmueller, *The National Charity Company*, pp. 240-1 (note 121).
[14] See Lyons, op. cit., pp. 24 ff. On Lyons's overall argument see also J. B. Stearns, 'Bentham on Public and Private Ethics', *Canadian Journal of Philosophy*, v (1975), 583-94; J. R. Dinwiddy, 'Bentham on Private Ethics and the Principle of Utility' (unpublished paper).

of the greatest happiness requires that only members of the political community be taken into consideration and not everyone affected by an action or practice. Nevertheless, it is doubtful that Lyons's argument can survive much scrutiny. For the parochial limitation seems to follow rather than precede the context in which the greatest happiness principle is applied. In the passage in question Bentham is concerned not with the 'end in view' of mankind, but with the 'end in view' of the constitution. Those subject to the constitution are the members of the political community. If the context of Bentham's discussion were universal legislation, the greatest happiness principle might very well apply universally. Thus, it is arguable that the parochial limitation follows from the fact that Bentham is directing the constitution to limited political communities. The limitation may rest on a general or universal premiss that the practice in question should aim to maximize the greatest happiness of those affected by it. In the *Code* those affected by the laws simply happen to be members of distinct political communities.

After stating in the passage in chapter II that the object of the constitution is the greatest happiness of individuals making up the political community, Bentham adds the proviso: 'strict regard being all along had to what is due to every other—as to which, see ch. vii. Legislator's Inaugural Declaration.'[15] The phrase contains more than a cross-reference to chapter VII. It refers to duties to other states, duties which should accompany the direction of the greatest happiness principle to the more limited political society. In the statement of the greatest happiness principle in chapter VII (quoted above) the limitation of the principle to the political community is also repeated, but the qualification about duties to other states is not included, most probably because the Legislator's Inaugural Declaration itself contains a section dealing with relations between states.[16] The reference in chapter II to 'what is due to every other' presumably refers to this section, the only major section in the *Code* dealing with general principles of international relations. We might be able to determine from this material how Bentham conceives the greatest happiness principle operating beyond the confines of the political community.

[15] Ch. II, Art. 1 (*CW*), pp. 18-19.   [16] Ch. VII, §8 (*CW*), pp. 142-4.

Most of the principles set forth are concerned with the legislator's duties to other states. He promises to observe the same standards of justice and impartiality in dealing with other states as he does with his own constituents and other citizens. He agrees to add to the power and wealth of his state only through friendly competition, where other states do not lose from his gain. This precludes conquest of other states, the acquisition of dominions, and war except where fought to defend his country. He also favours the free movement of persons from state to state.[17] Lyons's argument about the relationship between Bentham's 'parochial' standard and relations between states, i.e. that Bentham never adopts a universal orientation but believes that 'internationalism is really in each nation's best interest', seems at first glance to be confirmed in the *Code*.[18] None of the provisions goes beyond the 'parochial' limit. Nevertheless, in one important passage the legislator comes closest to possessing duties to all people. Bentham writes:

On every favourable occasion,—my endeavours shall be employed to the rendering, to the subjects, and for their sake to the constituted Authorities, of every foreign State, all such positive good offices, as can be rendered thereto, without its being at the expense of some other State or States, or against the rightly presumable inclination, as well as at the expense, of the majority of my fellow-countrymen, in this our State.[19]

It is true that the 'endeavours' of the legislator to the subjects of 'every foreign state' are restricted by the proviso that these are not done at the expense of the citizens of his own state. But Bentham also writes that these endeavours should not be at the expense of any other state. Although the former statement may support Lyons's 'parochial' standard and the principle on which it is based ('one ought to promote the happiness of those who are *subject to* one's direction, influence, or control—in other words, those under one's governance'),[20] the latter supports a universal outlook, that subject to the constraints imposed by one's constitution, one ought to promote as well the greatest happiness of the members of every foreign state. Bentham also constrains the legislator from acting in a way that causes expense to other

[17] Ibid.
[18] Lyons, op. cit., p. 103.
[19] Ch. VII, §8 (*CW*), p. 144.
[20] Lyons, op. cit., p. 85.

states. None of these people is subject to his direct governance. Nor can they be said to be, except in the vaguest way, under his influence and control. Although the context of the constitution necessarily limits the perspective of the legislator to a primary concern for the members of his own political society, the universalistic character of the greatest happiness principle impels him to look beyond this in his calculations. His interests may still remain constrained by the perspective of seeing not 'mankind' but a number of foreign states and members therein. Nevertheless, Bentham is saying more than, as Lyons claims, that 'internationalism is really in each nation's best interest'. Bentham's position amounts to a universalism qualified by the conditions of political existence. This position hardly amounts to a 'parochial' standard in international relations. In spite of the initial limitation of the *Code* to the members of the political community, Lyons's conception of a 'parochial' standard for Bentham's greatest happiness principle is not established.

III

Another aspect of Bentham's formulation of the greatest happiness principle concerns the status and significance of what has been called 'psychological egoism'. In his first major discussion of securities in the *Code*, Bentham provides an important (and generally overlooked) statement of his principles as a series of assumptions on which his conception of securities is based.[21] He first grants that in all human minds there are 'propensities' towards both self-regard and sympathy for others.[22] These may exist in different proportions in different people, and presumably some people would exhibit stronger sympathetic motives for action than others. Bentham then argues that self-regard is a more fundamental characteristic than sympathy.[23] Without basic self-regard he believes that sympathy cannot exist, because self-regard ensures the physical survival of the species. If Adam thought only of Eve and never of himself and Eve thought similarly of Adam, sooner or later (but not as long

---

[21] Ch. VI, § 31, Arts. 6 ff. (*CW*), pp. 118 ff.
[22] Ibid., Art. 7 (*CW*), p. 119.
[23] Ibid., Art. 8.

as twelve months) the two, Bentham contends, would have perished.[24]

Having stated these assumptions Bentham then defines the role of the utilitarian legislator:

> To give increase to the influence of sympathy at the expense of that of self-regard, and of sympathy for the greater number at the expense of sympathy for the lesser number,—is the constant and arduous task, as of every moralist, so of every legislator who deserves to be so.[25]

Bentham's conception of the task of the moralist and legislator may seem self-defeating. If he succeeds in his duty of replacing self-regard with sympathy as the sole motive and influence on conduct, his subjects will perish. Bentham himself does not reach this conclusion, largely because he feels that it is physically impossible to replace self-regard completely with sympathy, and, furthermore, it would be imprudent to attempt to do so. But why then should he be concerned with increasing sympathy? Part of the difficulty with answering this question stems from an ambiguity in his argument. At one level he postulates self-regard to ensure physical survival. Each person must satisfy his physical desires at a certain basic level or perish. If he ignores them and devotes his whole attention to the welfare of others (ceases to eat, drink, etc.) he will die. Obviously, at this level sympathy is dependent on physical survival. But the struggle in which the legislator is called upon to engage, to maximize sympathy at the expense of self-regard, is not at this level. On a different plane Bentham seems to be conceiving self-regard in terms of selfishness and self-aggrandizement. Here he is concerned more with morality than with what might be called the physical conditions for morality. At this level, sympathy does not appear to be based on self-regard; it forms an opposing term. To advance the greatest happiness, the legislator's 'constant and arduous task' is to increase 'the influence of sympathy at the expense of self-regard'. Bentham does not distinguish between self-regard and sympathy on each of these levels, and the result renders his argument somewhat incoherent. As it stands, however, the argument uses the ambiguity to provide the further assumption that

---

²⁴ Ibid., Art. 9.   ²⁵ Ibid., Art. 10.

sympathy will never prevail over self-regard.[26] Otherwise, beyond physical survival, it would seem that sympathetic motives would be as strong as self-regarding ones. At times Bentham seems to suggest that this is so, but he also argues the primacy of self-regard on the basis of physical survival, and then uses the latter to establish the primacy of self-regard over sympathy. He succeeds in his overall argument only through his exploitation of the ambiguity.[27]

Bentham postulates this rule to guide the legislator:

> whatsoever evil it is possible for man to do for the advancement of his own private and personal interest . . . at the expense of the public interest,—that evil, sooner or later, he will do, unless by some means or other, intentional or otherwise, prevented from doing it.[28]

To be successful the legislator will on the one hand assume that sympathy plays a small role in human action and on the other hand use arrangements based on the primacy of self-regard to generate actions contributing to the greatest happiness. And while a few individuals in every society will be distinguished by their sympathy and regard for the greatest happiness, the legislator must proceed on the assumption that the individuals for whom he legislates are not.

Bentham's *Constitutional Code* is not a scheme for enabling the most sympathetic and benevolent actions to be performed. He does not, as Aristotle does, see the public sphere as one where all of the virtues can be cultivated and brought to perfection.[29] Throughout his writings, including the *Code*, Bentham endeavours to distinguish between two kinds of sympathetic action. The first is positive and is based on

---

[26] Cf. W. Godwin, *Enquiry concerning Political Justice*, London, 1793, Bk IV, ch. X, where this assumption is not made.

[27] To clarify Bentham's argument we might distinguish between a physical egoism and a moral egoism. In each of these, Bentham assumes the primacy of self-regard, but he fails to make clear the status of sympathy. In relation to physical egoism a person's sympathy would be self-destructive; in relation to moral egoism, it would enhance his character and contribute to the greatest happiness of society. One might give up moral egoism while adhering to physical egoism in the sense of cultivating a benevolent disposition without jeopardizing physical existence. Nevertheless, Bentham's egoism (in either form) should not be conceived too narrowly. See S. R. Letwin, *The Pursuit of Certainty*, Cambridge, 1965, p. 141: 'the self-preference principle expressed, in an unusual, technical form, Bentham's awareness of an ultimate mystery and privacy about every man's view of life.'

[28] Ch. VI, § 31, Art. 11 (*CW*), p. 119.

[29] See Aristotle, *Nicomachean Ethics*, V, 1129b25 ff.

motives to enhance the happiness of others. The second is more negative and is manifest in forbearing to diminish the happiness of others.[30] Bentham's remarks on sympathy, which appear somewhat incoherent, may become more intelligible if this distinction is borne in mind. After he states that the legislator should act to increase sympathy as much as possible (see the quotation above), he adds the following:

But, in regard to sympathy, the less the proportion of it is, the natural and actual existence of which he assumes as and for the basis of his arrangements, the greater will be the success of whatever endeavours he uses to give increase to it.[31]

Bentham seems to be saying that if we assume that people will act without much sympathy and build on this assumption the various entities of the state, the institutions, having been built on solid foundations, will actually increase sympathy. At the minimum they will increase the negative form of sympathy. But if this is his argument, he does not need to discuss sympathy at all in relation to the work of the legislator. By creating institutions which appeal to self-interested men, and preventing them from harming one another he is (like Hobbes) creating a successful and stable state. Nevertheless, Bentham does not want to deny that men act from sympathetic motives, because empirically they claim that they do. But he also does not wish to claim that a constitutional system will induce men to act with positive benevolence towards one another. To aim at this sort of society is, for Bentham, to court disaster with one's constitutional arrangements. He does not jettison his concern with sympathy; he concentrates instead on enhancing negative benevolence which is manifest in the desire not to harm others. The institutions of his *Code* are designed so that power cannot be abused. Rulers are not trusted to behave wisely and benevolently; nor are they allowed to serve only themselves. They are induced to act benevolently in a limited sense by the threat of punishment or dismissal if they harm those they rule in order to serve themselves. The task of the legislator in designing securities is to enhance the limited,

[30] See ch. IX, § 21, Art. 26 (*CW*), p. 397; cf. *An Introduction to the Principles of Morals and Legislation*, XVII. 6–7 in *CW*, pp. 283–5.
[31] Ch. VI, § 31, Art. 10 (*CW*), p. 119.

negative benevolence of rulers. In this way, Bentham feels that the legislator will be successful.

Bentham reflects this negative attitude towards benevolence in the way he formulates his 'moral code' for legislators, the Legislator's Inaugural Declaration. He states many of the principles in negative terms, so that the promises of the legislator amount to his agreeing not to harm others. The legislator, for example, is placed on his guard:

against the power of all those appetites, to the sinister influence of which, the inalterable nature of my situation keeps me so constantly and perilously exposed: appetite for power, appetite for money, appetite for factitious honor and dignity, appetite for vengeance at the expense of opponents, appetite for ease at the expense of duty. [32]

Similarly, when the legislator promises to act with impartiality, which, as a positive principle, is difficult to reconcile with utility, Bentham again formulates the promise in a negative fashion:

On every occasion . . . sincere and anxious shall be my endeavour, to keep my mind as clear as may be, of undue partiality in every sense: of partiality in favour of any class or individual, to the injury of any other: of partiality, through self-regarding interest: of partiality, through interest inspired by sympathy: of partiality, through interest inspired by antipathy. [33]

In Bentham's formulation, impartiality is conceived as not harming others with partiality. It lacks the positive notions of reason and equality which are usually associated with impartiality.[34]

It is clear that in the *Code* Bentham's psychological egoism has an important effect on the way in which the greatest happiness principle is to be realized in terms of constitutional arrangements. The legislator is not encouraged to establish any scheme which will promote happiness; it must be conceived in terms which will allow for human selfishness and will control aggressiveness. This limits the scope of the legislator in one sense, but it also makes his work more demanding.

---

[32] Ch. VII, § 3 (*CW*), pp. 137-8.

[33] Ch. VII, § 9 (*CW*), p. 144.

[34] See, for example, D. D. Raphael, *Problems of Political Philosophy*, London, 1970, pp. 175 ff. Bentham's conception of negative benevolence reflects his conception of liberty as non-interference. See chapter IV above.

The legal system must create motives in self-regarding people to prevent them from oppressing others. The primacy of self-regard is compatible with this limited benevolence and Bentham sees here the key to successful legislation.

IV

A third aspect of Bentham's conception of the greatest happiness principle concerns the place of equality in its formulation. This is a complex and much debated problem, and most commentators accept A. J. Ayer's assertion that Bentham 'held, as he must have held to be at all consistent, that the right action was that which produced the greatest measure of happiness, no matter how it was distributed'.[35] Although the concept of equality can enter into utilitarian theory on a number of planes, we shall look first at the extent to which equality of distribution is part of Bentham's conception of the greatest happiness principle. To do this we shall examine again the three examples quoted above where Bentham sets forth his principle. In the first of these (chapter II of the *Code*) Bentham simply states that the object of the constitution is the greatest happiness of the greatest number of the individuals of the state in question. No reference to equality appears here, though in referring to the object of the constitution Bentham may have held implicitly that laws apply to all members of the state equally. Nevertheless, he does not develop this point.

In the second formulation of the greatest happiness principle (chapter VII), he adds the proviso that, where possible, the legislator should seek to maximize the greatest happiness of all, and, where not possible, that of the greatest number. This is a familiar contrast in Bentham, but it does not indicate whether or not he favours an equal distribution. One might be able to argue that in so far as he makes the contrast in the first place he favours the widest possible distribution. But this would depend on what he means when he says that the happiness of the greatest number is to be preferred to the greatest happiness of all 'on every occasion

---

[35] A. J. Ayer, 'The Principle of Utility' *Jeremy Bentham and the Law*, eds. G. W. Keeton and G. Schwarzenberger, London, 1948, p. 250. Goldworth, p. 317n confirms Ayer's argument.

on which the nature of the case renders it impossible, by rendering it matter of necessity to make sacrifice of a portion of the happiness of a few, to the greater happiness of the rest'. If Bentham simply means that the greatest happiness of the greatest number should be preferred to the happiness of all where a greater sum of happiness can be produced by greater inequality or by the sacrifice of pleasures of a few for the sake of very much greater pleasures of the rest, his interest in equality is minimal. Nevertheless, on this interpretation it is not clear why Bentham would use such words as 'impossible' and 'necessity'. What would be at stake is simply a calculation of the greater amount of happiness. However, one point is certain: the greatest happiness of the greatest number seems to be a second-best criterion for distribution to which the legislator resorts when it is not possible to distribute according to the greatest happiness of all. On this interpretation, the best distribution would be the one which most closely approximates the greatest happiness of all. But we have still not determined how the greatest happiness of all is linked to equality.[36]

In the third formulation of the greatest happiness principle in the revised form of chapter VII which appeared in 1831 Bentham uses the notion of equality to explain what is meant by the greatest happiness of all in relation to the greatest happiness of the greatest number. Government is to maximize the greatest happiness: 'of all of them, without exception, in so far as possible: the greatest happiness of the greatest number of them, on every occasion on which the nature of the case renders the provision of *an equal quantity of happiness for every one of them* impossible.'[37] Clearly, Bentham means here by a policy, which serves the greatest happiness of all, one which does so equally to all. And if the greatest happiness of the greatest number is to approximate as closely as possible the greatest happiness of all, it must maximize the greatest quantity of happiness to as many as possible on an equal basis.

Bentham's formulation of his principle in this third example

---

[36] In the passage under consideration Bentham does not directly speak of equality. Curiously, in his summary of principles he includes the maxim, 'equality maximized' even though equality is not discussed in the text he summarizes.

[37] *Parliamentary Candidate's Declaration*, p. 7 (my italics).

thus contains an explicit and conscious attempt to link the greatest happiness of all with equal distribution. The equality which he favours seems more than a formal equality, i.e. equal things for equal people depending on other principles, for example, need, desert, or ability, for the determination of how goods should be distributed. Nor is he referring to notions of 'equal respect' or 'equal rights' which are commonly invoked in discussions of equality but which may or may not entail a commitment to substantive equality in the distribution of goods.[38]

Bentham's overall position with regard to equal distribution as a substantive goal of legislation may be seen in the following passage:

on the supposition of a new constitution coming to be established, with the greatest happiness of the greatest number for its end in view, sufficient reason would have place for taking the matter of wealth from the richest and transferring it to the less rich, till the fortunes of all were reduced to an equality, or a system of inequality, so little different from perfect equality that the difference would not be worth calculating.[39]

This position is in turn reflected in his conception of the place of equality in the greatest happiness principle. Nevertheless, Bentham's conception of equality needs further elaboration to see how he deals with equal distribution. His various discussions of equality rest on several assumptions to which more critical scrutiny would be given today. He assumes firstly that what will make one man happy will by and large do the same for another. He also assumes that to increase wealth and power (as instruments of felicity) leads to an increase in happiness, and a decrease in wealth and power leads to a decrease in happiness.[40] He is not naïve in his use of these assumptions. The character of each individual, he admits, is unique and inscrutable and the circumstances of two men are never the same. Nevertheless, if assumptions like these are not made, he argues that no general propositions about equality can be advanced. It is sufficient, he believes, that they are closer to the truth

[38] Bentham includes some of these notions in his concept of security and in other concepts, including equality, but these need not concern us here.
[39] 'Pannomial Fragments' (Bowring, iii. 230).
[40] 'Principles of the Civil Code' (Bowring, i. 304-5).

than another set of propositions and that they can be of use to the legislator with less inconvenience than any other set of assumptions.[41] He thus does not try to avoid the problem of equality by saying that human variability and subjectivity make all discussion fruitless.

Bentham relies most on various conceptions of diminishing marginal utility in his arguments regarding equality. In the early 'Principles of the Civil Code', a translation of part of Dumont's *Traités* of 1802,[42] he considers three cases of the effect of wealth on happiness, and in each case he argues that there is greater happiness as wealth is more equally distributed in society.[43] The first is concerned with the possession of wealth. Here he starts with the argument that a portion of wealth corresponds to a portion of happiness, and he who possesses the greatest wealth will possess the greatest happiness. He rejects the view that there is a point beyond which the possession of wealth will no longer bring happiness and that people will be satisfied with a determinable amount of wealth. Nevertheless, the happiness of a very rich man is not exactly proportionable to his wealth. A king with the wealth of a thousand labourers with sufficient earnings for their needs 'and a trifle to spare' will not be a thousand times happier than the labourers; he is unlikely to be even five or ten times as happy. A man born to wealth, he argues, is not aware of the value of his fortune. 'It is the pleasure of acquiring, and not the satisfaction of possessing, which is productive of the greatest enjoyment.'[44] This sharper pleasure belongs to the artisan more than it does to the king who already possesses so much. Bentham uses this argument to assert that as fortunes approach more closely to equality, there will be a greater mass of happiness, because more will approach the condition of the artisan and fewer that of the king. As to the second case, the acquisition of wealth, Bentham argues that where fortunes are equal, it is best that an equal distribution is made, and where fortunes are unequal, the distribution should aim to increase equality.

[41] Ibid., p. 305.
[42] It is arguable that this work, though based on Bentham's manuscripts, is Dumont's rather than Bentham's. I have treated it as a work of Bentham, especially as the material discussed here does not conflict with similar arguments made directly by Bentham himself.
[43] Ibid., pp. 304-7.   [44] Ibid., p. 305.

In both of these instances the production of greater equality means the production of a greater total amount of happiness. Because of diminishing marginal utility, a movement towards increased inequality would not lead to a corresponding increase in happiness. Thus a condition of equality is preferable.

The third case is concerned with loss. Bentham begins by asserting that the loss of a given amount of wealth will produce a loss of happiness in proportion to the amount retained, so that a man who loses a fourth of his wealth will lose a fourth of his happiness. But he then qualifies this assertion by noting that loss beyond a certain stage becomes disproportionate to loss of happiness. If loss means the loss of the means of physical existence a slight loss at this level will produce a catastrophic loss of happiness. Bentham then advocates the equalization of loss or the distribution of loss so that the fortunes of those who suffer loss become more equal. He speaks favourably of schemes of insurance and compensation which distribute losses widely rather than have them fall heavily on a few. The argument for equality of outcome is presumably similar to those made earlier.

Bentham develops his argument further by examining some cases where one person profits at the expense of another. He presents a number of arguments to the effect that the person losing will suffer more pain than the person gaining will obtain pleasure. For example, if two men each have £1000 and one receives £500 from the other, the person who gains will gain a third more wealth, but the person who loses will lose half of his wealth. A redistribution according to the greatest happiness principle would favour a return to equality. Furthermore, the move back to equality would be favoured by weighing up the pain of disappointed expectations involved in the first loss against the pain of not having gained following the redistribution. Bentham feels that the former is much stronger than the latter; otherwise, 'every man would experience this evil with regard to every thing which he did not obtain'.[45] Finally, the pain of loss is stronger, Bentham believes, than the pleasure of gain. 'Mankind in general', he writes, 'appear to be more sensible of grief than pleasure from an equal cause.'[46] Where the person losing is poor and the gainer is

---

[45] Ibid., p. 307.   [46] Ibid.

rich, there are even stronger reasons for a return of the loss, as, in addition to the arguments above, the poor man may suffer greater pain from his loss in so far as it may affect his possession of the necessities of life. If a rich man suffers loss, he will also suffer the pains associated with a shock to his security, although Bentham admits that there will be some compensation in good arising from the movement towards equality.

Bentham does not depart very much from this early view of equality in his later writings. In *Leading Principles of the Constitutional Code*, he writes: 'In proportion as equality is departed from, inequality has place: and in proportion as inequality has place, evil has place.'[47] He also compares the happiness of the monarch with that of the artisan. Here, he reflects his later political radicalism in stating 'that the quantity of felicity habitually experienced by a gloomy, or ill-tempered or gouty, or otherwise habitually diseased monarch, is not so great as that habitually experienced by an habitually cheerful, and good tempered, and healthy, labourer' even though the monarch possesses the wealth of between 10,000 and 100,000 labourers.[48] In a body of late manuscript which was published posthumously in the Bowring edition under the title of 'Pannomial Fragments' he returns to the sort of arguments or 'axioms' he advances in the 'Principles of the Civil Code'.[49] To each particle of wealth, he begins, belongs a particle of happiness. The person with the most wealth must be regarded by the legislator as possessing the most happiness. But, as he argues earlier, happiness does not increase in the same proportion as wealth, and from this premiss (and others employed earlier) he reaches the same conclusion that with the greater equalization of wealth, a greater quantity of happiness will be produced. Furthermore,

---

[47] Bowring, ii. 271.   [48] Ibid.

[49] Bowring, iii. 228–30. Some commentators dwell on Bentham's early 'Essay on Representation' of 1788 (UC clxx, 114-16, 89-92) for remarks relevant to equality and democracy. See Halévy, *La Formation du radicalisme philosophique*, i, pp. 424–39; Mary Mack, op. cit., pp. 448–53. The essay contains the argument about diminishing marginal utility and the assumption that people have a roughly equal capacity for happiness. Although Bentham gives the impression (see Werner, op. cit., p. 239) that he is indifferent to the distribution of happiness, he does qualify his remarks in the next paragraph with observations about diminishing marginal utility. However, the essay does not contain an account of equality in relation to the greatest happiness principle.

in *Leading Principles*, he speaks of an equal distribution of power as well as wealth.[50] The greater the concentration of power in society (and hence the greater the inequality of power) the greater will be the tendency to abuse it. Hence, with a movement towards greater equality of power (presumably in the replacement of monarchy with representative democracy based on universal suffrage) there will be less opportunity for the abuse of power and consequently more happiness. There should be no doubt now that Bentham regards substantive equality in the distribution of wealth and power as producing the greatest happiness. From the point of view of equality, therefore, the greatest happiness requires equal distribution or a distribution that moves people towards a condition of equality.

It is true that Bentham places limits on equality, but these do not diminish his view of the desirability of equality as an end for legislation. He recognizes, however, that there are other ends, namely, security, subsistence, and abundance (as future security) which have a higher status. Although he believes, as we have seen, that under a new constitution a redistribution of wealth which would correspond as closely as possible to equality would be desirable in the first instance, he immediately qualifies his argument to bring in evils of a second and third order which would limit such an action. The evil of the second order is the threat to security caused by such a proposed redistribution. The evil of the third order is the threat to subsistence by the extinction of any inducement to labour produced by compulsory equalization of property. Related to this is the possibility that with equal distribution there will be no accumulations of abundance to provide security against famine, calamity, etc. in future years. With greater inequality the wealthier members of society would possess this superfluity.[51]

Throughout his writings it is security (and recall the connection between security and liberty) which Bentham places over all other ends of legislation. Equality as a co-ordinate end comes into conflict most often with security. In the 'Principles of the Civil Code' Bentham sees equality mostly in opposition to security. Security, 'under the name of

[50] Bowring, ii. 271.   [51] 'Pannomial Fragments' (Bowring, iii. 230).

justice', requires that the legislator 'maintain the distribution [of property] which is actually established', though it is fair to say that security is extended equally to all members of society.[52] But where security is threatened, Bentham argues, so is subsistence and abundance; society without security 'would relapse into the savage state from which it has arisen'.[53] What threatens security most is a sudden movement towards equality. Bentham then argues that to an extent security and equality can be reconciled.[54] Limitations can be placed on inheritance to prevent too great an accumulation of property, but most important is a gradual progress towards equality which will take place in a society which values security and free trade. This will allow the development of industry and trade and consequently a movement towards equality of wealth as opposed to the polarization of wealth and power found under feudalism.

Bentham also argues that security in some senses must give way to achieve security in others. He notes that taxation to pay for a standing army reduces security in one sense by taking the citizen's property but increases the means by which he can enhance his security in another sense by ensuring security against foreign enemies.[55] Thus, he can envisage a considerable redistribution of property for the sake of security. But he is strongly opposed to a general shock to security which would follow a sudden move to introduce equality of property.

With Bentham's emphasis on security and especially security of property, one might well wonder how he reconciles this with his political opposition to monarchy and aristocracy and the inequalities inherent in these regimes. Does his later political radicalism founder on the principle of security? Bentham's main insight which enables him to be radical in politics, a committed egalitarian, but not to abandon the primacy of security is his belief, which appears only in his later writings, that equality can be an important means to achieve security. Only through equality of power (approached in universal suffrage) is it possible to gain security from arbitrary and tyrannical government. Universal suffrage and representative democracy have additional advantages in

---

[52] Bowring, i. 311.   [53] Ibid., p. 312.
[54] Ibid., pp. 312-13.   [55] See Ibid., p. 313.

enabling security and equality to be advanced without disturbing security of property. This is the great achievement of democracy in America to which Bentham never tires of pointing.[56] The system of representative democracy also allows for reform which moves towards equality of property so long as there is no shock to security. The greatest happiness, as the 'end in view' means, as we have seen, equal happiness. In his later writings Bentham does not emphasize the maintenance of the existing distributions of property. The 'disappointment-prevention' principle allows for reform to take place towards equality so long as full compensation is paid for violations of 'fixed' expectations.[57] Although it is arguable that full compensation merely maintains the original distribution, in major projects of reform there are numerous consequences flowing from alterations of established states of affairs. Where the object is the production of the greatest happiness, the new arrangements may lead to a greater equality generally than existed before. Furthermore, we have seen in chapter VI that Bentham believes that government policies which require general taxation can be more readily justified if the benefits are distributed widely in society. He is highly critical of policies which tax the many and benefit the few.

Finally, one wonders whether Bentham would authorize the redistribution of property in circumstances where civil strife is prevalent and security can be re-established only with radical redistribution. In his early writings he notes that the overthrow of property by revolution, though of great importance, is transitory and leads usually to another system of property. It is far less dangerous than the direct attempt to establish permanently a system of equal property.[58] The former may provide only a temporary shock to security followed by enhanced security due to the benefits of the redistribution. The latter may constitute a permanent shock to security.

From this discussion, we might distinguish between the goal of equality of wealth and power in a substantive sense to which Bentham clearly subscribes and the means to achieve

---

[56] See, for example, *Radical Reform Bill* (Bowring, iii. 560).
[57] See ch. VI above.
[58] See 'Principles of the Civil Code' (Bowring, i. 311-12).

this end which are more limited. He recognizes, of course, that the goal can never be fully realized. The more egalitarian 'greatest happiness of all' must often give way to the 'greatest happiness of the greatest number'. The goal of equality must give way to security which has a higher status. Nevertheless, Bentham seems more apprehensive about the means to equality than the end. If a condition of equal wealth evolves in a stable representative democracy, he would see this condition as itself augmenting happiness. His great fear is the shock to security which any sudden move towards equality may cause. However, this fear about the means does not diminish the extent to which Bentham values the end of equality.

Having now seen the emphasis Bentham places on equality in his conception of the greatest happiness principle and generally in his thought, we must consider a remark, such as Parekh's, that 'in Bentham's view there is no prima-facie case for equality and fairness in the distribution of benefits or burdens', as mistaken.[59] There is indeed a prima-facie case made for equality, but not an absolute one. Similarly, John Rawls's comment that 'the striking feature of the utilitarian view of justice is that it does not matter, except indirectly, how this sum of satisfactions is distributed among individuals' a comment that leads him to the conclusion that 'utilitarianism does not take seriously the distinction between persons' will have to be revised.[60] In Bentham, at least, the principle of equality guides the distribution of benefits and burdens, providing a substantive goal within the framework of the greatest happiness principle.

[59] B. Parekh, 'Bentham's Theory of Equality', *Political Studies*, xviii (1970), 494.

[60] John Rawls, *A Theory of Justice*, pp. 26, 27.

Chapter XII

Democratic Theory

An assessment of Bentham's contribution to a theory of democracy might begin with the implications of his commitment to the strategy of reform. It is here, perhaps, that one can appreciate the depth of his radicalism and the extent of his vision. The strategy of reform looks for a middle way in politics between support for the status quo and advocacy of revolution.[1] It brings a critical politics, working largely through the Public Opinion Tribunal, to bear on those who find any settled political arrangement from which they benefit, however unjust, to be good and on those who promise what cannot be achieved. From Bentham's point of view both positions are false and dangerous. His detailed proposals for reform, based on empirical data and measured to appeal to fallible, self-interested men, contain their own rhetoric—persuading the 'ruling few' to accept reform for their own good and the 'subject many' that here is a programme which is in their interest to pursue. In its most rational form the rhetoric of the strategy of reform is expressed in the greatest happiness principle.

Bentham's vision is of a society where each individual can live his life in security, with adequate subsistence, the prospect of abundance and an ever-increasing equality. He also envisages a growing benevolence in society secured initially by the law which prohibits the oppression and exploitation of some by others and sustained to an extent by the development of genuine other-regarding sentiment. The security that he seeks to establish is not enslavement, but a realm of personal freedom where each person can define and pursue his own idea of happiness so long as he does not endanger the security and subsistence of others. It is also a realm of political action where the critical searching voices of the people deal with the transgressions of their rulers.

[1] See H. L. A. Hart, 'Bentham', *Proceedings of the British Academy*, xlviii (1960), 302.

I

If Bentham were to examine the problems of democracy today, he might reaffirm the strategy of reform as the middle way between the complacent of the right who say that democracy exists when they say it exists and those of the left who promise too much and bring only despotism. He might look at England again and argue that democracy has not been fully constituted. The survival of the House of Lords and monarchy and, more importantly, the survival of the Common Law and the absence of a written constitution would alert him to the existence of classes of the 'ruling few'—especially civil servants, the professions, the police, and the judiciary—who are not yet accountable to the governed. He might see in the political parties major obstacles to accountable government. The widespread opposition in the Labour Party to the modest proposal for the reselection of sitting members of parliament would increase immensely in the face of Bentham's proposal for 'temporary non-relocability'. The opposition to current proposals for 'open government' would be greatly enhanced by Bentham's more complete plans for publicity in government. Dare one even suggest pecuniary competition?

Bentham's radicalism might be addressed to 'democrats' of today in the same way as it was to the Whigs of his own day. He might accuse them of neglecting accountability in all spheres of administration. He would question the enormous expense of government, not only the costs which people must bear through taxation but also the additional costs to the individual of gaining access to the law through the courts. The strategy of reform would require that 'democrats' of today see what they take to be established democracy as government in many spheres without effective accountability.

Bentham's other important opponents would lie on the left among an assortment of critics of liberal democracy who include orthodox marxists, the 'new left', proponents of other forms of democracy (such as 'participatory democracy'), and anarchists. It is here that the strategy of reform is most strongly opposed, and one finds articulate criticism of Bentham's position. One recent criticism appears in C. B. Macpherson's *The Life and Times of Liberal Democracy*

where a brief, but important analysis is provided of the contributions of Bentham, James Mill, and J. S. Mill to democratic thought.[2] Macpherson begins by distinguishing between
liberal democracy (as in Bentham and James Mill) and pre-
liberal democracy (as in Jefferson and Rousseau) and argues
that the difference between the two is in the connection of
the democratic thought of Bentham and James Mill with 'the
assumptions of a capitalist market society and the laws of
classical political economy'.[3] Liberal democracy, unlike pre-
liberal democracy, begins in the 1820s with Bentham's *Code*
and Mill's *Essay on Government*.

Macpherson wishes to link Bentham and James Mill
closely together. He notes that James Mill 'often put the
Benthamite case more strikingly than the master himself'
and that 'it will do no injustice to either to treat them almost
as a unit'.[4] The consequence of Macpherson's uniting the
two writers (which has been strenuously opposed in this
book in chapter IX above) will be seen in due course. However, we shall first examine Macpherson's analysis of Bentham's theory and especially his analysis of the relationship
Bentham establishes between security and equality. Macpherson finds in Bentham's idea of security 'a case for a
system of unlimited private property and capitalist enterprise'.[5] To be a democrat Macpherson argues that Bentham
ought to be committed to equality. He admits that equality
is one of the four ends of legislation (as we have seen in
chapter XI) to which Bentham subscribes in his writings,
but he argues that he subverts his principle of equality by
arguing that equality must yield to security. In his discussion Macpherson relies wholly on the 'Principles of the
Civil Code', the English translation of Dumont's *Traités*,
published in 1802 some years before Bentham's conversion
to radicalism in 1809 and two decades before Bentham began
the *Code*.[6] Macpherson fails to take into account the most
important argument that Bentham develops in his later
writings, namely, that equality of power (achieved through
universal suffrage and representative government) actually

---

[2] Oxford, 1977. [3] Ibid., p. 24.
[4] Ibid., pp. 24, 25. [5] Ibid., p. 27.
[6] See chapter XI above, note 42, and the general discussion of equality.

enhances security by curbing the abuse of power by government officials. Bentham also believes that equality of power can contribute to a gradual movement towards equality of wealth. In his later radicalism, therefore, Bentham achieves an important reconciliation between security and equality. Furthermore, Bentham's early material on the Civil Code emphasizes property, because it is set in the context of a discussion of the civil law which is largely concerned with the law of property. Bentham's later constitutional writings do not contain an emphasis on security of property as the main object of security. Even in the 'Principles of the Civil Code' Bentham argues that security of property might be sacrificed for other kinds of security as when taxation takes property from the individual to protect the whole society against invasion by foreign enemies. In the later *Leading Principles* Bentham clearly distinguishes between actions against security which affect only the instruments of security (property, person, reputation, etc.) and actions which constitute a general 'shock to security'. This distinction opens the way for gradual reform towards equality of property so long as property is not confiscated or taken without adequate compensation. Bentham's development of the disappointment-prevention principle guides this process of reform with compensation towards greater equality. Macpherson's attempt to discredit Bentham's argument through his interpretation of the notion of security thus fails, because he relies on the early material as though Bentham's argument never develops with his conversion to radicalism.

Macpherson also finds invalid a shift in Bentham's argument from the view that the individual should be secure in possessing the fruits of his labour to the principle that each system of property should be maintained as it is actually established even though it does not produce the greatest sum of happiness. It is true that Bentham regards the overthrow of a system of property as such a threat to security producing so much pain that it cannot be justified by reference to the greatest happiness principle. But Macpherson writes:

His contention is, that to overthrow *any* existing system of property is to make impossible any other system of property. It does not need a profound knowledge of history to see that this is not so. For instance the destruction of the feudal system of property led to the establishment of an equally firm capitalist system of property; and the same might be said of many previous overthrows of an existing system.[7]

Macpherson, unfortunately, does not continue with Bentham's own argument in the chapters on the Civil Code from which he quotes. For Bentham himself distinguishes between the 'overthrow of property' due to revolution or conquest on the one hand and due to the imposition of equality on the other, and he finds the former less threatening than the latter. Where there is a revolution, 'it is a great calamity; but it is only transitory.'[8] 'Industry is a vigorous plant', he continues, 'which resists numerous loppings and in which the fruitful sap rises immediately upon the return of spring.'[9] However, the imposition of equality at the expense of security threatens industry itself. Under this system the governed would be unwise to pursue industry, as the fruits of their labour would be taken to give to those who dissipate theirs. They might better pursue prodigality, but at any rate the society would soon sink into a 'savage state'. Industry can repair the damage caused by revolution but not that resulting from the imposition of equality at the expense of security. Although Macpherson overlooks this material, Bentham clearly allows for the change from one system of property to another. Nevertheless, he opposes the change from a system based on security of property to one of equality of property at the expense of security. While neither change ought to be made since each involves greater pain in the general threat to security, the former is more acceptable where necessary. Macpherson objects also to Bentham's general conclusion that any established system of property should be maintained. He ignores Bentham's remarks on the 'means of reconciliation of security and equality'.[10] As we have seen in chapter XI, this consists largely of curbs on inheritance and the gradual movement towards equality in the development of trade and manufacturing. 'Hence we may conclude', writes Bentham, 'that *security*, by preserving its rank as the supreme principle, indirectly conducts to the establishment of *equality*.'[11]

---

[7] Macpherson, op. cit., pp. 31-2.
[9] Ibid., 311-12.
[11] Ibid., p. 313.

[8] Bowring, i. 311.
[10] Ibid., pp. 312-13.

Bentham's argument obviously depends to an extent on assumptions taken from political economy. But this is different from saying, as Macpherson does, that 'he was really concerned only with the rationale of the capitalist market society.'[12] The reason why Bentham's own position is different from that depicted by Macpherson is that Macpherson leaves out of his argument Bentham's overriding concern with reform. Bentham never denies the value of equality as an end to be sought in society. What he criticizes is not the end but the means to equality, that is to say, the destruction of settled, civilized society for the sake of equality. Macpherson thinks that Bentham's argument here is invalid, but when the whole argument is examined, it is neither illogical nor 'unhistorical'. In the early material, Bentham sees a movement towards equality in the development of trade and manufactures. In his later writings he sees equality as powerfully enhanced by the adoption of universal suffrage. Here is an equality of power which challenges privilege and corruption in a way that does not threaten security. Bentham recognizes that a widespread suffrage is the great achievement of the United States. It enhances equality but poses no threat to security. The strategy of reform finds a powerful ally in the movement towards universal, annual, secret and equal suffrage.

Macpherson sees Bentham as not being enthusiastic about the extension of the franchise supposedly because Bentham seeks *only* a government which would nurture the free market economy and would prevent oppression. That is to say, Macpherson does not take seriously Bentham's commitment to equality and to a gradual process of reform towards equality. We have seen that equality as the end and gradual reform as the means is at the heart of his system, and that Bentham is an enthusiastic supporter of virtual universal suffrage. Now Macpherson tries to establish his argument about Bentham's lack of enthusiasm for universal suffrage by quickly shifting the discussion to James Mill's *Essay on Government*. Here, having already linked Bentham with James Mill, he finds Mill's severe exclusions from suffrage evidence that 'it cannot be said that James Mill was enthusiastic

---

[12] Macpherson, op. cit., p. 33.

about democracy, any more than was Bentham'.[13] Macpherson sees in Mill's exclusions a subtle argument in support of political power in the middle classes expressed in a way which does not offend the working classes. For Macpherson, 'it is scarcely a spirit of equality.'[14]

At this point we must recall the manuscript discussed in chapter IX where Bentham dissents from Mill's exclusions from suffrage in the *Essay on Government*.[15] If Mill's exclusions are evidence for Macpherson of his lack of commitment to equality, Bentham's rejection of Mill's argument might be seen as an indication of his serious commitment to equality of suffrage and equality in society. And if Macpherson must grant the seriousness of Bentham's commitment to equality, he must also concede the importance of the strategy of reform which is based on the assumption that the 'powerless' people must act through the ballot and other public means to achieve competent and accountable government. Macpherson's model I ('Protective Democracy for Market Man') is seriously defective, once Bentham's position and his differences from Mill are fully appreciated.

Furthermore, the argument in chapter X that John Stuart Mill rejects Bentham's confidence in the people and tends to follow his father, rather than Bentham, would render the next stage of Macpherson's argument invalid. Although Macpherson appreciates that 'Mill's model ... is arithmetically a step backward from Model I [i.e. Bentham and James Mill], which had stipulated, in principle at least, "one person, one vote",' he argues that in providing for and encouraging moral development rather than treating man as 'infinite consumer and appropriator', it is a step forward.[16] But we have seen that Mill's 'moral' attitude towards the people, especially in their need to develop in quality to be worthy of self-government, is dangerous, and leads to paternalism and to the potential justification of colonialism on the grounds of backwardness. Bentham, on the other hand, while still upholding the importance of competence in office, avoids Mill's paternalism. Macpherson does not appreciate Bentham's theory of democracy,

[13] Ibid., p. 38.   [14] Ibid., p. 42.   [15] See chapter IX above.
[16] Macpherson, op. cit., p. 60. Many writers emphasize the differences between James Mill and John Stuart Mill. See, for example, A. Ryan, 'Two Concepts of Politics and Democracy: James and John Stuart Mill', *Machiavelli and the Nature of Political Thought*, ed. M. Fleisher, New York, 1972, pp. 109-11.

because he believes that Bentham sees man purely as a consumer and appropriator. He ignores the political dimension in Bentham which develops in the people a regard for the public interest as well as for their own narrow interests. He ignores this partly because he sees Bentham through James Mill but more importantly because he sees Bentham's political ideas as merely reflecting his economic ideas. In the end, it is Macpherson's 'method' which leaves him blind to the significance of Bentham's theory of constitutional democracy.

II

Although a chapter has been devoted to Bentham's discussion of the greatest happiness principle in the *Code* and related writings, his theory of democracy as a utilitarian work has not yet been assessed. Indeed, it is not clear what would constitute a utilitarian theory of democracy, especially as we have examined three different accounts of representative democracy set forth by three major utilitarian thinkers, Bentham, James Mill, and J. S. Mill. John Plamenatz depicts modern utilitarian theories of democracy in terms of the maximization of the satisfaction of wants, a close cousin of Bentham's theory of maximizing pleasure or happiness.[17] Plamenatz then rejects various versions of utilitarianism in favour of his own approach from the perspective of rights and duties.[18] But in Plamenatz's discussion, there is little that could not be easily incorporated into Bentham's theory. The theory, as we have seen, is not confined to the simple development of the implications of his belief in maximizing pleasure. Long before we discussed the greatest happiness principle we examined the notions of functions and securities for appropriate aptitude. These notions are Bentham's substitutes for traditional ideas of duties and rights. They play as important a role in Bentham's account of democracy as Plamenatz's conception of rights and duties plays in his theory. The question then arises of what is distinctively utilitarian about Bentham's theory of democracy.

Let us attempt to answer this question by concentrating on the differences between Bentham's notions of functions

[17] J. Plamenatz, *Democracy and Illusion*, London, 1973, pp. 10 ff., 16, 181-2.
[18] Ibid., pp. 180–212.

and securities and the more traditional ideas of rights and duties. We can see that securities and functions are not ends in themselves. They are employed as means to the 'all-comprehensive end in view', the greatest happiness. But Bentham does not intend, as many critics have alleged, to divest these notions of 'moral' meaning and to give them purely on 'instrumental' character. These are terms and categories which Bentham would reject. He simply intends that in addition to their being ends to be established, they also must serve as means to (or at least not be incompatible with) the greatest happiness as the overall end. The main issue between those who emphasize rights in their theories and Bentham is the extent to which Bentham's securities provide absolute protection for the individual against oppression by the government. So long as the greatest happiness of the greatest number remains the ultimate end, it may be thought that individual rights must give way to utilitarian calculations which may place these rights in jeopardy. But let us consider an example where such calculations might take place. Bentham establishes securities which should be sufficient to guarantee what in the language of rights is a right to a fair trial. That these securities exist amply serves the greatest happiness. Consider, however, the possibility that the use of these securities under certain circumstances in certain trials costs so much money that the burden of expense is not justified by the greatest happiness principle. Let us imagine that even Bentham (however improbable it may seem) cannot devise ways of maintaining the securities and at the same time reducing the expense. Presumably, the end of minimizing expense is closer to the greatest happiness principle, and consequently, the effectiveness of the securities might have to be reduced.

One cannot deny this possibility in Bentham's system. However desirable a practice may be, there must be the resources to pay for it so that the fairness of the outcome does not require an oppressive burden placed on the people through taxation. Nevertheless, let us consider more carefully another aspect of Bentham's system in the most important end next to the greatest happiness—that of security. If it can be established that the reduction of certain judicial services threatens the security of everyone in society, then the burden of expense will be outweighed by the benefits that maintaining a fair trial at any cost bring to society. A strong argument can be developed from within Bentham's system to support a right to a fair trial which cannot be easily compromised. Furthermore, Bentham's later elaboration of the disappointment-prevention principle, if extended to the constitutional provisions in the *Code*, might allow one to argue that there is a constitutional equivalent to a 'vested right' and that the removal of these judicial services constitutes a violation of this principle. The disappointment-prevention principle, as we saw in chapter VI, might be taken as a substitute for a principle of justice. Thus, from the perspective of security and through the further application of the disappointment-prevention principle, securities for appropriate aptitude can give in Bentham's theory the same protection from state oppression as we expect from a theory of rights. It may be argued, however, that Bentham's theory, in allowing the legislature to pass whatever laws it wishes, allows it easily to abolish the securities. Securities may not have the same standing as a constitutional bill of rights which cannot be altered directly by the legislature. It was suggested earlier that Bentham may have underestimated the importance and success of the Supreme Court in the Constitution of the United States in securing rights against the state and as a useful curb on legislative power. Nevertheless, in theory at least, even the US Constitution empowers the legislature to limit the power of the Supreme Court to hear certain kinds of cases.[19] And in Bentham's theory, it would be incorrect to see the legislature as totally unlimited by other authorities in the exercise of its powers.[20]

Bentham's securities are mainly enforced by political pressure and action. He does not trust one branch of government to curb the excesses and deficiencies of a superior and more powerful branch. More importantly, he believes that a determined government can easily destroy the constitution if it wishes, and no bill of rights will offer protection against this kind of subversion. The doctrine of securities, by trusting to political action, rather than to judicial remedies, may even be a better protection against such subversion.

[19] See Article III, Section 2 of the US Constitution.
[20] See above chapter III.

Let us now examine the notion of duties which Bentham conceives in terms of functions. Here, again, there is little to distinguish Bentham's treatment of functions (in chapter V) from an account of duties. We have seen that Bentham even develops a notion of political virtue. Of course, Bentham is not concerned in a constitutional document with moral doctrines such as 'not telling lies' and 'keeping promises'. But he would argue that his careful enumeration of functions, together with the use of securities, provide strong incentives for officials neither to lie nor to break their promises.

If Bentham's notions of securities and functions cover the same ground as traditional notions of rights and duties, it is still not clear why his ideas should be labelled 'utilitarian'. Admittedly, the words are different. Bentham talks of 'securities' and 'functions' rather than of 'rights' and 'duties'. This reflects his use of a technical language so that difficulties associated with the traditional language of rights and duties can be avoided. As we have seen, he believes that by talking about securities and functions he can depict these notions more clearly and fully than the traditional notions of rights and duties. Nevertheless, his care with the use of language is not necessarily the product of a utilitarian philosophy.

The difference between Bentham and more traditional theories lies less with the actual doctrines than with the arguments and evidence with which he establishes these doctrines. This is not to underestimate his claim that his conception of securities and functions goes far beyond what had ever been conceived with regard to constitutional rights and related duties. But this is characteristic of Bentham's inventiveness rather than of a utilitarian philosophy. As a utilitarian, his theories look more to the consequences of various arrangements than to any other arguments for their validity. And the theories are based where possible on empirical evidence. If, for example, it is contended that the institution of an established church would better teach men their duties than a careful definition of functions in a constitutional document, Bentham would characteristically argue that one must first determine whether or not such established churches have actually had this effect (by empirical investigation) and consider the cost to society of their success or failure (i.e. through taxation, oppression, censorship, etc.). Bentham's use of empirical data to establish the utility of practices plays an important role in his assessment of consequences. Where, as in the case of Bentham's theory of functions, there is little or no empirical data, as no society has actually adopted the scheme of functions and securities, he would use psychological or sociological arguments based on his conception of the human condition. He would contend that his theory of functions is better than a church, for example, for teaching men their duties, because it appeals to men as they are, basically self-interested and self-aggrandizing. If a practice can be shown to be better able to deal with 'men as they are' as opposed to 'men as they ought to be', this assessment would weigh strongly in its favour.

What Bentham rejects are arguments based on tradition, history, 'nature', or intuition which do not allow for weighing alternatives and calculating consequences. He also rejects rhetorical arguments which gain acceptance from the emotional appeal of terms like 'liberty' and 'natural rights'. He subjects such arguments to intense critical scrutiny by analysing the terminology, using relevant empirical data, referring generally to the human condition, and calculating the consequences of the adoption of policies based on such arguments. The different kinds of arguments show that Bentham has developed a more complex approach to political argument than is often discerned in accounts of his 'felicific calculus'.

In using empirical data and referring practices to the 'realities' of the human condition in an overall assessment of consequences, Bentham also uses his method to refine the substance of his theory. Thus, his theory of securities and functions appears in its present form partly as a result of his attempt to devise a system where self-interested men, bent on corruption and tyranny, will none the less be induced to follow the constitutional rules by their apprehension of the advantages of doing so.

III

If Bentham's utilitarian approach to democracy is different from what it has often been alleged to be, we must still deal with one of its characteristic doctrines which is usually considered defective. This is his conception of the way that the individual's interests can be reconciled with the general interest. It is a well-known view of Bentham that the general interest (or interest of the community) is 'the sum of the interests of the several members who compose it'.[21] What he means by this phrase is often misunderstood.[22] He does not mean that the legislator can determine what is in the general interest by adding up the sum of the wants and aspirations of each member of society. But, on the other hand, he rejects the view that the general interest can be established without any direct reference to individual interests. How Bentham achieves the reconciliation of general and individual interests might best be explored through an example. If a political leader decides to pursue a policy of military expansion which places at risk the lives and property of the people of the state, Bentham would say that this policy would not be in the general interest. He might even go further and say that it would not be in the general interest even though a vast majority of the people in the state elected the man to office and approved his policy. The people might thus see their leader as satisfying their wants and aspirations. The reason why Bentham can separate the general interest from what the people believe is in the general interest is that he possesses an objective and fairly definite account of what is in the general interest. This includes, as we have seen in chapter II, happiness in general terms as well as security, subsistence, abundance, and equality. It also includes the application of the disappointment-prevention principle as well as subsidiary ends in government such as maximizing aptitude and minimizing expense. Within this context the Legislator's Inaugural Declaration specifically precludes offensive war as being contrary to the general interest.[23]

How then can the general interest be the sum of the interests of the people in the society? Bentham would argue that his conception of the general interest is reducible (on a calculation of pains and pleasures) to the interests of particular individuals taken as individuals in society. An offensive

---

[21] *An Introduction to the Principles of Morals and Legislation*, I. 4 (*CW*), p. 12.
[22] See, for example, Thompson, op. cit., p. 25.
[23] See ch. VII, § 8 (*CW*), pp. 142-3.

war, if lost, would threaten each person's life and security and, if won, might none the less place heavy burdens on the people for the benefit of the rulers. These burdens may not be evident to the people at the outset of the war, but they would soon have to be recognized. Thus, Bentham would conclude that the burdens on each member of society would outweigh the benefits to each member. In this sense, the policy would not be in the interest of each particular member of society. And it follows that what is in the general interest (no offensive war) can be reduced to the interest of each member of the society, and is also the sum of their interests.

Bentham would also say that each person is none the less the best judge of his interests and that these interests should embrace the objects of his desires. How then are these interests to aggregate into the general interest? It seems that in the present example the people are not the best judges of their interests in supporting the policy of offensive war. Bentham would argue that they are mistaken or deluded, and when confronted by the truth, they will vote for the person and policies which will best preserve security. The important point for Bentham is that the individual himself must see that he is mistaken or deluded, and the process of gaining insight should not be presumed by another person or group. He also believes that this process is neither mysterious nor difficult. Without a fairly easy shift from subjective wants and judgements to interests which aggregate to form the objective general interest in security, etc., Bentham's argument would have to abandon the premiss that each person is the best judge of his own interests. With the ballot, a free press, and other institutions and practices which we have examined, Bentham believes that this process will be fairly straightforward. The problem is with rulers and not the ruled. They have an interest in misleading the people; the people do not.

Bentham does not expect that each person will consider *only* the general interest when he votes, but that each will identify some of his interests with the general interest because it is through this process of identification that his interests will be advanced. Each person has an interest in security and he can identify his interest with the general interest of society in security. He may think that he can best advance and secure his life and property by pursuing policies adverse to those of society in general. He will soon learn, however, that as security diminishes generally in society by his actions and those of others like him, his own security will diminish. But will he learn?

A superficial perusal of a daily newspaper might provide enough evidence to declare that Bentham's position is a false one. Many people pursue interests so detrimental to the security of society that the newspapers are full of accounts of war, terrorism, crime, and economic blackmail which benefit only a few. Furthermore, Jack Lively has argued that 'in any interest calculation, a man's role as a trade-unionist, property-owner, Catholic or black is likely to be of greater significance than his role as a member of the whole community deriving common benefits from governmental policies'.[24] Bentham does not deny these 'realities', and he would be foolish to do so. Nor is he so optimistic about his system of representative democracy that he expects war, crime, and terrorism to disappear with the advent of universal suffrage. We have seen in chapter II that for Bentham democracy is a fragile constitution needing constant protection and always under threat. All that he claims for the democratic system is that it allows the identification of interests to take place; in monarchy and aristocracy, the interests of rulers tend to be distinct from those of the ruled. Besides the representative system, however, is the strategy of reform. The strategy of reform, backed by the power of the Public Opinion Tribunal, persuades people that their interests should be identified with the general interest. The rich, as we noted, have to be persuaded to pursue their prosperity within the democratic system with the promise that their wealth will be more secure and of greater amount than if they seek increased wealth at the expense of the security of the community. The trade union leader must be persuaded that his attempt to achieve financial security for his members through an inflationary wage settlement at the expense of the security of the rest of the community will not be successful in the long run. Bentham recognizes that it may be difficult at times to persuade people that they will profit

---

[24] J. Lively, *Democracy*, Oxford, 1975, p. 115.

more by identifying their own interest in security and prosperity with that of the community. But this is the task of the Public Opinion Tribunal which for Bentham has a greater chance to do so in an atmosphere of free speech and the ballot than would be possible in any other form of government. For the criminal and terrorist who see themselves prospering only at the expense of society, Bentham proposes repression plus incentives established by the system of punishment to encourage them to pursue more conventional paths. Nevertheless, unless this process of identifying individual interests with the general interest takes place largely spontaneously or voluntarily, as the result of persuasion by the Public Opinion Tribunal, the democratic system cannot survive. And the democratic system, based on individual perceptions of interests, is the best environment for this identification to take place.

IV

In writing this book, this author has been guided by two aims: to establish that Bentham's *Constitutional Code* is the classic text of liberal democracy; and to show that many of those who analyse and criticize Bentham's ideas have usually mistaken part of his thought for the whole of it. Many of these partial views have been corrected. It may none the less be thought that this work has not been sufficiently critical of Bentham's theories. If his *Code* was actually adopted by a state (together with the whole *pannomion*) and an economy to complement the codes of law, the result might be quite different from what Bentham intended. Indolence and apathy, close cousins of self-interest and far more destructive, might soon make the most rigorous system of securities ineffective. The availability of all of the information needed for legislation may very well not produce wise legislation. Bentham could appreciate that his great work was a utopia.[25] He called it a utopia, because it existed only in printed form and had not been adopted by any state. He none the less intended it to be adopted and put into practice especially in new states. Many practices Bentham

[25] See Bowring, v. 278.

advocated have been adopted by various countries. When Bentham wrote, there was no state where competitive examinations for the civil service were widely employed. Nor was there much emphasis on records and bookkeeping in government. We need not be concerned with whether or not these practices were adopted because Bentham advocated them, but rather that his ideas were such that governments might adopt them. In spite of Bentham's idiosyncratic language and in spite of the bizarre character of some of his proposals, he is clearly speaking to the needs and aspirations of the modern industrial and democratic state. And if practices like pecuniary competition or temporary non-relocability seem remote today, if not absurd, it may be worth recalling that Bentham was above all committed to experiment and creativity in legislation. Without this commitment a work like the *Constitutional Code* could not have been written. Perhaps Bentham's approach to representative democracy may still inspire democrats to reform and improve. It may be the case that wisdom in legislation cannot be guaranteed by a system of registration and publicity. It may also be the case that indolence and apathy may defeat various securities. Yet, the strategy of reform together with creativity in legislation seem important securities against indolence, apathy, and even folly.

Appendix

L. J. Hume's *Bentham and Bureaucracy*, like the present work, emphasizes the importance of the *Constitutional Code* in Bentham's thought.[1] He approaches his subject, nominally confined to the evolution of Bentham's ideas on the organization of the administration and the judiciary (but in fact more wide-ranging), through a study of the evolution of Bentham's ideas, especially in his voluminous manuscripts. In contrast with Hume's book, the emphasis has been placed here on Bentham's text of the *Code* and the ideas which are contained in it as the fullest statement of his theory of democracy. Neither approach excludes the other (indeed, they should be complementary), but in this case the two approaches have led to differences in interpretation and emphasis. By looking to its origins, Hume's account of the *Code* seems to lack a full appreciation of the radical and democratic elements in Bentham's theory of administration which are fully evident only in the *Code* and other later writings. For example, in his concluding remarks on accountability, Hume stresses the hierarchical structure Bentham has evolved, beginning with the electorate, with the legislature subordinate to the electorate and the two co-ordinate branches, the administration and judiciary, subordinate to the legislature.[2] He suggests that Bentham 'might have achieved accountability most simply by prescribing that all offices, in all branches of government, should be filled by popular election'.[3] He claims that Bentham was attracted to this idea, but thought that it was impractical. Instead, Bentham gives to the electorate, he continues, only an indirect role of working through the elected legislature plus providing information and publicity about the performance of administrators and judges, and this leads to the hierarchical structure. Hume neglects to mention that although the electorate chooses only their legislators, Bentham gives

---

[1] Cambridge, 1981. See also chapter I above, note 1.
[2] Hume, op. cit., pp. 254–5.
[3] Ibid., p. 254.

it the power, to the chagrin of J. S. Mill in the *Considera-tions*, to dismiss directly a wide range of administrative and judicial officials including the prime minister, justice minister, ministers, local headmen, local registrars, judges, and judicial officers.[4] The effect of this grant of power is to establish very extensive democratic control which runs parallel to the establishment of administrative and judicial hierarchies. This example confirms my argument that Bentham provides a 'democratic dimension' in his approach to administration in numerous spheres. He not only anticipates scientific manage-ment, as Hume suggests, but he surpasses it with his insights into the relationship between bureaucracy and democracy. Hume fails to emphasize (though he describes Bentham's discussion of these themes) the later radicalism, because his research leads him backwards to the early writings prior to the full development of Bentham's democratic ideas. This perspective unduly limits Hume's argument and leads him to ignore some aspects of Bentham's theory.

Another difficulty in Hume's approach stems from too simple an account of Bentham's view of sovereignty and command. Like many Bentham scholars, Hume sees obvious connections between Bentham and Hobbes in their mutual emphases on the problem of reconciling self-interested individuals in the state.[5] Hume also argues that Bentham's theory of administration evolves directly out of the prob-lems associated with Hobbes's view of sovereignty.[6] In chapter III, however, we have seen that as early as the *Fragment on Government* Bentham turns away from a view of sovereignty based on simple command and obedience in favour of referring to conventions of obedience in a 'matter of fact' way. This allows him to develop the more flexible view of sovereignty which appears in the *Code*.[7] Hume, however, wishes to emphasize the importance of a simple model of command and obedience which lies behind and renders coherent the entire theory of administration. But

[4] Ch. V. §2, Art. 5 (*CW*), pp. 31-2.
[5] See, for example, Mary Mack, *Jeremy Bentham, An Odyssey of Ideas 1748-1792*, London, 1962, pp. 117 ff.; D. Long, *Bentham on Liberty*, Toronto, 1977, pp. 6, 40-4, 210-12; D. Manning, *The Mind of Jeremy Bentham*, London, 1968, p. 109.
[6] See Hume, op. cit., pp. 56-7.
[7] See chapter III above. See also Hume, op. cit., pp. 63 ff., 84.

he tends to ignore those aspects of Bentham's discussions of administration and politics which do not fit the model. We have examined in chapter II the crucial roles played by the Public Opinion Tribunal and by the strategy of reform in Bentham's theory of constitutional democracy. These are not simply extra-legal influences, but are the foundations of the legal and constitutional system, and they cannot be understood in terms of a simple model of legal command and obedience. What is interesting about Bentham's conception of sovereignty is that it allows these factors to play the role that they do. Hume does not utilize these aspects of Bentham's thought, because he sticks somewhat narrowly to Hobbes's notion of sovereignty.

In applying his model of command and obedience to administration, Hume asserts that Bentham 'knew about informal relationships and their ability to pervade an administrative agency, but it was precisely his aim to eliminate such forces and to make the working of his Executive depend entirely on the formal relations of command and obedience'.[8] In contrast to Hume we have seen that Bentham allows considerable scope for the operation of informal relationships in administration under the scrutiny of the Public Opinion Tribunal to achieve constitutional ends. For example, in chapter V, it has been argued that Bentham distinguishes between the power of an office and the powers which accrue to the individual (enhanced reputation, influence, etc.) by virtue of his office. The latter informal sources of power cannot be eliminated, but Bentham argues that remuneration (related to office) might be reduced (through pecuniary competition) because the individual possesses these additional sources of informal power as compensation. Hence, by recognizing both the existence and the utility of informal relationships, Bentham makes an important innovation in administrative theory. Another example appears in his discussion of procurement where contracts between government officials and close relatives are not prohibited. Bentham's civil service is encouraged to exploit informal ties with family members so long as the resulting contracts are based on the cheapest possible terms. Full publicity must be given

---

[8] Hume, op. cit., pp. 3-4.

to the contracts so that scrutiny by the Public Opinion Tribunal becomes possible.

It may be true, as Hume suggests, that Bentham's civil service is not designed to inspire a sense of loyalty, i.e. an *esprit de corps*, in the system, but even here an important consideration might be added. In the way the activities and attitudes of the Public Opinion Tribunal, representing the public interest, replace notions of civic virtue and patriotism, a similar spirit among officials who are under the influence of this body might come into existence.

The direct influence of Hobbes on Bentham is difficult to establish. Although Hobbes's influence has not been discussed to any extent, it has been assumed that Bentham read Hobbes indirectly through other writers such as Hume, Locke, and the French *philosophes.* This approach is confirmed somewhat by the fact that Bentham seldom mentions Hobbes and does not discuss him in detail in any printed text. It is true that the stature and influence of Hobbes is enormous in later English thought even where, as in Bentham's case, the influence is indirect. But Bentham was not limited by the fairly narrow range of concepts which would be available to him if he is interpreted too narrowly as a follower of Hobbes.

Hume's approach to Bentham's thought through the evolution of his ideas in the manuscripts has its successes and failures. One important achievement is his discussion of the evolution of Bentham's ideas on political economy and the role of government in the economy.[9] Hume shows historically what has been argued here, that Bentham 'did not regard political economy as a master-science or as providing a model for all social relationships.'[10] He goes on to establish that Bentham has a more flexible approach to the issue of government intervention in the economy than is found in other liberal thinkers. Less successful, however, is his approach to the development of Bentham's ideas on the relationship of government to the electorate. Hume emphasizes Bentham's belief that government is a trust established for the benefit of the subject.[11] Bentham may have used this Lockeian notion in his writings, but Hume

---

[9] Ibid., pp. 93 ff. [10] Ibid., p. 93. [11] Ibid., pp. 239, 244.

does not point out that the terminology of 'trust', 'trustee' etc. is conspicuously absent from the *Constitutional Code*. As with the term 'representative', it is probable than Bentham had by this late period found the notion of government as a 'trust' too vague and too open to abuse to be useful in the more precise language of the *Code*. This is not to deny that Bentham may have started from the notion of trust in his understanding of the relationship between rulers and ruled. But in the end, he chooses other language and other concepts to express this relationship. Hume fails to bring out the distinctive character of this relationship in the *Code*, because he concentrates on the evolution of the notion of trust from Bentham's early writings.

Bibliography

(Note: this bibliography is confined to works cited in the text and notes. For a more comprehensive list of works on Bentham, see *The Bentham Newsletter*, i (1978), 36-44; ii (1979), 52-61; iv (1980), 53-63; vi (1982), 47-54. Further instalments are planned for future issues.)

Manuscripts

Bentham Manuscripts in the University College, London Library.
Catalogue of the Manuscripts of Jeremy Bentham in the Library of University College, London. Compiled by A. Taylor Milne, London, 2nd ed. 1962.

Bentham Manuscripts in the British Library, Add. MSS 33, 537-64.

Brougham Manuscripts, University College, London.

Dumont Manuscripts, Bibliothèque Publique et Universitaire, Geneva.

Bentham's Works

'Anti-Senatica', ed. C. W. Everett, *Smith College Studies in History*, xi (1926), 209-67.

Bentham's Political Thought, ed. B. Parekh, London, 1973.

The Collected Works of Jeremy Bentham, general editors, J. H. Burns, J. R. Dinwiddy, London, 1968—(in progress):
  A Comment on the Commentaries and A Fragment on Government, eds. J. H. Burns and H. L. A. Hart, London, 1977.
  Constitutional Code, vol. I, eds. F. Rosen and J. H. Burns, Oxford, 1983.
  The Correspondence of Jeremy Bentham, 1752-1780, ed. T. L. S. Sprigge, 2 vols., London, 1968.
  The Correspondence of Jeremy Bentham, 1781-1788, ed. I. Christie, London, 1971.
  The Correspondence of Jeremy Bentham, 1788-1797, ed. A. T. Milne, 2 vols., London, 1981.
  An Introduction to the Principles of Morals and Legislation, eds. J. H. Burns and H. L. A. Hart, London, 1970.

Of Laws in General, ed. H. L. A. Hart, London, 1970.

A Fragment on Government, ed. F. C. Montague, Oxford, 1891.

The Iberian Correspondence of Jeremy Bentham, ed. P. Schwartz, 2 vols., London–Madrid, 1979.

Jeremy Bentham's Economic Writings, ed. W. Stark, 3 vols., London, 1952-4.

Parliamentary Candidate's proposed Declaration of Principles: or say, A Test proposed for Parliamentary Candidates, London, 1831.

Théorie des peines et des récompenses, ed. E. Dumont, 2 vols., London, 1811.

Traités de législation, civile et pénale, ed. E. Dumont, 3 vols., Paris, 1802.

Traités des preuves judiciares, ed. E. Dumont, 2 vols., Paris, 1823, translated as *A Treatise on Judicial Evidence*, London, 1825.

The Works of Jeremy Bentham. Published under the superintendence of . . . John Bowring, 11 vols., Edinburgh, 1838-43.

Other Books and Articles

Arendt, H., *The Human Condition*, Chicago, 1958.

Aristotle, *Nicomachean Ethics*, trans. H. Rackham, London, The Loeb Classical Library, 1962.

Aristotle, *Politics*, trans. H. Rackham, London, The Loeb Classical Library, 1967.

Ayer, A. J., 'The Principle of Utility', *Jeremy Bentham and the Law*, ed. G. W. Keeton and G. Schwarzenberger, London, 1948, pp. 245-59.

Bahmueller, C., *The National Charity Company*, Berkeley, Calif., 1981.

Ball, T., 'Was Bentham a Feminist?' and 'Bentham No Feminist: A Reply to Boralevi', *The Bentham Newsletter*, iv (1980), 25-32, 47-8.

Baumgardt, D., *Bentham and the Ethics of Today*, Princeton, 1952.

Benn, S. I., 'The Uses of "Sovereignty" ', *Political Studies*, iii (1955), 109-22, reprinted in *In Defense of Sovereignty*, ed. W. J. Stankiewicz, New York, 1969, pp. 67-85.

Berlin, I., *Four Essays on Liberty*, Oxford, 1969.

Birch, A. H., *Representation*, London, 1971.

Blackstone, W., *Commentaries on the Laws of England*, 4 vols., Oxford, 1765-9.

Boralevi, L. C., 'Bentham and the Oppressed', Ph.D. thesis, European University Institute, Florence, 1980.

Boralevi, L. C., 'In Defence of a Myth', *The Bentham Newsletter*, iv (1980), 33-46.

Brebner, J. B., 'Laissez Faire and State Intervention in Nineteenth-Century Britain', *Journal of Economic History*, viii (1948), 59-73.

Budge, I., 'Jeremy Bentham: A Re-evaluation in the Context of Empirical Social Science', *Political Studies*, xix (1971), 18-36.

Burns, J. H., 'Bentham and the French Revolution', *The Transactions of the Royal Historical Society*, 5th Series, xvi (1966), 95-114.

Burns, J. H., 'Bentham on Sovereignty: An Exploration', *Bentham and Legal Theory*, ed. M. H. James, Belfast, [1974], pp. 133-50, reprinted from the *Northern Ireland Legal Quarterly*, xxiv (1973).

Burns, J. H., *The Fabric of Felicity: the Legislator and the Human Condition*, London, 1967.

Burns, J. H., 'J. S. Mill and Democracy, 1829-61', *Political Studies*, v (1957), 158-75, 281-94, reprinted in *Mill, A Collection of Critical Essays* (Modern Studies in Philosophy), ed. J. B. Schneewind, London, 1969, pp. 280-328.

Burns, J. H., 'The Light of Reason', *James and John Stuart Mill*, eds. J. M. Robson and M. Laine, Toronto, 1976.

Cromwell, V., 'Interpretations of Nineteenth-Century Administration: An Analysis', *Victorian Studies*, ix (1966), 245-55.

Crook, D. P., *American Democracy in English Politics 1815-1850*, Oxford, 1965.

Davidson, W. I., *Political Thought in England, the Utilitarians from Bentham to J. S. Mill*, London, 1915.

de Avila-Martel, A., 'The Influence of Bentham on the Teaching of Penal Law in Chile', *The Bentham Newsletter*, v (1981), 22-8.

Dicey, A. V., *Introduction to the Study of the Law of the Constitution*, London, 5th ed. 1897.

Dinwiddy, J. R., 'Bentham on Private Ethics and the Principle of Utility', (unpublished paper).

Dinwiddy, J. R., 'Bentham's Transition to Political Radicalism, *Journal of the History of Ideas*, xxxvi (1975), 683-700.

Dunn, J., *Western Political Theory in the Face of the Future*, Cambridge, 1979.

Everett, C. W., 'The Constitutional Code of Jeremy Bentham', *Jeremy Bentham Bicentenary Celebrations*, London, 1948.

Godwin, W., *Enquiry concerning Political Justice*, ed. I. Kramnick, London, 1976.

Goldworth, A., 'The Meaning of Bentham's Greatest Happiness Principle', *Journal of the History of Philosophy*, vii (1969), 315-21.

Gunn, J. A. W., 'Jeremy Bentham and the Public Interest', *Canadian Journal of Political Science*, i (1968), 398-413.

Halévy, E., *La Formation du Radicalisme Philosophique*, 3 vols., Paris, 1901-4, translated as *The Growth of Philosophic Radicalism*, trans. M. Morris, London, 1928.

Halliday, R. J., *John Stuart Mill*, London, 1976.

Hamburger, J., *James Mill and the Art of Revolution*, New Haven, Conn., 1963.

Hare, T., *A Treatise on the Election of Representatives: Parliamentary and Municipal*, London, 1859.

Hart, H. L. A., 'Bentham' (Lecture on a Master Mind), from the *Proceedings of the British Academy*, xlviii (1960), 297-320.

Hart, H. L. A., 'Bentham on Sovereignty', *The Irish Jurist*, ii (1967), 327-35, reprinted in *Jeremy Bentham*, ed. B. Parekh, London, 1974, pp. 145-53.

Hart, H. L. A., 'Between Utility and Rights', *The Idea of Freedom*, ed. A. Ryan, Oxford, 1979, pp. 77-98.

Hart, J., 'Nineteenth-Century Social Reform: A Tory Interpretation of History', *Past and Present*, xxxi (1965), 39-61.

Himmelfarb, G., 'The Haunted House of Jeremy Bentham', *Victorian Minds*, London, 1968, pp. 32-81.

Hume, L. J., *Bentham and Bureaucracy*, Cambridge, 1981.

Hume, L. J., 'Jeremy Bentham and the Nineteenth Century Revolution in Government', *Historical Journal*, x (1967), 361-75.

Hume, L. J., 'Jeremy Bentham on Industrial Management', *The Yorkshire Bulletin of Economic and Social Research*, xxii (1970), 3-15.

Hume, L. J., 'The Political Functions of Bentham's Theory of Fictions', *The Bentham Newsletter*, iii (1979), 18-27.

Hume, L. J., 'Preparations for Civil War in Tripoli in the 1820s: Ali Karamanli, Hassuna D'Ghies and Jeremy Bentham', *Journal of African History*, xxi (1980), 311-22.

Hume, L. J., 'Revisionism in Bentham Studies', *The Bentham Newsletter*, i (1978), 3-20.

James, M. H., (ed.), *Bentham and Legal Theory*, Belfast, [1974], reprinted from the *Northern Ireland Legal Quarterly*, xxiv (1973).

James, M. H., 'Bentham's Political Writings 1788-95', *The Bentham Newsletter*, iv (1980), 22-4.

James, M. H., 'Public Interest and Majority Rule in Bentham's Democratic Theory', *Political Theory*, ix (1981), 49-64.

Letwin, S. R., *The Pursuit of Certainty*, Cambridge, 1965.

Lively, J., *Democracy*, Oxford, 1975.

Lively, J. and Rees, J., (eds.), *Utilitarian Logic and Politics*, Oxford, 1978.

Long, D., *Bentham on Liberty: Jeremy Bentham's Idea of Liberty in Relation to his Utilitarianism*, Toronto, 1977.

Long, D., 'Bentham on Property', *Theories of Property, Aristotle to the Present*, ed. A. Parel and T. Flanagan, Waterloo, Ontario, 1979, pp. 220-254.

Lyons, D., *In the Interest of the Governed*, Oxford, 1973.

MacDonagh, O., 'The Nineteenth-Century Revolution in Government: A Reappraisal', *Historical Journal*, i (1958), 52-67.

Mack, Mary, *Jeremy Bentham, An Odyssey of Ideas 1748-1792*, London, 1962.

Macpherson, C. B., *The Life and Times of Liberal Democracy*, Oxford, 1977.

Magid, H. M., 'Jeremy Bentham and James Mill', *History of Political Philosophy*, eds. L. Strauss and J. Cropsey, Chicago, Ill., 1963, pp. 621-7.

Manning, D., *The Mind of Jeremy Bentham*, London, 1968.

McKennan, T. L., 'Benthamism in Santander's Colombia', *The Bentham Newsletter*, v (1981), 29-43.

Mill, James, *Essays . . .* , London, n.d.

Mill, James, *On the Ballot; from the Westminster Review for July 1830*, London 3rd ed., 1830.

Mill, James, *Selected Economic Writings*, ed. D. Winch, Edinburgh, 1966.

Mill, J. S., 'Bentham', reprinted in *Jeremy Bentham*, ed. B. Parekh, London, 1974, pp. 1-40.

Mill, J. S., *The Collected Works of John Stuart Mill*, ed. J. M. Robson et al.

vol. x (*Essays on Ethics, Religion and Society*), Toronto, 1969.

vol. xix (*Essays on Politics and Society*), Toronto, 1977.

Mulgan, R. G., *Aristotle's Political Theory*, Oxford, 1977.

Nozick, R., *Anarchy, State and Utopia*, New York, 1974.

Parekh, B., 'Bentham's Theory of Equality', *Political Studies*, xviii (1970), 478-95.

Parekh, B. (ed.), *Jeremy Bentham, Ten Critical Essays*, London, 1974.
Parris, H., 'The Nineteenth-Century Revolution in Government: A Reappraisal Reappraised', *Historical Journal*, iii (1960), 17-37.
Pateman, C., *Participation and Democratic Theory*, Cambridge, 1970.
Peardon, T., 'Bentham's Ideal Republic', *Canadian Journal of Economic and Political Science*, xvii (1951), 184-203, reprinted in *Jeremy Bentham*, ed. B. Parekh, London, 1974, pp. 120-44.
Pérez Luño, Antonio-Enrique, 'Jeremy Bentham and Legal Education in the University of Salamanca during the Nineteenth Century', *The Bentham Newsletter*, v (1981), 44-54.
Plamenatz, J., *Democracy and Illusion*, London, 1973.
Plamenatz, J., *The English Utilitarians*, Oxford, 2nd ed. 1958.
Priestley, F. E. L., 'Introduction', *The Collected Works of John Stuart Mill*, ed. J. M. Robson, vol. x, Toronto, 1969.
Raphael, D. D., *Problems of Political Philosophy*, London, 1970.
Rawls, J., *A Theory of Justice*, Oxford, 1972.
Robbins, L., *Bentham in the Twentieth Century*, London, 1965.
Roberts, D., 'Jeremy Bentham and the Victorian Administrative State', *Victorian Studies*, ii (1959), 193-210, reprinted in *Jeremy Bentham*, ed. B. Parekh, London, 1974, pp. 187-204.
Roberts, W., 'Behavioural Factors in Bentham's Conception of Political Change', *Political Studies*, x (1962), 163-79.
Roberts, W., 'Bentham's Conception of Political Change: a Liberal Approach', *Political Studies*, ix (1961), 254-66.
Roberts, W., 'Bentham's Poor Law Proposals', *The Bentham Newsletter*, iii (1979), 28-45.
Robson, J. M., *The Improvement of Mankind*, London, 1968.
Robson, J. M., 'John Stuart Mill and Jeremy Bentham, with some Observations on James Mill', *Essays in English Literature from the Renaissance to the Victorian Age*, eds. M. MacLure and F. W. Watt, Toronto, 1964, pp. 245-68.
Rosen, F., 'Bentham's Letters and Manuscripts in Greece', *The Bentham Newsletter*, v (1981), 55-8.
Rosen, F., 'The Constitutional Code: The New Version', *The Bentham Newsletter*, ii (1979), 40-3.
Rosen, F., 'Jeremy Bentham and Democratic Theory', *The Bentham Newsletter*, iii (1979), 46-61.
Rousseau, J. J., *The Social Contract*, trans. M. Cranston, London, 1968.
Ryan, A., *J. S. Mill*, London, 1975.
Ryan, A., 'Two Concepts of Politics and Democracy: James and John Stuart Mill', *Machiavelli and the Nature of Political Thought*, ed. M. Fleisher, New York, 1972, pp. 76-113.
Sabine, G. H., *A History of Political Theory*, London, 3rd ed., 1963.
Schwartz, P., 'Bentham's Influence in Spain, Portugal and Latin America', *The Bentham Newsletter*, i (1978), 34-5.
Shackleton, R., 'The Greatest Happiness of the Greatest Number: the History of Bentham's Phrase', *Studies on Voltaire and the Eighteenth Century*, xc (1972), 1461-82.

Sidgwick, H., 'Bentham and Benthamism in Politics and Ethics', *Miscellaneous Essays and Addresses*, London, 1904, pp. 135-69.

Stankiewicz, W. J. (ed.), *In Defense of Sovereignty*, New York, 1969.

Stearns, J. B., 'Bentham on Public and Private Ethics', *Canadian Journal of Philosophy*, v (1975), 583-94.

Steintrager, J., *Bentham*, London, 1977.

Stephen, L., *The English Utilitarians*, 3 vols., London, 1900.

Stokes, E., *The English Utilitarians and India*, Oxford, 1959.

Thompson, D., *John Stuart Mill and Representative Government*, Princeton, N.J., 1976.

Werner, L., 'A Note about Bentham on Equality and about the Greatest Happiness Principle', *Journal of the History of Philosophy*, xi (1973), 237-51.

Williford, M., *Bentham on South America*, Baton Rouge, 1980.

Winch, D., *Classical Political Economy and Colonies*, London, 1965.

Wolin, S., *Politics and Vision*, Boston, Mass., 1960.

Index

Lightning Source UK Ltd.
Milton Keynes UK
UKOW04n2103101213

222753UK00005B/32/A